Christ the Representative

Studies in Systematic Theology

Edited by

Ashley Cocksworth (*University of Roehampton, UK*)
Hanna Reichel (*Princeton Theological Seminary, USA*)

Editorial Board

Trond Skard Dokka (*University of Oslo, Norway*)
Junius Johnson (*Baylor University, USA*)
Veli-Matti Kärkkäinen (*Fuller Theological Seminary, USA*)
Rachel Muers (*University of Leeds, UK*)
Eugene Rogers (*The University of North Carolina* at *Greensboro, USA*)
Katherine Sonderegger (*Virginia Theological Seminary, USA*)

VOLUME 27

The titles published in this series are listed at *brill.com/sist*

Christ the Representative

Toward a Representational Christology

By

Reinhold Bernhardt

Translated by

Tom Marshall

BRILL

LEIDEN | BOSTON

 This is an open access title distributed under the terms of the CC BY-NC-ND 4.0 license, which permits any non-commercial use, distribution, and reproduction in any medium, provided no alterations are made and the original author(s) and source are credited. Further information and the complete license text can be found at https://creativecommons.org/licenses/by-nc-nd/4.0/

The terms of the CC license apply only to the original material. The use of material from other sources (indicated by a reference) such as diagrams, illustrations, photos and text samples may require further permission from the respective copyright holder.

This work was originally published in German as *Jesus Christus—Repräsentant Gottes* by Theologischer Verlag Zürich (TVZ) in 2021. This English edition has been translated from the original and adapted to the context of Anglo-American theology and religious studies.

Cover illustration: Sieger Köder, Jesus begegnet seiner Mutter. IV. Station. Kreuzweg Bensberg
© Sieger Köder-Stiftung Kunst und Bibel, Ellwangen www.verlagsgruppe-patmos.de/rights/abdrucke.

The Library of Congress Cataloging-in-Publication Data is available online at https://catalog.loc.gov
LC record available at https://lccn.loc.gov/2025025866

Typeface for the Latin, Greek, and Cyrillic scripts: "Brill". See and download: brill.com/brill-typeface.

ISSN 1876-1518
ISBN 978-90-04-73419-7 (paperback)
ISBN 978-90-04-73420-3 (e-book)
DOI 10.1163/9789004734203

Copyright 2026 by Reinhold Bernhardt. Published by Koninklijke Brill BV, Plantijnstraat 2, 2321 JC Leiden, The Netherlands.
Koninklijke Brill BV incorporates the imprints Brill, Brill Nijhoff, Brill Schöningh, Brill Fink, Brill mentis, Brill Wageningen Academic, Vandenhoeck & Ruprecht, Böhlau and V&R unipress.
Koninklijke Brill BV reserves the right to protect this publication against unauthorized use.
For more information: info@brill.com.

This book is printed on acid-free paper and produced in a sustainable manner.

Contents

Preface IX

1 Preliminary Considerations: Contextual Christology 1
   1.1 The Religions as Context 6
   1.2 'Natural Self-Affirmation'? 10
   1.3 Outline of the Argument 12

2 The Problem: Christology and the Theology of Religions 14
   2.1 Interreligious Appreciation? 15
   2.2 Renunciation of Textual Justification? 18
   2.3 The Person and Mission of Jesus Christ 21
   2.4 Particularity and Universality 25
      2.4.1 *From Particularity to Particularism* 25
      2.4.2 *From Universality to Universalism* 27
      2.4.3 *Escape Clauses* 28
      2.4.4 *Christocentric Universalism* 32
   2.5 The Theology of Israel as a Precedent 34

3 The Agenda: 'Representation' as the Key Concept of Christology 39
   3.1 Clarification of the Term 'Representation' 39
   3.2 Application of the Concept of Representation to the Interpretation of Jesus Christ 43
      3.2.1 *Representation as 'Making Present'* 45
      3.2.2 *Whom Does Jesus Christ Represent?* 46
         3.2.2.1 Identification Christology 48
         3.2.2.2 Constitutive Christology 48
         3.2.2.3 Representational Christology as Dilution? 50
      3.2.3 *What/Whom Does Jesus Christ Represent?* 51
      3.2.4 *Not Only Showing, but Also Transforming* 53
      3.2.5 *The 'For Structure'* 56
      3.2.6 *'Salvation'* 57
      3.2.7 *Related Terms* 61
         3.2.7.1 Image; Icon; Parable 61
         3.2.7.2 Sacrament 64
         3.2.7.3 Symbol 68
         3.2.7.4 Revelation 75
         3.2.7.5 Substitution 78

4 Implementation: Unfolding Representational Christology 87
   4.1   Person and 'Work' of Jesus Christ   88
   4.2   Revisions of Logos-Incarnation-Nature Christology   92
       4.2.1   *Relationship Instead of Unity of Two Natures*   93
           4.2.1.1   Turning Away from the Concept of Substance   93
           4.2.1.2   'Relationship', 'Act', and 'Event' as Guiding Categories   95
           4.2.1.3   Representation as a Pattern of Relationships   95
       4.2.2   *Unity and Difference*   97
       4.2.3   *The Humanity of Jesus*   101
   4.3   Defining Relationships with Sensitivity to Difference   103
       4.3.1   *The Difference between God and the Logos or Word of God*   105
           4.3.1.1   The Logos of God in the Prologue of John   105
           4.3.1.2   The Philosophical and Religious Context: Philo of Alexandria   108
           4.3.1.3   Divine Beings besides God?   110
       4.3.2   *The Difference between the Logos and His Personification*   113
           4.3.2.1   'Incarnation of God'?   113
           4.3.2.2   Foundation in the New Testament   114
           4.3.2.3   Christ as *totus Deus* but Not as *totum Dei*   117
           4.3.2.4   Emphasis on the Unity between the Eternal and the Incarnate Logos   126
           4.3.2.5   'Incarnation' as a Metaphorical *modus loquendi* for 'Representation'   128
           4.3.2.6   Fullness as Wholeness   131
   4.4   Spirit Christology   133
       4.4.1   *Biblical Starting Points and Contemporary Approaches*   135
       4.4.2   *Avoiding the Minimization of Jesus' Humanity*   139
       4.4.3   *Compatibility with Contemporary Forms of Thought and Language*   141
       4.4.4   *'Before Him, in Him, through Him, and beyond Him'*   142
       4.4.5   *On the 'filioque'*   144
   4.5   Wisdom Christology   148
       4.5.1   *Biblical Approaches*   149
       4.5.2   *The Ambiguity of God's Wisdom in the World, Represented by the Cross*   152
   4.6   Word, Spirit, and Wisdom—an Interim Evaluation   154
   4.7   The Revelation and Withdrawal of God   158

4.8 The Work of Jesus Christ and Its Effects 163
 4.8.1 *The Death of Jesus as a Saving Event or as Desolation?* 165
  4.8.1.1 New Testament Interpretations of the Death of Jesus 166
  4.8.1.2 The Death of Jesus Christ as a Saving Event: Constitutive Soteriology 167
  4.8.1.3 The Death of Jesus as a Catastrophe 171
  4.8.1.4 The Death of Jesus as the Consequence of His Mission 173
 4.8.2 *'Resurrection' as a Reversal of Meaning* 174
 4.8.3 *A Paradigm Shift: Focusing on Suffering Instead of Sin* 177
4.9 Christ-Event and Christ-Content 180

5 Selected Approaches to a Representational Christology 186
5.1 Schubert M. Ogden's Concept of Representation 186
 5.1.1 *Jesus-Kerygma and Christ-Kerygma* 187
 5.1.2 *Connections and Demarcations* 189
 5.1.3 *Consequences for the Theology of Religions* 192
5.2 Roger Haight: Jesus as Symbol of God 194
 5.2.1 *The Term 'Symbol'* 196
 5.2.2 *Elaboration of Haight's Approach* 198
  5.2.2.1 Redemption 198
  5.2.2.2 Religions 199
  5.2.2.3 The Divinity of Jesus Christ 201
  5.2.2.4 Trinity 204
 5.2.3 *Questions* 205

6 Conclusions and Further Reflections 208
6.1 Soteriological Exclusivism? 208
6.2 *Solus Christus?* 211
6.3 An Application: the Qur'an as a Representation of God? 213
6.4 Closing Remarks 216

Bibliography 219
Index of Names 233

Preface

Since the beginning of my studies in theology, I have felt a burning need to relate 'my' Christian faith to other religions. My teachers in Germany offered little help, as they were focused primarily on the Christian tradition and contemporary Protestant theology. At that time, Barth's Christocentrism played a significant role in the theological arena. In my PhD thesis, I sought to determine both whether the 'claim of absoluteness' is an essential ingredient of Christian faith, and how it had been understood in the recent history of theology. This inquiry led me to the Anglo-American debate on the theology of religions, which at that time was dominated by discussions on the three models of relating Christianity to other religions: exclusivism, inclusivism, and pluralism. The 'Pluralist Theology of Religions' polarized the debate.

I participated in these discussions and contributed to them, but I increasingly felt the need to turn to the core issues of Christian dogmatics and pursue the question of how to relate not Christianity as a religion but God, Jesus Christ, and the Holy Spirit to non-Christians, to their religions, and to religious plurality in general. This led me to initiate this project. Over the course of more than twenty years of teaching in the Karl Barth chair in Basel, I developed a Christology in the context of the theology of religions debate. Another book on the doctrine of God in reference to theology of religions followed.[1] In those works I honor Barth's great heritage but go beyond and even contradict it in crucial respects. His understanding of God's presence as being mediated in its fullness only through Jesus Christ I found to be too narrow. I am aware that Barth would have strongly rejected such an understanding.

The book on Christology was published in German in 2021[2] and received both approval and—predictably—criticism. Anglo-American colleagues and friends encouraged me to have it translated and published in English. In doing so, I shortened and adapted it more closely to the Anglo-American debates in this field. The most significant reductions I made are in Chapter 5. In the German version, this chapter discussed Friedrich D. E. Schleiermacher, Alois Emanuel Biedermann, and Albrecht Ritschl, alongside Schubert M. Ogden and Roger Haight as pioneers of a representational Christology. With a heavy heart, I decided to omit the first three figures.

---

1 Bernhardt, Monotheismus und Trinität.
2 Bernhardt, Jesus Christus.

In October 2023, a symposium on the book was held at the University of Basel. The contributions from that symposium were published in 2025.[3]

I hope that this English edition will offer a fresh perspective on Jesus Christ by linking Christological reflections to issues of interreligious relations. The book also proposes a new interpretation of salvation that resonates with contemporary ways of thinking. It presents Christology in a non-exclusivist manner, avoiding both absolutization and relativization. It engages with biblical sources, overlooked strands of theological tradition, and current theological approaches. 'Incarnation' it interprets as 'representation.' Through these reflections, I hope to encourage the search for representations of God's universal and radical grace in other religious traditions and in secular contexts.

Many thanks are due to Dr. Katharina Merian, Dr. Gesine von Kloeden, and Kathrin Schäublin for their critical and constructive reviews of the manuscript; to Lea Stolz for assisting in shortening the German edition of the book; to Tom Marshall for translating this version into English; to Ulrike Guthrie for reviewing the translation; and to the editors of the *Studies in Systematic Theology* series, Hanna Reichel and Ashley Cocksworth, for accepting the volume for publication.

---

3   Merian, ed., *Repräsentation*.

CHAPTER 1

Preliminary Considerations: Contextual Christology

Christology is the focal point of dogmatics. This is where the threads of Christian theology converge and from where they spread out. But how should we understand this focal point? The history of theology constitutes a series of attempts to answer the question of how to view the person of Jesus in the light of his relationship with God; of what his mission consisted; and the significance of his suffering, death, and presence beyond death. In so doing, Christology addresses the central content of the Christian faith.

The material basis for this reflection comes from the New Testament and its interpretations in the history of theology. It unfolds in specific historical contexts, along with the things that shape each of these contexts in terms of historical experiences, current intellectual developments, cultural formations, and religious challenges. Christologies are always contextual; they are also always driven by particular interests. In the elaboration of these contexts and interests, certain starting points in the New Testament are singled out and foregrounded as leitmotifs, others are subordinated to this center of integration, and still others are marginalized. The claim to have developed a Christology that does full justice to the New Testament tradition and follows no other interest than to bring the timeless gospel to the fore has been made again and again, but itself comes under suspicion of ideology. It is a claim that absolutizes its own contextual Christology and shields it from questioning. The present proposal of a Christology therefore names right at the beginning both the context in which it unfolds and the motivation that guides it.

The religious-cultural context consists of the threefold challenge that the Christian faith is currently facing, especially in the Western world. These challenges are ever-continuing secularization, the transformation of Christian forms of religion from those guided by church tradition to those emphasizing individual experience, and the plurality of religious (and secular) worldviews. It is this third challenge in particular that constitutes the frame of reference for the Christological reflections developed here.

These reflections are motivated by a theology of religions but are not dependent on it. They can also be detached from it. Even those who do not share, or who reject, the perspectives expressed in this volume, should find in it a proposal of a Christology that strives to make the meaning of the person of Jesus understandable in a way that is anchored in the Bible, justified by the history of theology, and plausible in the present contexts of experiences, interpretations, and forms of thought.

This proposal is positioned within the plausibility structures that can be summarized under the (fuzzy) term 'postmodernity'. These are characterized by a pervasive historicization, contextualization and pluralization of thought; by a turning away from anthropocentrism, universal concepts of meaning ('grand narratives') and absolute claims to truth; by an awareness of the fragmentary—as well as of the fluid—nature of reality; by the insight that reality discloses itself symbolically and that the language that expresses it is highly metaphorical. This also includes a pronounced sensitivity for differences, an appreciation of alterity, and an advocacy for marginalized views. Thought develops in the ever-new circular movement of deconstruction and reconstruction, whereby the normative foundations of the formation of judgements are also always up for discussion in light of a critique of power, hierarchy, and ideology.

The present proposal is particularly aware of the problematic demands that have been imposed on Christology since the separation of dogmatic and historical perspectives in the nineteenth century and on which it has been working ever since. Its task is to make both the dogmatic determinations of the person of Jesus Christ, as well as the meaning of his revelation and salvation, understandable for the present. It seeks to do this in connection with New Testament testimony of Jesus' speech, action, and deeds, and to relate these to basic contemporary questions of human existence. Fundamentally, it is about Bonhoeffer's question of "who Christ really is, for us today".[1]

If 'today' is not only an *addendum* to Christology, a question of its *application*, but if Christology actually develops *from the beginning* as a 'responsive theology' (Tillich)—responding to the existential, social, cultural, and religious questions of the present—then it must have in view from the outset, and orient itself towards, questions posed by the diversity of religions. This will be reflected in the study's methodological approach.

In line with Protestant theology in the wake of Schleiermacher, the starting point is the radiance that the person and work of Jesus have generated, and continue to generate, towards his disciples, the people he encountered, and Christians, but also to non-Christians, throughout history.

I agree with Hermann Deuser's call for Christology not to dwell in "remote metaphysical museums", but rather "to read and understand the story of Jesus

---

[1] Bonhoeffer, *Letters and Papers from Prison*, 279.

and the closeness of God represented in it [...] in a much more naturalistic way than certain, only ostensibly 'Christian' systems of thought would have us believe".[2]

This is not a plea for a one-sided Christology 'from below' that represses the concerns of Christology 'from above'. This distinction involves two perspectives, both of which have their rightful place, and which should be held together in unity while also encompassing their contrasts. Christology 'from below' starts with the man Jesus, as the Synoptic Gospels above all witness to him, and such Christology interprets his mission as an expression of his intense relationship with God. By contrast, Christology 'from above' emphasizes his intrinsic divinity. Whenever one side of Christology is emphasized, the other must also be taken into account. Yet the question arises regarding from which side this dialectic is entered into—from the side of the human person of Jesus or from the side of the God who is revealed in Jesus? I prefer the first of these two possibilities: the starting point and the normative reference point lie in the person of Jesus Christ as described in the New Testament. The path of knowledge leads from Jesus to God and back to Jesus.

Christology is about the central self-understanding of the Christian faith; it is what makes the Christian faith 'Christian'. Christology is also about its credibility in the tension between biblical tradition and contemporary contexts of understanding. Credibility also includes intellectual plausibility. 'Fides quaerens intellectum' (Anselm of Canterbury)! Johannes Fischer states:

> For faith that is not knowledge, and neither comes from knowledge nor is based on knowledge is without contact with reality. Faith without contact with reality does not change the reality of the believer. It is without soteriological power.[3]

Paul Tillich rightly warned against repeating in the present the responses of faith of earlier centuries—and thus also the classical doctrinal decisions of Christology—without relating them to the existential questions and states of consciousness that arise today.[4] Instead, it is necessary to transform these responses in order to bring their original meaning to bear anew under the conditions of the present. Biblical and theological traditions offer many approaches to this.

---

2 Translated from Deuser, *Gottesinstinkt*, 166.
3 Translated from Fischer, *Vom Geheimnis der Stellvertretung*, 166. See also Fischer, *Glaube als Erkenntnis*, 31–35.
4 E.g., in Tillich, *Systematic Theology*, Vol. 2, 13ff.

Protestant theology in particular carries in its heritage the impulse to return again and again to the biblical sources. It is not bound to the ways of thinking that have become predominant in theological traditions, but rather can exploit the broad scope of interpretation inherent in biblical traditions. The doctrinal formulations of the early church councils, the great theological systems of the Middle Ages, the confessional writings of the Reformation, and the beacons of what Ernst Troeltsch called neo-Protestantism constitute important guidelines—but are not fixed as the core of theological thought. Every age must develop an understanding of Jesus Christ which it considers appropriate and responsible in relation to the testimony of the Bible and to the theological tradition. The norm of all Christology is not conformity with a classical doctrinal view, but rather the faithfulness of the Christological concepts to the original testimonies about the presence of God in Jesus Christ. Christology must make these testimonies plausible within the framework of contemporary understandings of God, the world, and the self; and it has to show how it transforms the contexts of contemporary life.

The principal points, both of departure and of reference, for Trinitarian and Christological doctrinal formation in the early Church were the Johannine writings of the New Testament. The divinity of Jesus Christ attested to in these texts was emphasized primarily because of soteriological interests; the theologians of that time stressed the uniqueness of God's revelation and the mediation of salvation in him. While doctrinal formation foregrounded these Johannine themes, it emphasized other strands of the New Testament's witness far less, notably the fundamentally theocentric feature of Jesus' proclamation and Spirit-Christology. In the following reflections, I bring such starting points back from the margins to the center. In doing so, I follow the methodological principle formulated by Wolfhart Pannenberg that Christological statements about Jesus Christ must explore the biblical origins of the confessional statements and Christological titles of the early Christian tradition and be oriented towards the testimonies of Jesus.[5]

The dual criteria of identity and relevance evaluate the various approaches to Christology. These two criteria require further introduction before they can be applied:

(a) The criterion of identity demands the greatest possible correlation with the original impulse of the Christian faith as it is embodied in the person of Jesus and witnessed to in the traditions of the New Testament. It thus demands

---

5 Pannenberg, *Systematic Theology*, Vol. 2, 282–3.

a 'reduction' of Christology in the literal sense of *re-ducere*: to lead back to the biblical origins. This is certainly not to be understood in the sense of biblicism, nor as disdain for the tradition of interpretation, but rather as a critical questioning of whether and to what extent the later interpretations, as they were elevated to a normative rank in the history of theology (such as the decisions of the early church councils or the confessional writings of the Reformation), narrow the variety of biblical perspectives depending on their own historical contexts. Today, such perspectives are, moreover, only comprehensible with guidelines to aid understanding, with the result that the spiritual power and truth inherent in the message of Christ is sometimes obscured rather than brought to the fore. This leads to the second criterion.

(b) The criterion of relevance asks how Christological statements measure up in contemporary social, cultural, and religious contexts. Various factors shape these contexts, and the contexts can be addressed in different ways. This book primarily foregrounds the situation of religious diversity as a challenge to Christological reflection. It demands a Christology whose axiomatic truths do not lead to a devaluation of non-Christian religions, but rather enable us to imagine that God's self-communication can also reach people in these religions and through these religions, so that it becomes necessary to encounter not only people but also their religions with theologically grounded appreciation.

The identity of the Christian faith should not be called into question in the pursuit of relevance. Nor should we cling to any particular form of Christology that has been established in the history of theology, thereby losing our ability to communicate with contemporary problems.

Against the first danger it should be noted that the effort to deliberate on Christology in the context of theology of religions is not about elevating interest in interreligious dialogue to the norm of Christian theology. Nor is it about adapting theological doctrines in eager subservience to the supposed requirements of consensus-oriented understanding so that they appear less objectionable to non-Christian dialogue partners. That would be a form of theological heteronomy. Rather, deliberating on Christology must be a matter of sounding out the interpretive scope of theology—especially Christology— to see whether its own foundational axioms suggest that non-Christian sources and streams of tradition can also mediate valid knowledge of God and salvific relationships with God. A responsible form of Christological doctrine cannot draw its criteria of validity from interreligious encounters. As much as encounters with other religions can help to *discover and develop* theological and Christological insights, they can hardly become a *source of their justification*. The appropriateness of Christological statements cannot be judged according to their pragmatic value in dialogue. Rather, it must be "measured by internal consistency and agreement with exegetical findings across the history of dogmatics".[6]

These opinions, however, have at all times in the history of theology been contentious and open to interpretation. Those possibilities of interpretation can be highlighted that most closely correspond to the standards of intellectual plausibility and the basic soteriological orientations of our cultural context. That applies not only to theology of religions, but to theology in general. It strives for a reasonable and faith-worthy contemporary interpretation of the Christian tradition. This does not make the present zeitgeist the norm for theological statements, but neither is that the case for the zeitgeist of the first, fourth and fifth, or sixteenth centuries. This is of particular note regarding the second of the above-mentioned dangers.

Critics sometimes refer to attempts to exploit the scope for interpretation offered in the biblical tradition and theology in order to unfold Christology in the face of current challenges in a way that is as intellectually convincing as possible (and thus also worthy of belief) as 'revisions of Christology'. This would not be contested if the term 'revision' were used in a non-pejorative way. Every Christological system undertakes such a re-vision. Such critics, however, associate this with the accusation of relativizing classical Christology, which they believe they are obliged to guard. Yet Christology has always been vital where it has resisted such hegemonic theological claims and has left well-trodden paths or made abandoned paths newly accessible.

1.1 The Religions as Context

The special focus of the Christological reflections developed in this volume lies in their relationship to the plurality of religions. It is a Christology in the context of the 'theology of religions'.[7] The theology of religions is not itself the subject so much as the question of the person and work of Jesus Christ—but that question about Jesus is dealt with in the context of the theology of religions. This volume is not about a theological interpretation of other religions, nor about the question of how *they* see and understand Jesus, nor is it about how they relate to the Christian understanding of Christ. No: It is about the self-understanding of the Christian faith in a religiously plural world.

The starting point is the following problem: If Jesus Christ is the 'only', or 'only-begotten' (μονογενής) Son of God (Jn. 1:14; Jn. 3:16, 18; 1 Jn. 4:9), if God's

---

[6] Translated from Schmidt-Leukel, *Theologie der Religionen*, 514.
[7] See Bernhardt, *Ende des Dialogs?*, 167–290; idem., *Inter-Religio*, 267–457.

eternal Logos alone became man in him, if the predicate 'vere Deus' belongs to him in a singular way, if Jesus' death on the cross laid the objective foundation for a salvific relationship with God, then there can be no redeeming relationship to God that is not bound to his name, his person, and his work. If this relationship is realized by *faith* in Christ—and only in him—then no theological value can be attributed to non-Christian references to the divine reality and to the forms of religiosity and religion related to them, no matter how open-minded one encounters their followers.

If God has assumed human personhood once and for all in the fullness of his being in Jesus Christ, so that this revelation is to be regarded as final and ultimately valid (i.e., unsurpassable), exhaustive (i.e., neither in need of nor capable of being supplemented in any way), and universal (i.e., applicable to all human beings), then the being of God in Christ is not only authentically revealed but authentically revealed *in an exclusive way*. But if Christ is understood in this way as the one and only eye of the needle[8] through which God's way leads to humanity and humanity's way leads to God,[9] then the testimonies to a presence of the 'Holy' in other religions are theologically worthless or at least deficient. It follows that those testimonies, and thus these religions as a whole, cannot be held in theological esteem. There is therefore no theological reason to engage seriously with the sources and streams of tradition of other religions, unless for apologetic and/or polemical and/or missionary interests.

To mitigate this consequence, a distinction has often been made between revelatory testimonies articulated *before* Christ in Israel's history and those that appeared *after* Christ and/or outside this stream of tradition. The former could be interpreted as a promise pointing towards Christ and thus granted relative validity, while the latter were usually rejected as erroneous beliefs. Thus Karl Hartenstein, who headed the Basel Mission from 1926 to 1939, interpreted *post*-Christian religions as *anti*-Christian: "Every religion after Christ must unfold against Christ, because after the revelation of God in Christ there is no new one".[10] Similarly, Emanuel Kellerhals asserts, "The *post Christum* can only be a *contra Christum*, an *anti Christum*".[11]

---

8   With reference to, e.g., Mt. 19:24, and parallels.
9   Like Calvin, Luther also invoked the *locus classicus* Jn. 14:6 to justify this claim: "Hear the absolute sentence: no one comes to the Father except through Christ" ("audis absolutam sententiam: Neminem nisi per Christum ad patrem venire") (Letter to Spalatin dated 12 February 1519: WA, Letters I, 329).
10 Translated from Hartenstein, *Die Kirche*, 11.
11 Translated from Kellerhals, *Der Islam*, 372. This sentence no longer appears in the shorter third edition of this book from 1981 (reprinted in Moers 2002). Kellerhals was Africa Secretary of the Basel Mission from 1933 to 1948 and Local Secretary of the "Mohammedan

Such Christocentric exclusivism, which equates *extra* or *post* Christum with *contra* or *anti* Christum, which interprets post-Christian or all non-Christian religions atheistically—as godless—is still found in many instantiations of worldwide Christianity. In Western academic theology, on the other hand, it is hardly represented at all any more. However, there are also hardly any forms of thought offered which, from the Christological and soteriological center of Christian theology, open up the possibility of also placing the sources and streams of non-Christian traditions in a positive relationship to God's revelation and salvation, possibilities that would allow us to think that there can also be an authentic communion with God *extra Christum*. Mostly one retreats into an agnostic form of theology of religions, which holds that this possibility and its realization must be entrusted to *God*, without this statement being reconciled with Christology; sometimes those who argue in such a way are referencing the hiddenness of God's action.

Lutheran theologians of the recent past distinguish between God's (hidden) action in the world and God's salvific action in Christ; they also see the former at work in religions. However, this only becomes recognizable as such in the light of Christ, and thus remains hidden from the followers of these religions themselves.

This position is questionable not only with regard to the theology of religions, but also because it sets apart the action of the second Trinitarian person from that of the first and thus violates the Trinitarian theological principle 'opera ad extra indivisa sunt'. Reformed theology, on the other hand, has insisted that all God's action is subject to an ultimately salvific purpose.

Roman Catholic theologians who are influenced by Karl Rahner also speak of both God's action in the world and God's salvific action in the religions, but they see this latter as grounded in Christ, emphasizing the universality of salvation in Jesus. According to Johannes Herzgsell, there may well be non-Christian mediators of salvation: "Moses, Lao-tzu, Confucius, Buddha, Muhammad and others, as genuine mediators of revelation, have also truly communicated God's salvation to other people".[12] However, these are 'mere' human mediators of salvation, whose partial mediation of salvation is only possible through participation in the whole and absolute mediation of salvation through Jesus

---

Mission" based in Basel from 1937 to 1948. He accuses Islam of "having denied and betrayed its own very essence and decisive message" (*ibid.*): "it has fought the divinity of Christ as a blasphemy—and has made a god out of its own prophet [...]. In this sense, as the one made Antichrist by his congregation, Muhammad is really the 'false prophet', as the Church has called him" (*ibid.*).

12   Translated from Herzgsell, *Das Christentum*, 564.

Christ. For Herzgsell, this results in the distinction between a first-order and a second-order mediation of salvation.[13]

Another strategy is to distinguish between theological epistemology and soteriology. For those who adopt this strategy, followers of other religions also have access to the general revelation of God and thus the possibility of at least a rudimentary knowledge of God. Salvation, however, lies in faith in Christ alone. This distinction is also problematic. Revelation—understood as God's self-communication—means not only that God makes Godself known but that God *gives Godself*, i.e., the establishing of a relationship, the 'opening' of God to humankind and thus the acceptance of humankind by God. This is, additionally, always a salvific act and event.[14]

But if it is to be conceded that God can also reveal Godself *extra Christum*, and if every revelation of God ultimately aims at a salvific relationship with God, then the question arises as to what this concession means for Christology. Can the person of Jesus, his work, and his impact, be understood in a way that admits the possibility that there is salvific revelation of God that is not mediated by Christ? In relation to Judaism, this concession has been made in various ways.[15] But can it be limited to Judaism, or does it push beyond it?

I intend my Christological proposal to offer an interpretation of the person and work of Jesus Christ, which assumes that God's salvific action is not constituted, realized, and/or mediated absolutely uniquely in and through Christ, but rather that there can also be other mediations which do not have to be declared theologically deficient *a priori*. This entails working out the contours of a Christology that neither denies the theological value of the sources and traditions of non-Christian religions from the outset nor includes them in a Christocentric approach.

This theological interest is (by no means only, but nonetheless) also motivated by experiences of interreligious encounters. Many (if by no means all) of these experiences teach that deep wisdom, ethical orientation, meaningful ways of living, spiritual powers for overcoming crises, reverent respect for other living beings and for nature, strong motivations for altruistic action, etc., can also flow from the sources of non-Christian religious traditions. Those who draw from these sources understand themselves to be anchored in the divine ground of all being. Impressive analogies to phenomena described by the Christian term 'sanctification' can also be found in non-Christian religions

---

13 *Ibid.*
14 See Chapter 4.7.
15 See Chapter 2.5.

(just as, conversely, 'unholiness' has been and continues to be found in abundance in Christianity).

Can this insight be rejected as theologically irrelevant? Is it a mere human experience compared to the revelation of God in Christ, one on which theology need not dwell any further? With such an attitude, theology would isolate itself from religious experience and thus lose its connection to people's lives—both the contexts in which they unfold and the meanings assigned to them. Religious experience cannot be normative for theology, but it is the field in which Christian faith encounters other faiths. In this field admirable (as well as terrible) fruits are produced—by Christians and by non-Christians. According to Jacques Dupuis, the recognition of other religions is "based on the fruits of the spirit that can be perceived in the believers of other religions".[16]

It is therefore not only a matter of individual non-Christians' relationships with God, but also about the sources and streams of non-Christian traditions. Is it possible to think that these are in a positive relationship—however this may be defined—to God's self-communication? And if so, what does this mean for Christology?

To declare there to be a 'positive relationship' is not the outcome of demonstrating similarities between Christianity and other religions. It works the other way round: determining similarities presupposes a positive stance on other religions. The crucial question is what these similarities mean theologically. This question cannot be answered by comparing religions, but only through theological reflection. It is a matter of the *theological prerequisite* of comparisons between religions and of *presuppositions* in interreligious encounters.

What we are striving for is a Christology which understand Jesus Christ as a unique but not the only manifestation of God's saving presence; a Christology which takes into account the universality of God's saving presence in all creation; a Christology which allows us to make use of other sources and ways of knowing this presence. Can there be knowledge of God and relationships with God that are not centered in Christ that can nonetheless be considered 'authentic' and in this sense 'true' from the perspective of Christian faith?

1.2   'Natural Self-Affirmation'?

The Christian faith, like all religions, is primarily focused on its own center of identity: in this case, on Christ, on faith in Christ, on Christian life, and on the community of believers in Christ. Only secondarily, and not infrequently

---

16   Translated from Dupuis, "Die Wahrheit wird euch frei machen", 47.

as a reaction to challenges it faces, does Christianity come to terms with its external relationships, which also include its relationship to other religions. This confrontation, moreover, always serves to define that which is "decisively and distinctively Christian".[17] Insofar as non-Christian religions are competing narratives, doctrines, and orientation systems, there is a somewhat 'natural' tendency to set oneself apart from them and to affirm one's own claim to truth by disputing competing claims to truth.

Looking back on his encounters with Buddhism in Japan, Paul Tillich wrote in 1961:

> If a group—or an individual—is convinced that it possesses the truth, it implicitly denies those claims to truth which conflict with that truth. I would call this the natural self-affirmation in the realm of knowledge.[18]

In this 'natural self-affirmation' Tillich recognized a characteristic of personal certainties.

That self-affirmation can be counterbalanced if there are reasons—taken from the core of the Christian faith—that allow us to regard appearances of non-Christian religions as potential manifestations of the Word, the Spirit, and the Wisdom of God. This still does not establish a definitive judgement on the theological value of those religions, for example in the sense that other forms of faith are certified as being of equal value to the Christian ones. Nor is it necessary to deny, or to harmonize, the profound differences, tensions, and even open contradictions between religions. Rather, my approach is about exploring the possibility that there can be other manifestations of God's presence independent of Christ. The interpretation of the Christian faith offered here seeks to justify christologically the assumption that there can also be (and indeed that there must be, according to the gospel proclaimed and embodied by Jesus Christ) salvific relationships with God outside of this faith.

If this assumption can be made plausible, then other ways of believing and other forms of religion need not be theologically rejected *a priori*. Nor do they have to be regarded as theologically inferior or irrelevant (which is the milder form of exclusivism within the theology of religions). Rather, a theologically justified motivation arises to enter into a constructively critical dialogue with these other forms of religion, from which theologically relevant insights can ensue.

---

17 Following the wording of the title of Jürgen Werbick's book, *Vom entscheidend und unterscheidend Christlichen*.
18 Tillich, *Christianity and the Encounter of the World Religions*, 28.

1.3 Outline of the Argument

The first, introductory part of this study (chapter 2) will offer some basic reflections on situating Christology within the context of theology of religions. Is Christian faith and Christology as its reflection necessarily connected with exclusive claims that make an appreciative attitude towards other religious communities and traditions impossible or at least difficult? Where is the potential to justify such an attitude theologically?

From chapter 3 onwards, the discussion revolves around the concept or motif of 'representation'. This term, which has not yet been exhausted theologically, I will illuminate from different angles and establish as a central concept of Christology. This is not connected with the claim to tread a completely new path in Christology. Rather, I try to arrange around this concept biblical approaches and interpretations of the history of theology in such a way as to generate a Christology that is both plausible and practical for understanding the Christian faith in the present.

The Christological approaches used for this purpose—from the Prologue of John to Christologies of the present day—are, for the most part, not based on the challenges of theology of religions but appear in other discourses. They therefore do not follow the same particular interest as the focus of this volume. But they should be related to it; the representational Christology developed here gains its contours by debating with them.

In chapter 3, I first consider the term 'representation' in general, i.e., independently of its theological application. Against this background, I then highlight the aspects that are relevant for its application to Christology. I further relate it to similar terms, such as 'symbol' or 'substitution'. Here—as in other parts of the book—I refer to Paul Tillich, whose Christological approach and reflection on symbols was and is an important inspiration for the development of a representational Christology.

After that part has outlined the concept of representation, the approach of representational Christology is then unfolded in chapter 4 with a view to the biblical tradition and the history of Christology. The distinction between the person and work of Jesus Christ, which was fundamental to the classical doctrinal form of Christology, largely loses its significance in this approach (4.1). A concept of relationship that focusses on Jesus' two basic relationships—to God and to humanity—replaces the ontology of the two-natures doctrine. Both I define in terms of a unity in difference. Particularly with regard to the relationship with God, I emphasize the aspect of difference, not least in order to bring Jesus' humanity fully to bear (4.2). Even in the Prologue of the Gospel of John, which played a central role in the development of early church theology, the relationship between God and the Word (or Logos) of God as well as the relationship between the Word of God and the Word as personified in Jesus is not defined in the sense of an undifferentiated sameness, but as a differentiated, personal, and relational unity. Chapter 4.3 selectively traces the debate about these two relationships from antiquity to the present, exploring what the expressions 'Incarnation of God' and 'divine Sonship' mean when applied to Jesus.

I answer the question of Jesus' 'being God' not only in terms of a revised Logos-Incarnation Christology as discussed in chapter 4.3. I place Spirit Christology (4.4) and Wisdom Christology (4.5) alongside Logos-Incarnation Christology—not as alternatives to it, but as differently accentuated approaches to the ultimately unfathomable mystery. This inscrutability I address more specifically in 4.7 with regard to the understanding of revelation.

Chapter 4.8 is dedicated to soteriology, i.e., the meaning of salvation through Jesus Christ. How is Jesus' violent death to be understood in light of that meaning? What does 'resurrection' mean? In this context, the concept of representation transforms traditional doctrines of reconciliation and thus gives their concerns fresh expression.

Chapter 4 concludes by addressing the question of how the historical 'Christ-event' relates to the 'Christ-content' which is significant across time (4.9). The whole project of representational Christology hinges on this distinction.

Chapter 5 consists of two individual studies on approaches to representational Christology from North American theology. These are the approaches of Schubert M. Ogden and Roger Haight.

In the final part of the study (chapter 6), I draw some theological consequences from the representational Christological approach. I offer one implementation by way of example, in addressing the question of whether the Qur'an can also be regarded as a representation of God.

When I speak of 'Jesus Christ', I am not only referring to the 'historical' person as he is recognizable in the biblical traditions, but also to his presence as grasped in faith: the *Christus praesens*. 'Jesus' refers rather to the historical person, 'Christ' to his presence and significance across time. And 'Jesus Christ' refers to the 'Christ-event' in which the historical and the kerygmatic perspectives coincide.

CHAPTER 2

The Problem: Christology and the Theology of Religions

The theology of religions, as I understand it, does not concern itself with making value judgements about the phenomena of other religions, or even about these religions in their entirety. Theological engagement with non-Christian religions rightly demands a constant abstention from judgement (ἐποχή/ epoché). However, such judgements may necessarily arise in the context of lived religion—in view of the many problematic phenomena that emerge in a religious guise.

However, the theology of religions as an academic discipline is a project which, in the words of Joseph Ratzinger/Pope Benedict XVI,

> would not straightaway concern itself with the value of these religions for eternity—thus imposing upon itself the burden of a question that can in fact be decided only by him who shall judge the world.[1]

As part of Christian theology, this project does not—as I practice it—start from philosophical questions about truth in (other) religions, but from the specific contents and manifestations of the Christian faith. The self-understanding of this faith, however, gives rise to (implicit or explicit) views, perceptions, and theological evaluations of other religions or of religious plurality overall. The more it is claimed that the Christian faith exclusively mediates truth and salvation, the less such a mediation can be granted to other religious traditions. Christology, soteriology, and the doctrine of revelation are inevitably connected with implicit or explicit theological assessments of other religions. These assessments influence the formation of relationships that exist with them or with their followers. If the Christian faith has an attendant exclusive claim to truth and salvation, then its relationship with those of other faiths can only be determined by the paradigm of mission, aiming at conversion, even if encounters with them are practiced in dialogic forms. A theologically based openness towards other religions cannot occur without an appreciation— however this may be expressed—of each one's relation to the Transcendent.

How can the Christian faith's self-understanding be developed such that it does not necessarily lead *a priori* to rejecting or devaluing other religious

---

1 Ratzinger, *Truth and Tolerance*, 18.

claims to truth, without abandoning or relativizing its own? How can we understand the person and significance of Jesus Christ in a way that is both true to itself and also open to pluralism? There are types of Christology that permit, or perhaps even demand, this, and others that impede or even preclude it. Approaches focused on the Incarnation or the Cross tend more toward the latter. Must this be the case? Or do they, too, offer room for interpretation that can help to break down interreligious boundaries? Are there other approaches that can be fruitful in this respect? Such theological re-visions have also been sought given the many other challenges that have confronted theology in recent decades, challenges such as the reformulation of relations with other Christian denominations or with Judaism.

A practical interest in peaceful coexistence, a better understanding of the Other, and a collaborative, dialogic exchange that enriches its participants have always motivated such re-visions. Beyond that, however, we must ask whether there are not also genuinely *theological* reasons for such a new interpretation. This question leads to the heart of the Christian faith: How is the Gospel to be understood? Every exercise in Christology is ultimately concerned with this question. This book is no exception.

The theology of religions tries to sound out ways of thinking that account for the changed requirements of this, our age of religious pluralism, without departing from the normative framework of the Christian traditions. It is not a matter of developing a religio-philosophical bird's-eye view that determines "how God can save without detracting from the uniqueness of Christ".[2] Rather, it is a matter of drawing on the potential that is inherent in the self-understanding of Christianity to identify a way of understanding Jesus Christ which nourishes the expectation that we can discover also in non-Christian religions "manifestations of [God's] grace"[3]—the grace which, according to the Christian creed, is decisively and essentially personified in Jesus Christ.

2.1   Interreligious Appreciation?

In 1961, Heinrich Bornkamm, referring to the Reformation period, wrote,

> at that time, the idea that, for its own sake, faith should grant freedom of belief and worship to those who think differently was inconceivable and has remained so in part to this day.[4]

---

2   Ratzinger, *Truth and Tolerance*, 44; and elsewhere.
3   Translated from Tillich, *Protestantische Gestaltung*, 57–61.
4   Translated from Bornkamm, *Das Problem*, 376.

Recent discussions of ecumenism and the theology of religions have dared to think this 'inconceivable' thought, and that will also be the case in this volume.

When he wrote this sentence, Bornkamm had in mind *intra-Christian* struggles within which intolerance was directed toward those who were considered heretics. Today, the focus of the theological debate with those who think and believe differently has shifted to the *interreligious* sphere. It is no longer just about granting persons the freedom to hold different beliefs in a different way, but about the possibility that those who believe differently can be recognized appreciatively *along with* their faith—rather than *apart from* or *despite* their faith. Thus, it is also about the relationship of the Christian faith to non-Christian beliefs, forms of faith, religious communities, and traditions. But this raises even more pointedly the question implied in Bornkamm's statement: Is it possible for the Christian faith, *for its own sake*, to give space to other forms of faith alongside it? What's more, is it possible and conceivable to do this with an attitude, not of grudging tolerance or detached indifference, but of appreciation based on theological foundations?

The real challenge, which is handled in various ways in the various approaches to a theology of religions, is to regard with theological appreciation not only *persons* of other faiths but also their *religions*. That *persons* of other faiths are to be treated according to the Christian ethos of love of neighbour, stranger, and enemy, and that among them there can even be those chosen and called by God ('holy pagans'), was widely recognized in the history of the Church and theology, despite the occurrence of persecutions of Jews, crusades against Muslims, and the burning of heretics. But the idea that non-Christian *religions* can lead to an authentic relationship with God was and is in large parts of the theological tradition virtually 'inconceivable': it stands in obvious tension with the conviction that such a relationship with God can only exist 'in Christ', i.e., in the Christian faith.

In the history of Christian piety and theology, the desire to know that one's own relationship with God was founded on as unshakeable a foundation as possible led to confessions of faith in Christ being repeatedly elevated to bold exclusivistic statements. Such statements left no room for theological recognition of other ways of believing. One can see in this the striving for certainty of salvation, but also a kind of 'salvation egoism'. However, the content of Christology should be determined neither by commitment to dialogue nor by concern with one's own salvation.

The first question this raises is: Why should Christians define the theological relationship to other religions as an appreciative recognition at all? Throughout theological history, it was the theology of sin or even demonology that quite often undergirded the prevailing polemical and apologetic patterns of defining relationships (demarcation, denial, condemnation, etc.). At best, the religious Other was regarded as an opponent in a debate, the purpose of which was to demonstrate publicly one's own faith's claim to truth. In many cases, however, there were harsh interreligious disputes based on exclusive truth claims for one's own religion.

In view of the history of interreligious hostilities, the need not only to practice a peaceful coexistence of religious communities but also to justify it philosophically and theologically, arose even in earlier times—e.g., during the Enlightenment. But especially after the Shoah and the growing awareness of Christianity's history of guilt toward Jews and Judaism, this need was felt so strongly that far-reaching theological revisions were made in relations with Judaism. It became clear that mere tolerance was not enough, but that a theological and especially a christological rethinking was necessary. There is a need for a theologically founded appreciation from within one's own Christian faith not only of biblical Israel as the historical and theological root of the Christian faith, but also of post-biblical Judaism. This was the case not only out of ethical considerations—for the sake of peaceful coexistence—but also to reap the benefits of the fruitful influence of rabbinic Jewish traditions on biblical interpretation and of scholarly Jewish dialogue partners on thought around Christian beliefs.

This impulse could not be limited to Judaism, despite its special relationship with Christianity, because it also dealt with basic questions about the theology of religions, and so came to concern itself with Islam and Eastern religions too, as well as with types of religion not classed among the so-called 'world religions'.[5] Christians discovered the value and dignity of the wisdom and spirituality accumulated and practiced in these other traditions and found in them a source of inspiration for their own Christian faith. In the encounter with these forms of religion, people's horizons were broadened, and Christian practice and theological reflection were enriched.

An attitude towards people of other faiths and other religions that is open to dialogue and based on theological appreciation is therefore not so much required for pragmatic reasons, since peaceful coexistence with their followers could also be achieved through tolerance and respect. Appreciative recognition goes beyond this. It correlates with positive interest in the religious Other and refers not only to their person but also to their religion. It seeks both to discover and to understand better these religious worlds, and in this process

---

5 For more on this questionable term, see Masuzawa, *The Invention*.

it expects that Christian faith and theological reflections will be enriched and deepened.

Such an attitude requires a theological appreciation of non-Christian religious traditions, for on the other hand theological appreciation makes fruitful encounters possible. As is true in life more generally, ideational presupposition and practical experience are mutually dependent.

'Appreciation' here does not mean a blanket and uncritical recognition of other religions in all their manifestations, just as there can be no such recognition of all historical forms of the Christian faith. Rather, it means a basically positive stance that relates the sources and streams of non-Christian traditions to the salvific presence of God, as the Christian faith witnesses to this regarding Jesus Christ. Firstly, this means taking into account the possibility that God's self-communication goes beyond the revelation in Jesus Christ. In the power of the Spirit, God can also make use of the spiritual sources of non-Christian religions in order to be creatively present among their adherents to bring salvation and enlightenment. Accordingly, testimonies to God's authentic self-revelation can also be discovered in other religions' traditional sources. There are not only numerous experiences of encounters with followers of other religions that support this hypothesis; there are also *theological* reasons for it, which I map out below.

2.2 Renunciation of Textual Justification?

But does such an appreciation need a *substantive* theological justification at all? Is it not sufficient to define a formal framework in terms of the philosophy of religion within which the Greek philosophical principle for distributive justice applies to religious faith and practice: '*suum cuique*' ('to each his/her own')?[6] In other words, everyone lives in their own religious cosmos, which they consider to be the only true one, and concedes the same right to others.

According to this 'formal' model of pluralism, religious perspectives of faith lie side by side like unconnected and thus non-communicating tubes. Each of these perspectives is entitled to hold on to its truth claim in full but must remain aware that this truth claim is an expression of its distinct faith, which does not apply to those who believe differently. The truth claim is thus placed in a hermeneutical bracket that identifies it as an internal confessional statement of a particular faith tradition, form, and community. Accordingly,

---

6 E.g., Plato (in reference to action): *Republic* IV 433a; and especially Vol. 5 of Aristotle's *Nicomachean Ethics* (1131).

the exclusive claims made for Jesus Christ which refer to Jn. 14:6 or Acts 4:12, among others, are self-assurances of the *Christian* faith which always remain bound to this internal perspective, i.e., to a specific hermeneutical circle. The statement that the Qur'an is the ultimate word of God and Muhammad the seal of prophecy expresses the specifically *Islamic* perspective of faith. Within this internal perspective, however, its truth applies universally. These claims to truth do not collide because they do not come together in a *single* frame of reference. They coexist in their unavoidable differences. One dispenses with any attempt to determine the content of the relationship. The two claims therefore cannot become a mutual challenge to each other.

The distinctive religious internal perspectives can thus be understood as resembling language games or languages that are meaningful for those who speak them. The statements formulated in them, however, cannot pretend to be applicable to a range of other perspectives or to transcend the limitations of a single perspective. They are required to undergo a hermeneutical self-relativization. They can absolutize themselves *within* their own hermeneutical circle.[7]

The question has thus been shifted from the material, dogmatic level to a matter of a philosophical theory of religion. The Christian doctrinal content remains unaffected. It can maintain the boldest truth claims so long as it places them within hermeneutical parentheses, explaining that 'the content within these parentheses is a self-expression of the Christian faith'.

A theory of religious pluralism from the perspective of philosophy of religion allows and demands the *formal* recognition of other religions. But it does not guide the different religions to develop substantive approaches for an appreciation of these other religions on the basis of their self-understanding. They can develop their self-understanding in a self-referential way, whether it be with complete disregard of these others, apologetically outperforming them, or rejecting them through polemic.

In recent Protestant theological and ecclesiastical commentary, a line of argumentation has been introduced into the discussion that neither goes beyond such a formal definition of the relationship between the religions nor intends to do so. It starts from the understanding of religious faith as personal certainty and connects this definition with the basic ethical law of reciprocity, thereby arriving at a recognition of religious plurality.[8] The argument runs that

---

7 Approaches of this kind are related to Hans Frei and George Lindbeck's post-liberal conception of theology.
8 This position was advocated, for example, by the "Protestant Church in Germany" in the document "Christlicher Glaube und religiöse Vielfalt in evangelischer Perspektive" (2015).

an individual who advocates a religious belief must also grant the same right to others who hold other beliefs.

This approach permits the peaceful coexistence of different religious communities—the value of which we should not underestimate. It is certainly a justified demand that the religious Other be granted the right 'to be blessed according to his own fashion', as the Prussian King Frederick II urged. However, at best this approach arrives at a formal tolerance and respect for the Other but makes no reference to the content of the Christian faith, shows no interest in a substantive discussion of other religious traditions, and yields no motivation to engage with these topics. In addition, it assumes a specifically Christian—Protestant-inflected—understanding of religion, centered on the concept of 'faith'.

Approaches of this kind are expressions of a *theory of religion* rather than of a *theology of religions*. They revolve around the *theoretical, philosophical,* or *ethical* underpinning of religion, but not around the theological content. They merely unfold the principle of freedom of religion as freedom of faith or of conscience. They cannot even be said to work on the basis of a 'hermeneutic of difference' since there can be no differences on display if the Christian faith is not placed into a substantive relationship to other religions. The religious traditions and the different individual religious attitudes are left to stand side by side.

Yet the self-conceptions of theistic religions are not related to 'religion' but to the reality of God and to the reality of both humanity and the world in the light of God's revelation. This is also true for the Christian faith: it does not want to speak about itself or about Christianity as a religion, but to give voice to the significance of Jesus Christ for the relationship of humankind with God. In doing so, however, it faces the challenge of having to relate its content to relationships with God that are not mediated by Jesus Christ. The confrontation with this challenge no longer takes place only on the margins of religious thought, but in its midst. It has become an integral part of theological reflection in the present, religiously plural age. One's relationship with transcendent, divine reality can only be established in the awareness that there also exist references which orientate themselves differently. That raises questions about the self-evident validity of one's own faith.

To answer this questioning simply by allowing this variety to stand (according to the motto 'others just believe differently') is unsatisfactory because it avoids all arguments about content. It leaves open the question of what this different faith means for the relationships of others with God, as well as for our own. Dealing with this question, however, involves religious thinking in continuous processes of negotiation and leads to constant transformations of one's own understanding of faith.

Interreligiosity has become an integral part of one's own religiosity. So, too, must the Christian faith make the revelatory and salvific significance of Jesus Christ explicit in the face of religious history and contemporary religious plurality. This is a question that arises not only through interreligious communication in the external relations of the Christian faith community but is also pervasive within it.

A merely formal classification of different forms of religion cannot provide the foundations of a basic attitude of interreligious appreciation. A hermeneutical, theoretical pluralism of faith perspectives at best leads to the demand to accept other religious loyalties as given. If the attitude of appreciation toward the sources and streams of tradition of other religions cannot be justified from the central contents of the Christian faith, it remains an external imposition which we cannot expect the faith community to accept.

The justification of an attitude of interreligious appreciation requires a substantive argument, which is primarily concerned with Christology. It is necessary to ask about the contents of the Christian faith which make it possible to put the normative sources and the central contents of other religions in a fundamentally positive relationship to God—as Godself has made known in Jesus Christ according to Christian understanding.

Questions arise about the understanding of revelation, the mediation of salvation, and the person and meaning of Jesus Christ. The *content* of the hermeneutical circle is up for debate. However, every attempt to determine this content also transforms it.

2.3 The Person and Mission of Jesus Christ

Is it even possible to justify a fundamental theological appreciation of other religious traditions and communities—one which stems from the center of the Christian faith? The question at stake is this: How are the individual non-Christians and the non-Christian religions to be related to the Christian belief that God's universal and unconditional self-communication is personified in Jesus Christ?

The decisive point for the theology of religions in understanding the *person* of Jesus Christ concerns the affirmation of his divinity; the decisive point for understanding the *work* of Jesus Christ is his unique function as mediator to God. The stronger the emphasis on the person of Jesus Christ's unity with

God, and the bolder the assertion of God's revelation and mediation of salvation being singularly accomplished in the 'Christ-event', the more theologically irrelevant we must declare other religions' revelations. On the other hand, if we assume that God's actions of revelation and salvation have or could also have taken place through them, in whatever way that might be, then they *do* become relevant. If we exclude even *this possibility*, then they can at best be engaged as part of religious studies, rather than theologically, excepting only through an apologetic engagement.

To put it another way, the more exclusively the constitution and mediation of God's grace is tied to the person of Jesus Christ and to the Christian faith, the less room there is for theologically founded appreciation of other religions to develop. There is greater leeway, however, if a distinction is made between the *person* of Jesus and the *mission* of Jesus. The *missio Dei* is the 'Christ-content', the 'cause' that Jesus proclaimed and practiced as the Christ, for which he went to his death and which was vindicated by God after his death.[9] Jesus made the 'cause of God' his own cause, and it permeated him so completely that it determined his whole person. He was so committed to the *missio Dei* that he could be experienced and understood as its personification.

'Person' according to the literal sense of 'per-sonare'—means 'to sound through'. Through the person of Jesus, the Word of God 'resounds'. God's will to be in covenant with humankind communicates itself *through* the person of Jesus Christ. The *acoustic* metaphor used in 'sounding' can also have an *optical* translation or connotation. Then it means: in him the essence of God appears, he is the image of God and the form of true humanity. This, in turn, can be linked to *functional* expressions: he is on God's mission, practicing God's will for the community, exerting a salutary influence over humanity's basic relationships (especially with God), etc. As I will show below, the concept of representation offers room for these and other fields of metaphor.

Jesus' 'cause' is the subject of soteriology. It can be defined in different ways and called different things; in the representational Christology developed here it refers not only to Jesus' speech and action but also to the salvific presence of God made present in him in his whole being. Accordingly, the 'Gospel' consists of the 'good news' of the universality and unconditionality of God's salvific will and actions.

But if this *will* is *un*conditional, it cannot be dependent on a historical event like the death of Jesus on the cross. Then this event would be the condition of it. God's salvific will would be *constituted* by it. God's will for salvation,

---

9 The expression "Jesus' cause" goes back to Marxsen, *Die Auferstehung*, 25; *id.*, *Die Sache Jesu geht weiter*.

however, is unconditional because it is rooted in the *essence* of God, i.e., in God's self-identification in terms of grace.

If God's salvific *actions* are unconditional, they cannot depend on any condition for human beings to fulfil, whether actively or passively, such as on a particular (external) religious affiliation or an (internal) religious attitude.

If God's salvific will and actions are both *universal*, then they must also include those who have not been or will not be reached by God's self-communication in Christ, for example because they lived before Jesus was born or because the proclamation of Christ did not reach them.

God's will for salvation becomes effective through God's presence in the world. This is expressed in the biblical tradition and in theology in a variety of differently inflected perspectives and phrases, for example, in the language of 'revelation', 'incarnation', 'indwelling', 'presence of the spirit', etc. All of these are based on *kenosis* (κένωσις, the *emptying* of God), whereby God makes Godself present to the Other. That presence must also touch the historical realities of non-Christian religions.

The possibility of God making himself salvifically present in these religions can be thought of either as the hidden presence of Christ in the whole cosmos (the 'cosmic Christ'), which is not recognized as such by their followers, or as an indication that God can also have a salvific relationship with people *extra Christum*. It is the second of these options which the present Christological approach takes up: it refrains from trying to develop a theology that goes beyond the self-understanding of people of other faiths. Their self-understanding, their individuality and otherness, are to be respected as far as possible.

The salvific presence of God is given priority over the personification of this presence in the person of Jesus. For it is prior to this person and can also occur where the person is not known and recognized as the bearer of this revelation. If the 'Christ-content' represented in the 'Christ-event' consists in God's presence embodied in Jesus, and if the 'Christ revelation' consists in the message that God wants the salvation of all people and that this salvation is not linked to religious preconditions, then it can and must be assumed that God lets the light of his self-communication shine beyond the historical influence of the Christian message and thus beyond the Christian tradition. *Jesus Christ is the decisive, but not the exhaustive, representation of the 'Word of God'.* He is the Logos of God in person, the manifestation of the infinite saving presence of God in a finite form that is rooted in its cultural and religious context. It is fully sufficient for a salvific relationship with God. But there might also be salvific relationships with God that are not mediated by him.

Jesus' 'cause', the realization of which constitutes his dignity as Christ, does not consist in the proclamation of his own divinity, but in the representation of the unconditional and universal grace of God. Therein lies the transtemporal core of the Gospel, as is also expressed in the message of justification: in the good news of God's near presence, of God's unconditional and unrestricted (and thus necessarily trans-religious) devotion to humanity. This 'Christ-content' became manifest in the way in which Jesus transcended social, ethnic, and religious boundaries and even singled out Gentiles—the Roman centurion of Capernaum (Mt. 8:5–13), the Syro-Phoenician woman (Mt. 15:21–28), or the Samaritan woman at the well (Jn. 4:1–45)—as models of faith in God. At the center of Jesus' mission was the proclamation and practice of this boundary-breaking, unconditional, and universal devotion of God.

The decision taken at the Apostles' Council (Acts 15:1–29; Gal. 2) to carry the Christian faith beyond Judaism to all nations is a consequence of this universality and unconditionality. This provided the basic impulse through which Christianity could become a universal or 'world' religion.

To declare faith in Christ to be the only way to participate in God's presence of salvation, and the only way to be assured of this participation, is in tension with the basic conviction of the Christian faith—that God's devotion is unconditional and universal, and that it applies to all people of all times, without them having to do religious works or show a particular religious affiliation.

A soteriological Christomonism proves to be a contradiction in terms for Christological reasons because it truncates or even denies the decisive dimension of the meaning of salvation in Jesus Christ—the proclamation and embodiment of God's unconditional and universal will of salvation. But if this interpretation of salvation extends beyond his person and work, then it opens up the possibility of relating the sources and streams of other religious traditions to the Christian faith—and, in principle, of doing so positively.

To summarize: the distinction between the person and the 'cause' of Jesus plays a central role in theologically justifying the appreciation of non-Christian religions. The more one emphasizes that Jesus' 'cause' cannot be distinguished from the person because it exists in this person himself, and the more one emphasizes the divinity of this person and reinforces it with claims of exclusivity, the narrower the available space becomes for a theologically justified appreciation for those relationships with God taught and practiced by other religions (including Judaism). However, the New Testament traditions testify that Jesus himself distinguished his person from God as the one in whose name and authority he spoke and acted.[10] That is what makes him the Christ:

---

10   See Chapter 4.2.2.

that dignity consists in the suffusing of the person of Jesus Christ with the presence of God and in his mission anchored therein.

2.4 Particularity and Universality

Christology stands in the tension between universality and particularity. This tension is already inherent in the 'Christ-event', which is simultaneously a historical and a theological one. As a concrete historical event, it is integrated into its contemporary historical context. As an event of God's self-communication, it is accorded a soteriological relevance that transcends time, even though Jesus knew himself to be sent only to the people of Israel (Mt. 15:24). Jesus Christ is the *'universale concretum'* (Hans Urs von Balthasar) who reveals the universal dimension of God's soteriological activity in a concrete historical way. Both of these—the universal significance and the historical concreteness—belong together. The Christian faith sees in the person and mission of Jesus the event of God's transhistorical presence of salvation and ascribes universal significance to this participatory event. The righteousness of God given in it benefits all people—as justification (in the theological sense of the term). The entire project of Christian mission is rooted in this awareness of universality.

The tension between universality and particularity also exists in the reaffirmation of the 'Christ-event' in the history of the Christian faith. All forms of faith are historically particular; that is, they are phenomena of the history of religion. But they express the consciousness of being anchored in the transhistorical ground of all existence.

Indeed, the entire field of theology of religions revolves around the tension between these two poles: the supposition of the unconditionality and universality of salvation and the proclamation that this salvation is given in the historically *particular* person of Jesus Christ. Depending on whether this tension has been resolved on one side or the other, the result has been either a soteriological universalism or a Christocentric (or even ecclesiocentric) particularization of the salvific relationship with God.

2.4.1 *From Particularity to Particularism*
Where the emphasis on the historically particular salvation event develops into to a *particularism* that is combined with an *exclusivism*, the following applies: only through faith in Christ can there be a salvific relationship with God. As Calvin puts it:

We see that our whole salvation and all its parts are comprehended in Christ (Acts 4:12). We should therefore take care not to derive the least portion of it from anywhere else. [...] Those who, not satisfied with him alone, [...] deviate from the right path.[11]

In baptism, humans are 'ordained' into this relationship, and it is cultivated further in the Church. This has led to the view that both baptism and belonging to the Church (according to pre-conciliar Catholic understanding[12] and Calvin's own opinion[13]) are necessary for salvation. If it is true that a saving relationship with God is possible only through a believing participation in the 'Christ-event', that this faith must be grasped in a reflexive way, be articulated in an explicit profession of faith, and be sealed by baptism, then only believing and baptized Christians can be in a saving relationship with God. If it is further assumed that baptism constitutes initiation into the community of believers, and that this community is manifested in the Christian religion, then the salvific community of God is in fact bound to Christianity as a religion. But can it be that saving relationships with God exist only in *one* strand of the history of religion, which, moreover, began only about 2000 years ago, meaning that both people who lived before that and those who live outside this particular historical strand would be excluded from it?

If God grants divine grace completely or on a preferential basis to people who lived *after* Christ and in the sphere of influence of Christ's proclamation, then we must conclude that that grace or at least its allocation is not universal and unconditional. The question of theodicy then arises as an interrogation of God's justice, not only in the face of innocent suffering in the world, but also from a theology-of-religions perspective as a question of 'soteriological equality of opportunity'.

A specifically Reformed version of particularism consists in the doctrine of (double) predestination, according to which God wants not so much the salvation of *all* as the salvation only of the chosen.[14] Thus, the basic problem of the

---

11 Calvin, *Institutes* II, 16,19, pp. 527–8.
12 Fourth Council of the Lateran (DH 802); Papal bull "Unam Sanctam" (DH 875); Council of Florence (DH 1351).
13 In *Institutes* IV (1,1), Calvin adopts as his own the words of Cyprian: "He who does not have the church as his mother can no longer have God as his father" (Cyprian of Carthage, *On the Unity of the Catholic Church* [BKV 34/1] § 6; similar wording in ep.74,7 [BKV 60]).
14 The starting point for this can be found in Calvin, *Institutes* III, 24,6. Theodor Beza sharpened the argument by shifting this doctrine from soteriology to the doctrine of providence and starting *a posteriori* with the effects of election or non-election rather than *a priori* with the eternal decree.

theology of religions—mediation between the particularity of the presence of salvation in Christ and the universality of God's will and act of salvation—no longer arises since the latter is denied. This doctrine intends to preserve God's sovereignty or freedom and to exclude any human contribution to salvation. In his sovereignty it is therefore quite possible for God to raise up children for Abraham even from stones (Mt. 3:9). God's righteousness, which takes place in the free choice of grace, goes beyond human ideas of justice and is ultimately not transparent (Rm. 9:1ff.).

This reduces the universality of God's grace to a mere option that can be claimed arbitrarily by God. This is opposed by the biblical statements that testify to God's *general* will to save as a trait of God's nature (such as 1 Tim. 2:4).

2.4.2 From Universality to Universalism

On the other hand, a one-sided emphasis on *universality* can lead to a 'global theology', i.e., to a trans-religious globalization in which relationship to Christ is declared contingent. Pluralism, from the perspective of the theology of religions, assumes that there is a plurality of authentic and, in principle, equally valid salvific relationships to the divine ground of being. It can also—or in connection with a pluralistic approach—present itself as a mystical spirituality that seeks to renounce all historical mediations and leave all religious traditions behind in order to strive for a direct relationship with God. But if, along with the historical dimension, the concrete humanity of Jesus Christ recedes too far (including his being a Jew in a certain context at a certain time), then Christology loses its historical grounding. Turning to the exalted Christ or to the unhistorical mystery of Christ then pushes back against the rootedness of the Christian faith in Old Testament Israel and thus also the Jewish context of the message of Christ. If, however, the message of Christ is not to be gnostically spiritualized, then it needs to be connected back to the historically particular, i.e., to the human Jesus in his particular historical context.

If there is an overemphasis on the historically particular, however, then not only the universality but also the relevance of the message of Christ that transcends both time and context can be called into question. This then becomes factually bound to a certain strand of religious history—to the history of the proclamation of the Christian faith beginning in biblical Israel and thus also to the Christian religion.

In contrast, the universality of the message of Christ must be maintained: the Logos of God is God's universal 'Word' of creation and salvation. Jesus was so committed to this 'Word' that his followers recognized in him the human expression of this Logos. In the particularity of his life and work, the proclamation of this universal 'Word' occurs as a consolidation of the powerful presence of God. This presence reaches beyond the historical sphere of adherence to Jesus Christ and manifests itself also outside this sphere.

2.4.3 Escape Clauses

Wherever attempts have been made in the history of theology to mediate between the twin poles of particularity and universality, rather than to resolve the polarity in one side's favour, the suggestion has arisen of inserting escape clauses into the particularity pole, typically by invoking the freedom of God's work of grace, with the goal of universalizing it to some extent. The following strategies have attempted this:

(a) By *universalizing the understanding of the community of faith (Church)*. This approach emphasizes the difference between the potentially universal spiritual community of believers (Church in the spiritual sense) and the empirically constituted and thus factually always particular religious community (Church in the institutional sense). This approach emphasizes that belonging to the Body of Christ can go beyond belonging to the institutional Church and can also occur through the gracious work of the Holy Spirit.

Approaches to a universal understanding of the church can already be found in the writings of Church Fathers such as Justin, Irenaeus, Origen, and Augustine, according to whom the Church does not begin with Christ and the apostles or at Pentecost, but rather as early as the creation (*ecclesia ab initio* or *ab Abel*). All those human beings who are regarded as righteous are incorporated into that spiritual body of Christ. Among the Reformers, Ulrich Zwingli particularly emphasized the invisibility—and thus potential universality—of the Church; he considered that Greek poets and philosophers could also belong to it.[15] More recently, Paul Tillich has notably unfolded an understanding of the Church as a universal community of spirit.[16]

The Second Vatican Council, while continuing to assert that one's salvation depends on one belonging to the church,[17] adopted a graduated notion of church membership, so that even people who are not members and do not know about the significance of the Church can be understood as being a part of it.[18]

---

15 In his "Fidei Christianae Expositio" (1531), Zwingli wrote: "There has never been a good human, there will never be a holy soul, there is no believing soul, since the creation of the world until its fall, that you will not see here [in heaven, R. B.] together with God" (*Collected Works* VI/5, CR 93, 132).
16 Cf. Paul Tillich's reflections on the "community of the spirit": *Systematic Theology*, Vol. 3, 149–244.
17 The Holy See, *Lumen gentium* 14a; *Ad gentes* 7a.
18 Especially in *The Holy See, Lumen gentium* 15f.

(b) By *universalizing the understanding of faith*. According to this argumentation, the relationship to Christ or the relationship to God mediated in Christ does not necessarily have to be grasped in a *conscious* faith and articulated in an *explicit* creed. It can also be realized in a way that is implicit, anonymous, latent, prospective, or preconscious. Accordingly, people who lived temporally *before* Christ, or who lived after Christ but whom the proclamation of the gospel did not reach, can nonetheless have a relationship with Christ.

Following this argument, it is possible on the one hand to maintain that Christ is the one and only mediator to God, and on the other hand to assume that all people—regardless of their religious affiliation—can participate in his mediation of salvation. Therefore, they have a relationship to Christ without having explicit faith in Christ.

Wolfhart Pannenberg goes even further and identifies yet another way in which a salvific relationship with God can be possible without explicit and even latent faith in Christ—notably in a situation in which a person *acts* in conformity with the proclamation of Jesus:

> It is true enough that the event of a personal encounter with Jesus through the Christian message and a response of faith to it cannot be the universal criterion for participation in salvation or exclusion from it if we take seriously what the NT says about the love of God for the world that embraces all people. Many have never been reached by the proclamation of the gospel. For them the fact of personal encounter with Jesus through the church's preaching, which depends on contingent and historical factors, cannot be decisive for eternal salvation. In their case what counts is whether their individual conduct actually agrees with the will of God that Jesus proclaimed. The message of Jesus is the norm by which God judges even in the case of those who never meet Jesus personally.[19]

As biblical evidence for this, one can point not only—as Pannenberg does—to the parable of the Last Judgment in Mt. 25 and to the Beatitudes (Mt. 5:3ff.; Lk. 6:20ff.), but also to Mt. 7:21 and to Mk. 12:18–34. In the latter pericope, Jesus tells the Jewish scribe who confesses one God (but not Jesus) that he is not far from the kingdom of God.

(c) By *universalizing the understanding of Christ*. The universalization of the understanding of Christ took place mostly in light of the Logos theology of John's Gospel and the Colossian hymn. Characteristic of this universal

---

19   Pannenberg, *Systematic Theology*, Vol. 3, 615.

Christology is the idea of the pre-existence of the Logos and the exaltation of Jesus to the Pantocrator Christ. The Johannine Christ is the eternal, incarnate 'Creator-Word', creatively and re-creatively (reconcilingly, salvifically) active from the beginning through all times in history. It is the light that enlightens all people (Jn. 1:9). Nothing, and no one, remains excluded from it except through their own fault.

The line of argumentation starting from here and running through the history of theology led to the idea of the 'cosmic Christ', which became fruitful for the determination of relations with non-Western Christianities and non-Christian religions, for example, at the Third Assembly of the WCC in New Delhi in 1961.[20] John Macquarrie echoes this line of reasoning:

> It is surely not impossible for a believer to profess Christ wholeheartedly and exclusively and yet at the same time have sufficient openness to the fact that the truth of God is to be found in non-Christian religions as well. Yes, such a conclusion is almost compelling if one admits that Christ is the eternal Logos through whom all things are created and who therefore manifests Himself in some way and to some degree in all things. The believer may then even be willing to admit that followers of another faith see some aspects of God's truth more clearly than he does, and then he may also be willing to engage in a dialogue that can help both him and the follower of the other faith to penetrate more deeply to the truth.[21]

In terms of theological anthropology, the postulated universality of Jesus Christ corresponds to the notion that every human as a creature of God is already oriented toward Christ. Justin developed the doctrine of the 'seeds of divine truth' implanted in all human souls. He concluded that Christ dwells within *every* human:[22] "in Christ, the firstborn of God, *the whole human race has a share*".[23] Tertullian spoke of the "witness of the soul, in its very nature Christian!".[24] In twentieth-century Catholic theology, the representatives of 'Nouvelle Théologie', the pioneers of the Second Vatican Council, and Karl Rahner were able to build on this anthropological anchoring of faith in God

---

20   In the context of Indian intellectual culture, the program of a "cosmic Christology" was proclaimed at the WCC's Third Assembly in New Delhi in 1961, drawing primarily on the Epistles to the Ephesians and Colossians. See Lüpsen, ed., *Neu Delhi Dokumente.*, especially the speeches of Paul Devanandan ("Called to Witness") and Joseph Sittler ("Called to Unity").
21   Macquarrie, "Jesus Christus, VII. *Dogmatic*", 60.
22   Justin Martyr, *The Second Apology*, 10 (emphasis mine).
23   Justin Martyr, *The First Apology*, 46 (emphasis mine).
24   "testimonium animae naturaliter christianae" *Apology*, 17, 6, pp. 88–89.

and Christ. Rahner unfolded the doctrine of a 'supernatural existential' that is inherent in the nature of the human.[25]

(d) By *universalizing the understanding of revelation*. The New Testament speaks of God's revelation in the works of creation (Rom. 1:18–20) and writing the (moral) law on the heart of all humans (Rom. 2:14f.), of not leaving Godself without witness even to the nations (Acts 14:15–17), and of not being distant even from the non-Jewish and non-Christian Greeks, so that indeed they belong to his race (Acts 17:27ff.). Taken together, such passages have led to the idea of a *revelatio generalis*, a general revelation of God to all people. Compared to the biblically attested revelation of God in Christ, however, this was regarded as deficient: as a revelation of God's existence and will, but not of God's very being, as a revelation of the law, but not of the Gospel, as a revelation that reveals human sinfulness, but not God's justifying grace; and as a revelation that is limited to man's *knowledge* of God and himself, but does not convey a message of salvation. At best, it prepares a person to receive this message, but it is soteriologically ineffective in itself.

But at least the universalized understanding of revelation could lead to an inclusivism which in principle grants all humans, as God's creatures, the possibility of a knowledge of God, however rudimentary. On this basis, the Old Testament tradition and pre-Christian philosophies could be understood as preliminary stages in the history of revelation, as *'praeparatio Evangelii'* (Eusebius of Caesarea[26]), which can prepare for the reception of the Gospel. In the Second Vatican Council, this approach was extended beyond individual non-Christians to non-Christian religions. The proclamation of the Gospel can take up the general revelation and lead it to the special revelation in Christ as its end and completion. The mediation of a salvific relationship with God remains bound to Christ and faith in Christ, but the knowledge of God reaches beyond that.

The attempts outlined above mediate between the historically particular and limited occurrences of the 'Christ-event' and Christian faith on the one hand and the universality of God's saving will and actions on the other. They position:
- the institutional Church in the context of a spiritual community of Christ encompassing humanity;
- explicit Christian faith and confession of Christ in the context of a theological anthropology, whose starting point is a universal human orientation toward God's self-communication in Christ;

---

25 See Bernhardt, *Klassiker*, 219–57.
26 Eusebius of Caesarea, *Praeparatio Evangelica*.

- Jesus of Nazareth as the historical origin of the Christian community of followers in the context of the cosmic Christ who is present in all of history and thus also in all of religious history;
- the revelation of Christ in the context of a universal revelation of God (*revelatio generalis et continua*).

2.4.4 *Christocentric Universalism*

The various attempts made to widen or universalize the significance of the 'Christ-event' described in chapter 2.4.3 can be summarized by the key phrase 'Christocentric universalism'. When applied to other religions, this position usually leads to one tracing the relationships with God developed there back to Christ or relating them to him, e.g., by assuming that he is at work there *incognito*—in an unrecognized way.

One can and must ask about the theological persuasiveness of the above concepts of Christocentric universalism. Each one distinguishes between proper and improper relationships with God—the latter set up as an exceptional decree founded on grace—and then makes contrived distinctions between these categories. This smacks of an ideological construction that serves the purpose of establishing the superiority of one's own relationship with the divine. But because a spiritual relationship with God only ever exists in the 'flesh' of a religion, the spiritual claim to superiority is followed by the religious one.

Aside from this criticism, one can also object that Christocentric universalist approaches either ignore or eclipse the self-understanding of non-Christian religious traditions. This leads to theological appropriations of these religions and of their followers. They can be positively appreciated—as 'anonymous Christians', for example—but they always remain deficient compared to those who participate in the revelation and transmission of salvation in the full and real sense. Such an interpretation is in tension with a fundamental demand not only of dialogic relations between religions, but also of proper scholarly work within the field of theology of religions: the demand to take the religious Other seriously in their self-understanding, to perceive their religion in its uniqueness, and *on that basis* to relate it to the Christian faith.

A *hermeneutic* inclusivism can certainly not be avoided in the way in which one's relationship to other religions is defined; every attempt to see the religious Other in the light of one's own faith will involve a kind of appropriation. Examples might include a Christian also seeing a Muslim—against their self-understanding—as a human, created in the image of God, or a Mahāyāna Buddhist seeing a Christian as permeated with Buddha's nature. There is nothing problematic about this—so long as it happens with the awareness that it is a matter of 'seeing' in a certain religious perspective; so long as the Other is also granted the same right, i.e., a plurality of justified perspectives is allowed; and, above all, so long as the intent is to appreciate the Other and not to devalue the Other's religious attitude in principle.

The problem only begins when there is a loss of perspectivity and when hermeneutic inclusivism develops into religious inclusivism. This shifts the appropriation of the Other and his or her religion from the level of cognition and understanding to the level of being. The other religion is thus inevitably fundamentally devalued. Its center of identity is subordinated to that of one's own religion or displaced by it.

Interreligious appreciation consists in renouncing not only an religious *exclusivism*, which *a priori* does not allow such an appreciation, but also in a renunciation of a religious *inclusivism*, which makes sweeping claims of superiority over other faiths. On the one hand, the universal claim connected with the Christian faith suggests a view of the history of salvation that also extends over the entire history of religion and thus places non-Christian religions in this perspective. On the other hand, it is important to include the self-understanding of other religious communities and traditions as far as possible in debates about the self-understanding of the Christian faith, i.e., to welcome non-Christian voices as guest speakers in matters of Christian theology and to develop these dialogically. This requires a step beyond Christocentric universalism.

The reflections presented in this book start from the assumption that the particular realization of God's salvific presence in Christ is the representation of God's universal and unconditional salvific will and action, goodness and justice. This historical representation points to a divine reality that precedes it and is authentically revealed in it. But in its revelation, this divine reality also retains its freedom to be represented outside of Jesus Christ, so that God's wider presences in non-Christian religions do not come up in the proclamation of Christ, are not grasped in the Christian faith, and are not communicated in the church.

From a soteriological aspect—in terms of participation in the saving presence of God—I can also describe the basic idea of this book as follows: Faith in Christ and membership in the Christian Church are not *necessary* conditions for this participation. There can also be other ways of being assured of God's saving presence. What is more, there is ultimately *no* condition that human beings are to fulfil which grants them this participation. It happens *sola gratia*.

This position, however, does not lead to a pluralistic theology of religions. It does not postulate the *existence* of specific authentic mediations of salvation outside the presence of God in Christ but wants only to show the *possibility* of it. Therefore, it cannot (and does not seek to) determine the values of the 'ways of salvation' taught by the religions, nor does it assert an equivalence between them—as do representatives of the pluralistic theology of religions. The assumption that the creatively and salvifically effective presence of God exceeds the manifestation of this presence that is decisive for the Christian faith does not in any way intrinsically or automatically lead to the consequence that communion with God is accessible in several equivalent revelations and mediators.

2.5 The Theology of Israel as a Precedent

Over the course of the profound revisions to the theology of Israel since the 1960s, it has been conceded, whether explicitly or implicitly, that there can be a fully valid communion with God by way of the Torah … without faith in Christ. It follows that there is no need for Jews to turn to Christ, and thus also no need for a Christian mission with such a goal in mind.

The Pontifical Council (now: Dicastery) for Promoting Christian Unity, which is also responsible for the Roman Catholic Church's relations with Judaism, states:

> that the Jews are participants in God's salvation is theologically unquestionable, but how that can be possible without confessing Christ explicitly, is and remains an unfathomable divine mystery.[27]

On November 9, 2016, the Synod of the Protestant Church in Germany stated, "Christians—regardless of their mission to the world—are not called to show Israel the way to God and his salvation".[28] It is left unsaid how this programmatic renunciation of the 'mission to the Jews' relates to the unquestioned conviction that the way to God and his salvation is through Christ alone: "the fact that Jews do not share this confession [of Jesus Christ as Messiah of Israel and Savior of the world], we leave up to God".[29]

The renunciation of Christian mission among Jews can be justified theologically only by the assumption that Jews are in covenant with God even without faith in, and confession of, Christ. If the continuing covenant with Israel does not require fulfillment through Christ, if it is rather regarded as theologically

---

27 Pontifical Council for Promoting Christian Unity / Commission for Religious Relations with the Jews: "The Gifts", 31.
28 Protestant Church in Germany. Proclamation of the 12th Synod.
29 *Ibid.*

THE PROBLEM: CHRISTOLOGY AND THE THEOLOGY OF RELIGIONS

and soteriologically sufficient, then Christian mission among Jews is indeed unnecessary. This does not rule out mutual witnessing, but it does rule out any attempt to persuade Jews to convert.

The well-known words of Franz Rosenzweig, as he expressed them in a letter to Rudolf Ehrenberg with reference to Jn. 14:6, apply here:

> what Christ and his church mean in the world, we agree on—no one comes to the Father except through him. No one *comes* to the Father— but it is different when one no longer needs to come to the Father because one is already with him. And this is now the case of the people of Israel.[30]

According to this, Jesus is not the Christ of the Jews; the goal of their election is not to enter into the covenant of Christ. Martin Buber shared this view. It can also be found in the National Jewish Scholars Project's 'Jewish Statement on Christians and Christianity', published in the USA in 2000 under the title 'Dabru emet' ('Speak Truth') and written by more than 200 Jewish scholars and rabbis. It states, "Christians know and serve God through Jesus Christ and the Christian tradition. Jews know and serve God through Torah and the Jewish tradition".[31]

The representatives of a two-covenant theory in the theological relationship between Judaism and Christianity, or Israel and the church, assume *de jure* or *de facto* that God's salvific presence has opened up and continues to be opened up in Christ; and, in addition, that this presence becomes a reality by following the path of the Torah and that it even goes beyond this. This assumption applies all the more to those who assume that God is also connected with other 'peoples' or religious communities within the framework of the Abrahamic covenant and the universal covenant with Noah.

Klaus Wengst expresses this view particularly clearly when writes:

> what we gain through Jesus Christ in trust in God, experience in forgiveness of sins, mercy and justification, Judaism knows and experiences in the past and present even without Jesus.[32]

According to Wengst, Jesus is the Messiah only for the nations. This position is quite in keeping with the theological view of Judaism that Paul unfolds in

---

30   Translated from Letter dated 1. Nov. 1913, cited in Franz Rosenzweig. *Der Mensch und sein Werk*, 134ff.
31   National Jewish Scholars Project, Dabru emet. See also Frankemölle, ed., *Juden und Christen*.
32   Translated from Wengst, *Jesus*, 135.

Rom. 9–11. The apostle to the nations assumes that Jews and Christians walk on parallel paths toward God's salvation. This is due to God's grace, which allows the Jews, in view of their refusal to confess Christ, to continue their way without Christ. Only at the Parousia will the paths merge. But then Christ will also submit to God and hand over his dominion to Godself (1 Cor. 15:28), at which point there can be no more salvation 'in Christ', but only in God. According to Erwin Dirscherl, in Rom. 9–11 Paul advances more and more clearly 'from Christocentrism to Patrocentrism' and emphasizes the will of the Father as the ultimate reason for the salvation of all of Israel.[33]

The theological basis for the recent revision of Christian theological attitudes towards Israel was the conviction, derived from Rom. 9:6a, 11:1f. and 11:29, that the Sinai covenant with the people of Israel has not become invalid, but rather has been renewed and extended by the Christ covenant.

The revision of the definition of Christianity's theological relationship to Judaism was possible not least through recourse to the Hebrew concept of truth (אמת/emet), according to which truth is to be understood as faithfulness or as the reliability of God's promise. But since God stands by and does not abandon promises and covenants, does this appeal to God's faithfulness apply only to the Sinai covenant? Does it not also apply to earlier examples, such as the Noahic covenant with all creation and the Abrahamic covenant, which includes Hagar and Ishmael?[34] According to the testimony of the Qu'ran, Ishmael is among the series of prophets which leads to Muhammad (Q. 21:85–86). But if the relation of the Sinai covenant to the Christ covenant—the former being not replaced by the latter but renewed by it—is also true of covenants *before* Sinai, then those, too, remain valid. This raises the question of whether there cannot also be a genuine people of God beyond Judaism without faith in Christ, and of how this wider people of God relates to Christ.

In addition to this *theological* reflection, it is also important to look at this matter from the perspective of the *history of religion*. As much as the Christian faith is historically and theologically rooted in biblical Israel, it is also true that post-biblical rabbinic Judaism, which followed the Talmud, is not a *pre-*Christian religion but a religion *alongside* Christianity. It does not stand in unbroken continuity with the biblical people of Israel but reconstituted itself after the destruction of the temple in 70 AD in the process of the 'parting of the ways'[35]—a process of self-definition over against Christianity—and

---

33 Translated from Dirscherl, *Die Herausforderung*, 225.
34 See Naumann, *Ismael*.
35 Dunn, *The Parting of the Ways*; id., ed., *Jews and Christians*. That interpretation, however, became disputed, giving rise to critical discussions about it. See Becker and Reed, eds. *The Ways that Never Parted*.

therefore one can speak of a "birth of Judaism out of the spirit of Christianity".[36] Talmudic Judaism has developed into a religion of its own, clearly distinct from Christianity, and therefore it is problematic to speak of a continuous 'Jewish-Christian tradition'. Jews not infrequently see this as an appropriation, and consequently distance themselves from Christianity, emphasize the independence of their religion, and demand that Christians respect this difference. Christianity should not be seen as an extension of Judaism.[37] But if Judaism as we know it today cannot be considered a *pre*-Christian religion, but must be seen as a sister religion *alongside* Christianity; if inclusion of the Jewish into the Christian tradition is renounced; if instead it is conceded that God's covenant with the Jews is sufficient in itself and does not need to be supplemented or fulfilled; if one holds that there is a fully valid Jewish reading of the Hebrew Bible alongside the Christian one; then the *solus Christus* and also the '*sola fide*' are set aside, at least for Jews. Jews are a chosen people of God, but a people not founded by Christ and not mediated by faith in Christ. This has consequences for Christology.

However, the task thus defined cannot be limited to the relationship with Judaism when it comes to the question of the *universal* significance of Christ. For even as early as the Old Testament tradition, the promise of salvation applies not only to the chosen people, but also to other peoples. Isaiah 19:25 refers to Israel as God's 'inheritance', Egypt as the 'people of God', and Assyria as 'the work of my hands'. According to Amos 9:7, the Philistines and the Arameans are also mentioned as peoples to whom God's liberating action applies. Deutero-Isaiah in particular emphasizes the extension of the promise of salvation to the peoples (Isa 45: 22f.; 51: 4ff. and more) using words like 'saving' and 'healing'.

The Hebrew verb yāša' (ישע) and its derivatives found in 353 places in the Old Testament denote God's salvific action. The word's basic meaning is 'to give space' or 'to remove restrictions'.[38] Here, 'salvation' is understood in a broad sense that goes beyond the spiritual dimension and extends to all dimensions of life. The promise of salvation aims at conditions of life in which freedom, peace, and justice prevail. In contrast to the later apocalyptic interpretation, this does not mean the eschatological overcoming of creaturely reality, but its continuously renewed transformations in this world towards conditions that are conducive to the unfolding of life. It is not about the *end* of time, but about the *turn* of times towards the consummation of creation. In this broad sense, eschatologies focused on the present ('realized eschatologies') and those

---

36 Translated from Schäfer, *Die Geburt des Judentums*.
37 As expressed in the National Jewish Scholars Project, *Dabru emet*.
38 Liefeld, "Salvation", 288.

focused on the future are then no longer opposed to each other; they belong together, albeit as opposite poles. The same applies to the dimensions of the individual and the cosmic.

If one wants to renounce a *Christocentric* interpretation of the Old Testament promises of salvation to the nations, according to which they find their fulfillment in Christ and the Christian mission, one must see these promises not as pointing ahead toward Christ, but as independent revelations of God's universal will for salvation. From the perspective of Christian theology, therefore, we must concede the possibility that these other peoples of God can have genuine fellowship with God, a fellowship which the Christian tradition has not previously perceived.

This all comes down to the *solus Christus* concept—not, however, viewed primarily in terms of the theology of justification but in a theology-of-religions light: the question of the uniqueness, singularity, and exclusivity of Jesus Christ's mediation of salvation. Is God's saving action focused on the life, suffering, death, and 'resurrection'[39] of Jesus Christ in such a way as even to be limited to these? Or is it decisively represented in the 'Christ-event' *while also* working beyond it? If it *does* also work beyond it, is the mode in which it does so necessarily deficient? This question concerns not only—and indeed not even primarily—the theology of Israel, nor only the theology of religions more generally, but Christology and soteriology in themselves, and thus ultimately the understanding of God.

Without obscuring the specificity of the theological definition of Christianity's relations with Judaism, the revisions made there can be fruitfully applied to the theology of religions at large. We need to work out the specifics of God's making Godself present in Jesus Christ, without simultaneously understanding this determination of the center as a drawing of boundaries which leaves no room for other modes of God's self-communication or declares them to be deficient. The revelation of God in Christ does not consist in something completely new, but in the renewal and intensification of the promise that God's salvific will to relate to human beings overrides everything that separates them from God and is thus revealed in the fullness of its universality and unconditionality.

---

39 I put the term 'resurrection' in inverted commas to indicate not a purely historical but rather a theological event of entering into an eternal relationship to God. It is described in analogy to being woken up, to standing up, becoming newly born etc. The latin *resurgo* means to rise again, be restored, be rebuilt, be revived.

CHAPTER 3

The Agenda: 'Representation' as the Key Concept of Christology

The Christological reflections I unfold in this book have to do with the concept of *representation*. This concept I first clarify in general, and then more particularly regarding its application to Jesus Christ. Does it fit into the classical structure of Christology, that is, into the distinction between the doctrine of the person and the 'ministry' (the 'work') of Jesus Christ? Or does it transform this structure? How is it expressed, and how does it interact with other semantically related concepts?

3.1 Clarification of the Term 'Representation'

In considering the history of philosophy and psychology, Eckart Scheerer draws a distinction between four different meanings of the term 'representation':

> 1) 'imagination' [*Vorstellung*] in the broader sense, i.e., mental state with cognitive content; 2) 'imagination' in the narrower sense, i.e., a mental state that reproduces, is derived from, or refers to an earlier mental state; 3) 'depiction' [*Darstellung*], i.e., structure-preserving mapping using images, symbols, and signs of all kinds; 4) and 'substitution' [*Stellvertretung*].[1]

The German terms *Vorstellung* ('imagination'), *Darstellung* ('depiction'), and *Stellvertretung* ('substitution') intersect semantically in the intra- and extramental process of positioning/placing [*stellen*]. In thought, in speech, or by means of an external medium, a reference to something or someone is established: an object is brought to mind (*Vorstellung*), an issue becomes depicted (*Darstellung*), X is *taking the place of* Y or X is *standing for/is signifying* Y (*Stellvertretung*).

---

1 Translated from Scheerer, et al., "Repräsentation", 790. See also Hofmann, *Repräsentation*; Schaede, *Stellvertretung*, 171–238.

© REINHOLD BERNHARDT, 2026 | DOI:10.1163/9789004734203_004
This is an open access chapter distributed under the terms of the CC BY-NC-ND 4.0 license.

Paul Tillich notes, "The Latin word *praesentia*, like the German word *Gegenwart*, contains a spatial image: 'A thing which stands before one'".[2] 'Prae-sens' originally meant 'to be in front of' in a spatial sense. Thus, the noun 'praesentia' means 'that which stands before/in front of one'. The temporal meaning of 'presence' is already inherently contained within it, because what is spatially before one's eyes is also temporally there. 'Representation' therefore means 'making present' in a spatio-temporal sense.

In today's usage the term's basic meaning is 'someone or something standing for another person or for something else'. It is a relation between a represented and a representing entity. This basic meaning can encompass a variety of different content in view of different spheres of reality. For our purposes, we must first prepare the term for application to Christology, while also excluding certain possible meanings. This I do in the following by highlighting various distinctions and selecting constituent elements of meaning.

An important distinction is that between mental (internal to one's consciousness), communicative (linguistic, pictorial, symbolic depictions), and personal (social) representations. This distinction is related to the 'what' (the *repraesentandum*) and the 'how' (the mode) of representation. Much of the philosophical and psychological debate around 'representation' relates to the first two categories, while personal representation tends to be the subject of jurisprudence and the social and political sciences.

If one applies the distinction between personal and non-personal representations to both the represented and to the representing entities, four possible combinations emerge:

– some*thing* (non-personal) represents some*one* (a personal entity), e.g., a coat of arms represents an aristocratic family, the name or a picture of a person represents that person;
– some*thing* represents some*thing*, e.g., in a metaphor standing for a meaning, or in a picture standing for what is depicted, or in a simulation standing for the simulated reality, or in a coin standing for a value;
– some*one* represents some*thing*, e.g., the emperor represents the state; the minister represents the ministry and takes political responsibility for the work done there;
– some*one* represents some*one*, e.g., in a guardianship, or in the theatre when a performer represents the person being portrayed.

In the case of personal representation, its implementation consists in a stand-in/proxy for a person or institution, whereby this substitute may not

---

2   Tillich, *Systematic Theology*, Vol. 1, 278, footnote 9.

only embody that which they are representing but is also authorized to act on behalf of it/them. The relationship between the represented and the representing person can be a hierarchical one, e.g., the representation of a high-ranking public official by one who is authorized by them or, in the reverse case, when the holder of an office represents those who are subordinate to them. But there are also egalitarian relations of representation between persons.

Non-personal representation, on the other hand, can only consist in the referential depiction of an actual or ideal reality lying 'behind' it. This can, however, take place in a personal-communicative context, e.g., when the meaning of a certain sign (as in the case of a traffic sign) is established by convention.

In all these cases it is true that the representation can only be understood and be valid as such in a certain frame of reference. That a coin represents a certain value is in the frame of reference of finance; that a lawyer represents their clients in court, in the frame of reference of jurisprudence; that bread represents the body of Christ, in the frame of reference of Christian faith or theology.

In contrast to such intentional representations of an entity or thing, there are also unintentional, natural representations, such as the cry that indicates pain. In these cases, the instance of the intended addressee is absent. The representation is not made to someone, as is the case with intentional representations. It occurs in a causal context and is perceived as an indicator of a physical state.

The determinations of the relationships between representing and represented entities differ accordingly. In the case of a non-personal representation, this relation may be *causal* (such as in the representation of mental states in the brain) or *analogical*, i.e., based on similarity (such as of a sign to the reality it denotes). In the case of personal representation, it is *actual*—that is, it is accomplished by an action. This may be an *implicit* representation (as in the case of a work of art representing not only what it depicts but also the artist who created it), or an *explicit* one (as in the case of a monarch or a president representing a state).

In this second case of a personal, intentional, explicit representation, the representational relation is constituted by an act of delegation of authority to the representing entity from the represented entity. This empowerment, legitimation, and transfer of rights and duties consists in the acts of appointing, calling, and commissioning. It may be based on an act of selection (such as an election or appointment based on an acquired qualification). But the worthiness to assume this function can also be derived from succession, a natural disposition, divine election, or one's own merits. In any case, even if it is a matter of representation one has claimed for oneself, legitimation is needed.

The forms of non-personal representation, as well as the entire domain of semiotic signification, have no role to play anymore in what follows. The concept of representation is used in a *personal, relational,* and *functional* sense; thereby it denotes both a particular *pattern* of relations and a relational *occurrence*. The relational pattern consists of three personal entities, which stand in relation to each other in two ways:

(a) These three entities are:
- the person who is represented (subject of the representation);
- the representative, who represents/stands in for the subject; and
- the person, community, or institution to whom the representation is made and who must recognize and acknowledge it as such.

The subject or 'principal' of the representation can be an individual person, a community of persons, or a (social, economic, political) institution. In the case of an institution, representation is usually tied to an office established for this purpose. This office is relatively independent of the person who holds it (the representative) and can also be filled by another person. The representative then represents this institution 'officially' (ex officio).

(b) The three entities are connected to each other in two ways. The representative is in relation to both the one he/she represents and to the one for whom (or towards whom) he/she performs the representation. *From* the one side the representative receives his/her authority, commission, and legitimation; *to* the other side he/she appears with it and brings it to bear. He/she is loyal and accountable to the one he/she represents. But if the authority of the subject of the representation (the authority conferred on the representative) is not recognized by the recipients of the representation, the *repraesentandum* cannot come into effect.

(c) The relational *occurrence* consists in the function that the representative performs. He/she not only represents the contracting entity (person or institution) but also carries out its will, thus acting in its name and on its mandate. This brings the fourth element into play: the *repraesentandum*, the content to be represented, the 'what' of the representation. This can coincide with the 'who', i.e., the subject of the representation. Then the representative represents the person for whom they are standing in, or at least that person's will (as is the case with, e.g., a conservatorship). But the *repraesentandum* can also possess a certain function which is to be distinguished (though not separated) from this person and their overall will. This is the case, for example, when the representative stands in for the subject who entrusts them in a specific respect, when they are endowed with a limited power of attorney for the execution of a particular order, or when they execute a particular act of the subject's will on their behalf.

The represented subject is not passive in the relational occurrence, but both directly and indirectly active. In the act of commissioning the representative, they act directly, unmediated; on the other hand, in the execution of that representation, they act indirectly, mediated *through* the representative. If they change the assignment or demand accountability, they once again act directly and in an unmediated way. The representative is also not a passive medium of representation, but an active intermediary/mediator of the one whom they represent. They embody the subject's presence in terms of that subject's will and thus, in a certain sense, their being. They act 'in their spirit'.

The peculiarity of *religious* representations consists in the fact that they not only make manifest the unmanifest Divine but they establish a relation to it, while at the same time respecting its hiddenness. The French classical philologist, historian of religion and culture, and anthropologist Jean-Pierre Vernant expresses this as follows:

> The religious sign does not present itself as a simple tool of thought. It does not aim exclusively to make present in the human mind the sacred power to which it refers. It always wants to establish a real connection, a conversation with it, to make it present in the world of humans. But in its effort to build a bridge to the divine, it must at the same time make clear the distance, the incommensurability between the sacred power and all that makes it visible—necessarily inadequately—in the eyes of humans.[3]

3.2 Application of the Concept of Representation to the Interpretation of Jesus Christ

The application of the concept of representation to Christology, as attempted in the present study, sees in Jesus Christ the representative of God towards humans and the representative of humans towards God. Thus, the representation takes place in Jesus Christ in a twofold direction: from God toward humans and from humans toward God.

The distinctiveness of the representation model presented here consists in this double relationality.

Within German-speaking theology, Hermann Deuser is one of the few who have applied the concept of representation to Christology—or, more precisely, to the interpretation of 'incarnation'.[4] He derives his concept of representation

---

3 Vernant, *Mythe*, 264, cited in: Ginzburg, *Repräsentation*, 12–3.
4 Deuser, *Gottesinstinkt*. See also *id.*, *Kleine Einführung*, 101–105.

from the semiotics of Charles Sanders Peirce and therefore understands it as a signifying process. Within this process there are three connected moments: an initial moment of creativity; a specifying reference to objects; and the act of understanding that recognizes in the object the creativity of its representation.[5] With reference to theology and more precisely Christology, in this process God is this creative ground, and Jesus is the 'object' in which God comes to be represented. In Christian understanding this representation is recognized as God's representation. The creative ground is thereby—as in every representational relationship—qualitatively preordered to the object of representation. The object is still undetermined and is available for representation, through which it attains its determination. Only in this way can it become accessible to knowledge and understanding; and only through knowledge and understanding does the representation actually become such. It does not exist in an objective way before understanding and interpretation accrue to it: "this third element of mental reception and constructiveness belongs to complete representation".[6]

The concept of representation I am developing in this book is distinct from Deuser's approach in at least three ways. Firstly, in contrast to him I am emphasizing the doublesidedness of the representational relationship: from humans to God and from God to humans. Secondly, I see representation not only as signification or depiction but as an occurrence that exerts a transformative impact.[7] In the representative, the creative ground not only comes to light, it also manifests itself in its powerful presence. Representation is more than a semiotic process. The third difference is that Deuser's approach is related only to the interpretation of 'incarnation', not to Christology as a whole, that his ideas remain largely at the programmatic level, and that he unfolds the indicated program rather allusively in terms of its content.

In his reflections on the 'vicarious substitution' (*Stellvertretung*) of Jesus Christ, Christof Gestrich likewise assumes a double representational relationship. He begins with the question of what constitutes a good ambassador. Such a messenger represents not only his employer, but also those to whom he has been sent. He acts as a mediator, especially when it comes to reconciliation. If necessary, he is even prepared to lay down his life for this purpose.

> In the vicariousness of Jesus Christ, God shows himself 'abroad' in the realm of humanity, but also humanity 'at home' in the realm of God.

---

5 Deuser, *Gottesinstinkt*, 163–4.
6 Deuser, *Gottesinstinkt*, 164.
7 See chapter 3.2.4.

Jesus' divine mission in vicariousness requires that in him the real and true God becomes visible, as does the real and true human.[8]

Stephan Schaede likewise considers the soteriological relevance of the concept of representation in terms of 'double representation'.[9] He summarizes this in three points:

> (a) Christ, by taking the place of the sinner, is the person in whom God allows sinful human beings to be present in their sin, in order to overcome sin in this person. (b) Christ, having taken our place as the righteous one, is the one in whom the sinner becomes present to God as a justified human. (c) In Christ, God becomes present to the human as the one who forgives and justifies their sins.[10]

That means: Jesus Christ represents the sinner, the justified sinner, and the justifying God. Thus, representation is traced back to substitution and further defined in the context of the theology of sin and of justification (following 2 Cor. 5:21).

In contrast, I seek (a) to apply the concept of representation not only soteriologically in view of the salvific significance of Jesus Christ, but more fundamentally also to the understanding of his person; and (b) to relate this concept not only to sin and forgiveness, but also to the saving presence of God in suffering as well as in all other states of existence.

3.2.1   *Representation as 'Making Present'*

In medieval Latin, as well as in English, French, and Italian, the concept of representation has a wide range of meanings.[11] Above all, this range includes the meaning of 'making present', which is of fundamental importance for representational Christology. This aspect of meaning results from the translation of the Latin term *representatio*. Here I understand the prefix 're' not so much in the temporal sense of 'to make present *again*' as in the ontic sense of making present someone who is already present (not someone who is absent), but who is withdrawn from sensory perception. It is thus about the manifestation of presence in a person.

---

8   Translated from Gestrich, *Unterscheidung*, 233.
9   Schaede, *Stellvertretung*, 227, see also 630–1, 634.
10 Translated from Schaede, *Stellvertretung*, 227.
11 Scheerer, et al., "Repräsentation", 790.

'Being-there' [*Da-sein*] is God's fundamental mode of being. This is already stated explicitly by God's self-communication as Yhwh in Exod. 3:14b, 'I am there', or, in the mode of a promise, 'I will be there' or 'I will be with you' (cf. Exod. 3:12). God's existence is not 'empty' but filled with God's intention for salvation (Exod. 34:6ff. and more). Presence is not to be understood as a static resting in itself, but instead as something dynamic, as a 'coming' that is always new. It has the character of an occurrence.

'Representation', then, in relation to Christ, does not mean 'substitution' in the sense of being commissioned to represent *an absent Other*, to play their role, to speak and act on their behalf. Christ as God's representative is *more* than a delegate, deputy, envoy, ambassador, agent, vicar, functionary, etc. He is the presence of God in person. He represents God and God represents Godself in him.

The representation of God to the human being can also be described (in epistemic terms) as 'revelation', as the self-revelation of God, who reveals Godself in Jesus to humans as the addressees of revelation.[12] In soteriological terms it can be expressed as mediation of salvation for the benefit of humans. If one understands 'mediator' from the Latin 'interpres', one can say along with Gregor Maria Hoff: "in Jesus Christ [...] God interprets himself humanly and the human 'divinely': his [human's] possibilities of life are 'defined' anew".[13]

If the relationship between God's self-revelation and the historical medium in which it takes place is understood as a representational relationship, the possibility emerges that God's presence can also make itself present in other representational forms. For the Christian faith, Jesus Christ is the authoritative representative of God's unconditional and universal salvific presence, but this does not exclude that God's presence also taking on forms other than representation through Christ. Rather, that possibility is a consequence of the unconditionality and universality of God's salvific presence. In Christ God has *identified* in the intention to offer salvation, but has not *de-fined* Godself in the sense of setting 'limits' (Latin: 'finis') to represent Godself.

3.2.2 *Whom Does Jesus Christ Represent?*

Chapter 3.1 examined the structure of relations inherent in the concept of representation. 'Representation' describes a tripartite relationship which maps out and distinguishes between three entities: (a) that which is represented, (b) the representative, and (c) the addressee(s) toward whom the representation is made. If we apply this structure to Christology, the meaning of Jesus

---

12 See Chapter 4.7.
13 Translated from Hoff, *Wer ist Christus?*, 198.

Christ is brought up in view of the two basic relationships that determine his person: on the one hand with regard to his relationship to God or to God's Word, Wisdom, Spirit which are expressions for the self-communicating saving presence of God, and on the other with regard to his relationship to human beings, to humanity:

(a) In Jesus' relationship with *humans*, the entity represented by him (and thus the subject of representation) is *God*. The act of representation is made to *humanity*. The core of representational Christology in this regard is the simple statement that "God was in him" (2 Cor. 5:19). Of equal significance is the Roman centurion's confessional statement recorded in Mk. 15:39b: "Yes, this human was truly the Son of God!" All titles given to Jesus in the New Testament express this being-in, this 'indwelling' of God being in Jesus, albeit with different emphases and alluding to different traditions. In sum they can all be interpreted in line with the concept of representation: "representation means: as Jesus Christ is, so is God",[14] and, even more, "where Jesus [is], there [is] Godself".[15] The certainty that Jesus Christ represents God has constituted, spread, and sustained his community of followers over two millennia. This community gathers in his name because he acted in the name of God and thus represented that name.

The question of how to think of God's presence in Jesus the Christ is answered in three ways in the Christological approach offered in this volume (see chapters 4.3, 4.4, and 4.5), following the biblical and early Christian ways of speaking of the 'Word' which became flesh, of the 'Spirit' who inspired him, and of the 'Wisdom' which dwelt in him. The presence of God is expressed in these three notions in different ways, each with its own emphasis. In contrast to the dominance of the Logos-Incarnation Christology in the history of theology, my approach pays greater attention to Spirit- and Wisdom-Christologies.

(b) In Jesus' relationship to *God*, the entities represented by him are *humanity* or *human existence*. This representation is made to *God*. The fact that Jesus himself was part of humanity and had the experience of being human—up to his appalling death on the cross—enables him to present that experience to God.

In view of the *person* of Jesus Christ I will now distinguish the representational approach to Christology from what I call 'identification Christology'. In view of his '*work*' and *impact* or his *salvific significance*, I then distinguish it from a 'constitutive Christology and soteriology'.

---

14 Translated from Deuser, *Kleine Einführung*, 100.
15 Translated from Joest, *Dogmatik* I, 234.

3.2.2.1 Identification Christology

Representational Christology differs from Christological approaches that tend to identify Jesus without a significant distinction either with God or with humanity.

On the one hand, identification Christology includes approaches that underdefine God's presence in Jesus and see in him merely a human 'functionary' commissioned by God to act in God's service. Here he is identified so much with being human that the relationship with God that shapes his personality is reduced to his belief in God, i.e., to a psychological act or state.

On the other hand, it includes those approaches which minimize or eliminate Jesus' distinctiveness from God (or from the 'Word' of God) and which emphasize his unity with God. This tended to be the case in the Alexandrian Christology of the Early Church, which conceived of this unity as a substantial (or physical) one. In the extreme position of Mono- or Miaphysitism (rejected by the Council of Chalcedon, but still held by some Oriental Orthodox churches), there came to be a complete identification of Jesus Christ with God.

This view continues to be held to the present day, for example, in parts of Orthodox and Evangelical theology, where Jesus is referred to simply as 'God' without adding qualifications that distinguish him from God (qualifications such as 'he is the incarnation of the Word of God').

In soteriology, identification Christology is expressed by proclaiming that Jesus Christ *is* the salvific presence of God. The greater the emphasis on the unity between Jesus Christ and God (or the salvation of God), the less room there is for the acceptance of other manifestations of the Word, Spirit, and Wisdom of God besides the one personified in Jesus. This leads to a soteriological exclusivism.

The relationship between Jesus Christ and God (or God's salvation) as well as the relationship between Jesus Christ and humanity, to whom his mission of imparting salvation applies, are defined by representational Christology, however, as a unity in difference,[16] as a realization that 'makes present', without stating a complete identification.

3.2.2.2 Constitutive Christology

In terms of the *work and impact* or the *salvific significance* of Jesus Christ, representational Christology differs from the Christological approaches that can be called 'constitutive' or 'causative' Christology. These assume that Jesus, by laying down his life, is not the representative but the cause or necessary condition of the salvation of humans or even of God's will and act of salvation—because

---

16   See also chapter 4.2.2.

the death on the cross was an atoning sacrifice necessary for the reconciliation of humans with God or even for the reconciliation of God. Christ's self-sacrifice healed the obstructed relationship between God and human beings, lifted the burden of original sin from humanity, and removed the penalty of sin imposed by God for it. According to this interpretation, with his death on the cross, sin was deprived of its power and salvation for humans was achieved. Thus, the crucifixion is the culmination of the history of salvation. It turned God's wrath to grace.

The main lines of Western soteriological thought before the Enlightenment follow constitutive Christology. They run from Paul through Augustine, Anselm of Canterbury (who interpreted the death on the cross as a vicarious satisfaction), and Luther (who saw in Jesus' passion a vicarious penal suffering for the salvation of humans). It is not important here to consider these approaches in detail.[17] What they have in common is their focus on the cross of Jesus. Constitutive Christological approaches are theologies of the Cross.

As a rule, such theologies are connected with an 'infralapsarian' view of God's intention and work to redeem humanity, which would see this intention and work as having become necessary through the original sin of mankind. As opposed to a 'supralapsarian' view, which assumes that God's salvific will exists from eternity and has not been overshadowed by the 'Fall' (*lapsus*) of humanity, 'infralapsarian' (literally: 'under the Fall') soteriology supposes that God's intention and work to redeem humankind had become necessary as a response to original sin. In this response, God decided to 'heal' the broken covenant, rehabilitate sinful humanity, and establish a 'New Covenant'. That took place in the 'Christ-event', particularly in the crucifixion.

Here, too, the consequences for the theology of religions are obvious: if the decisive act of God's salvation took place in Jesus—above all in his death on the cross—then there can be no healed relationship with God without Christ (*remoto Christo*). If participation in this act takes place through Christian faith, then it is only accessible to believers in Christ. If faith finds its social realization in the church, then membership in this community is necessary for salvation. Though escape clauses can be built into this exclusivism,[18] even at their best they cannot rise above being graciously granted exceptions to the rule.

In contrast to constitutive Christological approaches and causative soteriology, representative Christology and soteriology is closer to a 'supralapsarian' position. It assumes that God's unconditional and universal will for salvation is constituted *from eternity* in the very being of God, and that Jesus' blood

---

17   See chapter 4.8.1.2.
18   See chapter 2.4.3.

sacrifice was not a divinely ordered necessity to overcome human alienation from God. It was not humanity's 'fall into sin' (as in 'infralapsarian' thinking) that prompted the salvific work of God, which intended to remedy that fall's consequences. Rather, that salvific work was the achievement of the divine purpose already present from creation onwards for the consummation of creation. There is no fundamental sinful barrier to God's saving will that needs to be removed. Even if repeatedly irritated and disturbed by the machinations of creatures, God ultimately overrules everything put in the way. This type of Christology finds connections with modern Protestantism, especially in Hegel and Schleiermacher. Since the nineteenth century, it has been developed in different ways.

Representative Christology and soteriology understand the 'Christ-event' as the historical realization of the salvation that comes from eternity (the protological perspective) and is realized in its full form at the end of time (the eschatological perspective). God's salvation is represented in Christ, i.e., *revealed, communicated*, and thus *effective*. Paul Tillich phrased it like this: "It is the *eternal* relation of God to man which is manifest in the Christ".[19] This representation takes place not only in the passion and death of Jesus on the cross, but in the overall context of his life, work, suffering, death, and 'resurrection'.

God is salvifically present in Jesus Christ and works in and through him in the power of God's Spirit. But this power also works beyond the representative figure and the effect emanating from it. The possibility is thus kept open that there can also be other representative figures which point away from themselves and toward the divine reality of salvation which is made present in them. Only in this broadening can we convincingly conceive of the unconditionality and universality of God's will for salvation. The Christian faith is related to Christ and only to him. But as the "mirror of the paternal heart" (as Luther puts it),[20] Christ stands for the breadth of this heart.

3.2.2.3 Representational Christology as Dilution?

If one takes identification and constitutive Christologies as yardsticks, then representational Christology may appear somewhat watered down in contrast. A representation seems to have less content of being than the represented reality. Compared to 'actual' reality it seems 'inauthentic' at best. This objection, however, only arises within a framework of ontic thought which quantifies the substance of being, i.e., establishes greater or lesser degrees of being (in this case God-being). But representational Christology is not based on ontic thought but placed in a *relational* frame of reference. Moreover, representation

---

19   Tillich, *Systematic Theology*, Vol. 2, 96 (emphasis mine).
20   Luther, *The Large Catechism*, 2nd part, 3rd article.

indicates what Jesus *does* rather that what he *is* in his very being. According to it, there is not much meaning to be had in making an ontological gradation between the represented reality and the representative. This reality manifests itself in the representative; it comes into effect through him/her. One can even see in this reality the representative's 'greater degree of being' compared to the one represented, because he/she *realizes* what he/she represents. But such ontic quantifications do not lead further.

Some critics, however, first present this approach in a watered-down form so as then to accuse it of dilution. I, however, insist that representational Christology contains no less normative force than other Christological approaches. Critics who see representational Christology as a dilution should show constructively how *they* intend to take up the theological challenge posed by relating God's universal grace to the particularity of salvation in Christ.

Representational Christology is not antithetical to, or incapable of communicating with, identification and constitutive Christologies. It can take up their concerns and bring them to bear within its framework and in its own modified way. This should become clear as the present Christological approach develops below.

3.2.3 What/Whom Does Jesus Christ Represent?
In view of the two relationships of Jesus—to God and to humanity—the *repraesentandum*, the *content* of the representation should be defined differently:

(a) In his relationship to *humanity*, Jesus represents the salvific presence of God, the divine will for salvation, and the salvific action of God. Since it is not only a matter of acts of *will* (which would have to be distinguished from and subordinated to the *essence* of God) but also of the essential self-communication of God, the *content* of the representation coincides with its *subject*. Displaying that content characterizes the subject: God.

According to the testimony of the Synoptic Gospels in particular, Jesus does not proclaim his own Messiahship, his sonship with God, or even his being God, but rather the power of God's presence (symbolized as 'kingdom of God' or as 'reign of God'). He lays claim to finality and normativity, not for his own person, but for the mission embodied by him in his speech and action. The title of Christ expresses this transparency of the person to the 'cause of God' and God's powerful presence. Therein lies the 'Christ-content' that Jesus represents. However, he also gives the titles attached to him (like 'Messiah') a new meaning directed to this content.

The *repraesentandum* thus consists in the unconditional and universal goodness and justice of God which is intended to be made manifest in history. Like the significance of the *person* of Christ, the *content*, too, which determines this person, his 'works', his proclamation, and his passion can all be labelled in the New Testament with different terms. In each case other aspects of meaning come to the fore: in John as God's 'love' (ἀγάπη), in Paul in a more juridical metaphor as 'justifying grace' (χάρις), and in Luke as 'God's mercy' (ἔλεος). All these terms convey God's essential self-communication as unconditional and universally bestowed goodness and justice. They are to be understood in the sense of a realized, or future-oriented, eschatology, as that which is already present and simultaneously awaiting completion.

In both his proclamation of God's close presence and his practice that makes this presence tangible, Jesus was largely in agreement with the Pharisees. For all that he differed from their Torah observance, he was in agreement with them in the intention to align the entire practice of life with the all-encompassing presence of God. In this way, humans—according to the Pharisees—participate in the divine activity and thus in God's intention to complete God's work of creation for the good and salvation of creatures. The decisive difference to the Pharisees, however, is that Jesus not only proclaims and practices the presence of God but carries it within himself and in this way represents it as something 'real'.

In view of Luther's talk of the hidden God, however, one might ask whether the nature of God can be described unilaterally in terms such as 'love' or 'salvific affection'. What about the 'dark sides of God', which in the biblical tradition were associated with terms such as 'wrath' or 'retribution' and in which God's will for justice is expressed? These traits are unmistakably recognizable in Jesus' speeches and actions (e.g., Mk. 3:5; Lk. 3:7; Jn. 3:36 or in his appearance in the temple: Mt. 21:12ff. and parallel passages). They can be interpreted as a confrontation with human resistance and opposition to God's saving action. This confrontation takes place in the context of God's salvific action with the goal of overcoming this resistance.

(b) With regard to the relationship of the person of Jesus *to God*, representational Christology says: Jesus represents the fundamental existential situation of the human being to God—the real human being with all their creaturely mortality, neediness, and limitation, including the suffering of death, despair, and lamentations about the sense of being abandoned by God. What's more, he represents not only what he experienced (the suffering he endured), but also what caused these experiences. This includes humanity's self-centeredness and hubris; selfish striving for power to the point of violence; injustice; religious arrogance; sadistic lust; hypocrisy; betrayal; indifference to the suffering of others, and everything else that is expressed in the term 'sin'. He represents this in a negative way, as it were, as that to which he has fallen victim. He represents the sinful behavior of humans in his wounds. As a victim, he became the representative of that which is common in the human world, but which contradicts head-on the divine purpose in human life and which constitutes man's need for redemption.

This thought ties in with 2 Cor. 5:21 ("God made him who had no sin to be sin for us"). Jesus not only takes the 'foreign' place of the sinner so that, untainted by sin, he can ultimately justify the sinner before God, he also falls under the ramifications of sin and suffers its deadly power. His death is the wages of sin.

All suffering humans can find in him a symbol for their misery. In this regard, the Alexandrian notion of the 'human nature' of Jesus Christ becomes important: Christology is not solely about the individual person Jesus, but about him as a representative of humanity. In his commentary on Gal. 3:13, Luther could even see Christ as commissioned by God to *commit* the sins of all human beings, as a work virtually foreign to him, in place of humanity. According to Luther, God says to Christ: "you shall be the person of all humans, who have committed the transgressions of all humans".[21] Luther stated that, based on the Law, Jesus had to be crucified, because he not only assumed the personality of a sinner but even *was* the collective person of all sinners, thieves, and criminals. He, who himself was without sin, became *the* sinner.

Looking at both sides of this process of representation together, one can conclude that by representing God to human beings Jesus becomes the representative of *true* human existence, i.e., that which completely corresponds to God. According to the Adam-Christ typology in Paul, he is the new human, the one in whom the vocation of humanity to be in communion with God becomes clear. Applying the terminology of the two natures in Christ one can say: as representative of God, Christ is *vere Deus* who manifests 'true' humanity (= *verus homo*). As representative of the 'real' humanity, Christ is *vere homo*, and as such represents humanity in all its fallenness with respect to God. As *verus homo*, however, he represents the divine destiny of the human beings and God's salvific presence towards them.

3.2.4 *Not Only Showing, but Also Transforming*

'Representation', as I understand it here, is more than just *showing, displaying*, or *proclaiming* the powerful presence of God. It is about its *enactment*. It *realizes* this presence in Jesus' person. 'Realization' here does not mean the realization of that which was hitherto non-real. It is also not about the 'actualization' of a

---

21   "tu sis omnium hominum persona, qui feceris omnium hominum peccata" (WA 40/1, 437).

potential. Rather, it means the transition from an unexperienced to an experienced presence. By manifesting the presence of God, Jesus represents and also mediates it. One can apply a term from the theology of the Eucharist: Jesus is the 'real presence' of God. He manifests God's salvific presence, already existent in the power of his Spirit, in a historical and personal form. The presence effective in the power of God's Spirit obtains in and through the representative a 'corporeality' in which it becomes vivid and from which it radiates powerfully. The representative of God imparts this presence and is in this way the medium of the divine presence of salvation. Through him, God's eternal will of reconciliation and communion is effectively 'staged' and quintessentially executed. Through this reification in historical form God's saving presence is revealed to human paths of understanding.

The representative acts through radiating presence. That includes acting but goes further than this. Representation is an active 'being-there' [*Da-Sein*]. It is more than a particular action or a web of activities (which could also include self-withdrawal and conscious renunciation of action). The fundamental process of representation is mere presence—the presence of the representative, and the power of his presence. Jesus' 'works' consist not only of specific actions but also of the radiance of his presence as God's presence in him—which underlies these actions. Hebrews 1:3 describes this radiance as the 'reflection' of God's glory (ἀπαύγασμα τῆς δόξης). The presence of God in him makes him Christ. His being Christ means God's being in him and his being in God. However, this is not to be understood in the sense of a unity of substance, but in the sense of a unity of relationship.[22]

The self-communication of God in Jesus Christ is therefore to be understood not just in a significative sense, which merely gestures at meaning. It is an effective impact that transforms the relationship between God and human beings. In the force field of his radiance human beings are seized by this force and become for their part centers radiating God's presence, and thus those who themselves make God present. The representation of God in Jesus brings about that which it represents: the ever-new restitution of the relationship of humans to God.

This is not a supernatural (or 'magic') event, but an event of personal *resonance*. Christian faith is the experience of resonance with Jesus Christ, or with his relationship with God, and tuning into it. In Christians who enter into the relationship with God mediated by Jesus Christ there arises a resonance with Jesus; in this way they are connected to him and through him to God. The

---

22   See chapter 4.2.1.

impetus for this resonance goes beyond the call to discipleship or the evocation of 'imitation' (μίμησις); it comes to the human being from the outside and above all concerns their self-understanding and their orientation to action. The experience of this resonance, however, touches the human being in their innermost center and transforms them from within. It 'awakens' them. It leads them into the community of believers. 'Spiritual' resonances can also occur between the members of this community. Moreover, a bond can develop in this way with humans outside the community of faith.

For those who stand in this resonant relationship with Jesus, then, he is not only the *revealer* of God's will for salvation, but its powerfully manifested *archetype*, which provides the impetus for this resonance. To couch this in the terms of biblical metaphor, he not only announces the dawn of God's reign—like a prophet—but brings it about.

'Representation', therefore, refers to a performative presence in which the represented reality comes into effect. The reality of God's salvific presence, which precedes the act of representation, takes effect in this act and through this act in the reality of the world. Thus, representation also means mediation and historical manifestation. In the re-presentation of the will for salvation that is God's essential self-identification salvation becomes a present reality.

This *performative* presence means, on the one hand, that in Christ God puts into effect the reality of salvation and thus makes it effective, but on the other hand it also means that this reality always lies beyond the form it has so far taken and transcends it protologically as well as eschatologically. God's presence is completely *in* Jesus Christ and at the same time it remains distinct from him. It is *in* this form of its manifestation and at the same time *behind it and underlying it*.

Where one uses the metaphor of 'speaking' to describe this *praesentia operosa* [active presence] or speaks of the 'word of God', this is to be understood as *per*formative speaking, i.e., speaking *through* a medium. It is comparable to the jurisdiction of a judge, who establishes law in their verdict, but in doing so gives validity to a legal order that owes itself to the preceding legislation and ultimately to the principles of justice. The judge represents the legal order. In view of God's grace, representation does not mean the generation of a previously non-existent reality, but the *re*-presentation of God's gracious being, which precedes the presentation, makes it possible, and takes place in it.

The historical realization of this spiritual reality of God's presence refers not only to that reality externally, as is characteristic for the relationship between a sign and its meaning; rather, it gives it a real historical shape and thus brings it to reality and to effect. Jesus Christ made present the living, potent presence of God in such an intense form that he was called (in Col. 1:15, cf. 2 Cor. 4:4) 'the image of the invisible God' (εἰκὼν τοῦ θεοῦ τοῦ ἀοράτου).

Through the 'indwelling of God' he embodied the presence of God and radiated it, like a source of power or light, to those who followed him. As a human being who lived entirely out of relationship with God, he embodied true humanity, open to God. Jesus Christ is not only the proclaimer, but also the embodiment of the message of God's all-embracing and unconditional love and justice for creation.

This perspective enables us to maintain the uniqueness, the centrality, and the normativity of Jesus Christ for the Christian faith without making the exclusivist point that the gift of God's grace is granted only to those who participate in the Christ-event by faith.

3.2.5 *The 'For Structure'*
In the relational event inherent in the concept of representation, the preposition 'for' occurs with three different meanings:

(a) The person who represents someone stands *for* the one whom he or she represents. The preposition 'for' here means 'in the place of' or 'from ... to', 'in relation to'. A person speaks and acts 'in the name of' and 'on behalf of' another; that is, 'for' a person, community, or institution. This definition can be further delineated in two ways:

Firstly, 'in the place of' does not mean 'instead of' in the sense of substitution. 'Replacement', as a term, contrasts with 'representation', as I understand it here. When a person replaces another, then first person takes the latter's place for themselves and no longer represents the other.[23] This latter person is then, as it were, taken out of the game and no longer plays a role. The 'for' is removed. A representative, however, does not replace the person they represent, but brings that latter person's role, meaning, and agency to bear.

Yet we must, on the other hand, distinguish the performance of this function from that of a mere service for a client. The representative is more than a servant or messenger. Although they do not act autonomously, they do act on their own responsibility in the name of another. Representation is an assignment to be fulfilled on one's own responsibility. If a 'substitute' goes too far in taking the person to be represented out of the picture, someone who merely 'provides a service' does not go far enough; it leaves the representative underdefined.

(b) The representation is made 'for' an (individual or collective) addressee. It applies to this addressee, and they should let it apply to them, i.e., the

---

23   See chapter 3.2.7.5.

addressee should recognize the represented person or institution in the representative and acknowledge their or its authority. The preposition 'for' here means 'being directed toward someone'.

(c) The preposition 'for' can have the still further meaning of 'in favour of'. This meaning is highly significant for the Christological profiling of the concept of representation. It is not, however, a necessary implication of this concept in general—but it can be connected with it. This is indispensable in view of the representation of God in Christ because it is part of the essence and thus in the intention of the represented subject (God) to be in a relationship with the addressee of the representation (the human) that is salutary for the latter. This is expressed by the designation of Jesus as 'Immanuel'—God with us/among us—which is especially anchored in the Gospel of Matthew (Mt. 1:23).

Wherever the representative (Jesus) makes the represented subject (God) present in this essential self-identification (any other course of action being impossible for him, because this self-identification has become his own), the 'for' means an 'existence for' the addressee, an 'advocacy for' them, thus an act of *procuratio* (ministration). Christology or soteriology is not merely about the presence of God *as such*, but about the presence of God's salvific presence, salvific will, and salvific action. God does not exist *a se* (in pure being for Godself), in the sense that his will of salvation would be added as secondary. God *is* salvific presence. God's being is *pro nobis* (for us).

Jesus was completely focused on God and the already present but not yet fully realized presence of salvation. His 'being for' in the relationship with humans is based on this being not centered on himself. By relying completely on God he made God's salvific attention to humans present 'for' them. This relational dynamic can also be described as a double devotion—to God and to humans. Jesus' existence was ex-centric, centered in God. That allowed him not to live centripetally centred on himself, but centrifugally towards others.

With the interpretation of 'for' in the sense of 'in favour of', Christology coincides with soteriology. Jesus represents the salvific presence, the salvific will, and the salvific action of God towards humans.

3.2.6 *'Salvation'*

This chapter clarifies the concept of 'salvation'—a not unproblematic term that is susceptible to abuse and often misused, but one which plays a central role in the definition of the *repraesentandum*.[24] For this, too, I propose an existential and relational interpretation. Salvation is about the healing (or renewal) of the four fundamental relationships of the human: to oneself, to one's social

---

24   See chapter 3.2.3.

environment (i.e., fellow human beings), to one's natural environment, and to God as the foundation of all and thus also as the foundation of one's own being.²⁵ The inherent tendency of being human is to seek to establish these relationships on one's own power and interests, but this leads to these relationships being disturbed and disrupted; to selfishness. It leads also to the instrumentalization of fellow human beings; to reckless extravagance in one's use of natural resources; and to wanting to be like God. Beyond merely affecting each of the fundamental relationships, these disturbances can also affect the *balance* between them, e.g., when the relationship to oneself becomes dominant at the expense of the relationship to fellow human beings. Religious fanaticism also represents such a disturbance, in that it turns the relationship to God against those who believe differently.

The theological term 'sin' refers to fundamental disturbances in the constitution and practice of these relationships and in their relationship to each other. These ultimately lead to relational disengagement, i.e., relational death. The Greek word *hamartia* (ἁμαρτία), translated as 'sin', means 'falling short' of one's goal or purpose. In the context of an existential-relational understanding of sin, it means falling short of the type of basic relations that are salvific for human beings. Following Christof Gestrich, this falling short can be understood as a failure in dignity:

> to sin means in essence to be able to dignify no one and nothing. Sin is the inability to accept fellow creatures as they are by virtue of their creaturely dignity. The sinner is also unable to appreciate himself in this way.²⁶

Human existence stands in the polarity of creatureliness and the rejection of the dignity and responsibility given with it. God calls a responsive counterpart into being and gives him a living environment and orientation for the unfolding of life towards its fullness and perfection. In human beings, however, there is a tendency to turn away from their own reason for existing and from their proper orientation towards God's purposes for creation.

This 'original sinfulness' is paradigmatically expressed in the suffering inflicted on Jesus. The religious and political authorities responsible for this followed their own interests in maintaining their power in a repressive system. The motive of the Roman occupiers (represented by Pontius Pilate) was to nip all resistance in the bud quite brutally. The Sanhedrin and the temple aristocracy around the high priest Caiaphas tried to walk a tightrope between

---

25   See also Jüngel, *Hoffen*, 19.
26   Translated from Gestrich, *Die Wiederkehr*, 232.

collaboration and self-assertion. To them, Jesus was a blasphemer (Mk. 2:7, 14:61–64; Jn. 10:33), to whom the precept of Lev. 24:16 was to be applied. The commandment 'You shall not kill' took a back seat.

The figurative phrase 'being raised' (in the image of 'resurrection') refers to the fact that God takes away the definitive element of this 'original sinfulness' which is given with being human. His salvific action overrides its manifestations and their effects. God's relationship with Jesus continued through Jesus' suffering, through his despair at feeling abandoned by God (Mk. 15:34), and through his death by torture. Believing participation in this event is grounded in the certainty Paul expresses in Rom. 8:38:

> neither death, nor life, nor angels, nor rulers, nor things present, nor things to come, nor powers, nor height, nor depth, nor anything else in all creation, will be able to separate us from the love of God in Christ Jesus our Lord.

This is the core of the Gospel as a message of God's saving purposes, which determine the whole of reality—on this side and on the other side of the frontier of death. The 'us' in Rom. 8:38 applies not only to Christians, but to all who make this promise of salvation their own. The promise of salvation itself applies to all.

Against a triumphalist assurance of salvation, with an unbalanced sense of its having already been realized—such as Paul obviously encountered in Corinth[27]—salvation is ultimately the object of eschatological promise and hope. In history and under the conditions of human existence salvation only ever happens fragmentarily, and in an anticipatory mode, 'under the cross'. It stands in the eternal dialectic of being already-present and simultaneously still-pending. 'Salvation' describes a state that is an aim, a target. God's salvific action does not consist in the bestowal of salvation as a state of being, but in ever-new impulses toward salvation as a process of becoming. This entails the ever-new vanquishing of obstacles: liberation ('redemption') from dependencies, compulsions, imprisonments; healing of separations ('reconciliation'); processing of guilt ('forgiveness'); granting of dignity ('justification'); assurance of being in relation to God even beyond death ('resurrection'); and distinction between that which is precious before God and that which may appear important but is ultimately worthless ('judgment'). The ways of salvation are ways 'under the cross'. They run on the stony ground of existential contingencies

---

27 See Horn, *Das Angeld des Geistes*, 160–301.

and ambiguities, on the field of power struggles, unjust distribution of opportunities in life and social dislocations, in the face of global threats, and so on. They are not triumphs. They include protest and struggle against everything that stands in the way of the unfolding of life and of just orders of life and that thus causes suffering.

Discussion of the universality and unconditionality of God's saving presence, which is so central for the present account of Christology, must therefore not be understood as if the reality and power of 'sin'—and thus the human need for redemption—were denied or weakened. A realistic view of humanity and the world absolutely must include a view of this reality. The message of salvation applies to an unsaved world. Unconditional acceptance by God must not be understood as uncritical acceptance. This is expressed in the Reformation polarity of law and gospel. Here, 'law' stands for the uncovering of all that alienates and separates humans from God, from fellow human beings, from the world around them, and from themselves. 'Gospel' stands for the liberating promise that "nothing can separate us from the love of God that is in Christ Jesus our Lord" (Rom. 8:38).

In the life, speech, action, suffering, death, and 'resurrection' of Jesus Christ, God's will for salvation, which has existed from all eternity and which exudes these impulses, has come to normative self-expression. Therein lies the basic impetus of the Christian life of faith. In the salvific presence of God, the damaged or broken basic relationships of humankind can experience healing energy. This healing also applies to the (mutually supportive) interaction of these basic relationships. In this context, the healing of the relationship with *God* is of fundamental importance, because the bond given with it leads to ultimate freedom in the other relationships. 'Salvation' means being saved in the divine ground of all being; free from all that separates us from that ground, and trusting that this relationship will last even beyond death. This liberating bond is represented in Jesus Christ.

This discussion of perdition and salvation, however, should not only be related to humans, even if they are the focus of it. It also has cosmic dimensions. The world is called into being by God and allowed to function within its own dynamics, i.e., it is endowed with freedom. By orienting themselves to their own natural and historical dynamics and to human self-interest, human and worldly affairs often oppose the realization of God's saving purposes in many ways. That makes salvation necessary; according to Rom. 8:22, the world "groans and is in birth pangs to this day". But the world is also endowed with a salvific purpose. God's purposes in creation are directed towards salvation. God's salvific action finds expression in the creative and redemptive efficacy always emanating from it (*creatio et salvatio continua*). In view of the necessity of salvation, God's presence is always connected with 'overcoming the world', as it is represented in Christ (Jn. 16:33). 'Overcoming the world' is not to be understood as the apocalyptic end of the world, but as its constantly renewed liberation from bonds which are inimical to life.

3.2.7 Related Terms

Every Christology faces the task of linking the historical particularity of the person of Jesus with the universal divine ground of all reality, which—according to biblical testimony—has provided reality with its destiny and which has promised this destiny's realization despite all obstacles. It must make Jesus understandable as the Christ, i.e., as the one who stands for this promise and is of central importance for its realization. For this purpose, it must on the one hand determine the relationship in which this person stands to God, and on the other hand present his function or mission in the world and toward humans.

Different conceptual forms and terms lend themselves to defining the relationship between Jesus Christ and God. This chapter considers those terms that touch on or partly overlap with the idea of 'representation' favoured here, which will gain sharper contours in contrast with these terms. In doing so, I limit myself to theologically coined terms and leave aside those that have a rather unspecific and broader meaning (such as 'personification' or 'manifestation')—although they, too, express important shades of meaning when it comes to the concept of representation—and I will therefore use them repeatedly.

3.2.7.1 Image; Icon; Parable

Paul and the Deutero-Pauline writings call Christ the *eikon* (εἰκών: image, likeness) of God (2 Cor. 4:4; Col. 1:15). According to Heb. 1:3, he is "the reflection of God's glory and the exact imprint of God's very being". In him the image of God is realized as the dignity, destiny, and mission of human existence (according to Gen. 1:26–28). Believers are to be transformed into this image (Rom. 8:29; 1 Cor. 15:49; 2 Cor. 3:18). Christ thus appears as the archetype of the human, who is his likeness and is to live as such.

Jewish wisdom theology stands in the background of the 'image Christology' of Col. 1:15 and Heb. 1:3. The 'firstborn of all creation' addressed in Col. 1:15 is the Wisdom of God which, according to Prov. 8:22–36 was created by God and was with him before the creation of the cosmos. Heb. 1:3 alludes to Wis. 7:25ff., which calls the preexistent Wisdom "a breath of the power of God and a pure emanation of the glory of the Almighty" as well as "a reflection of the eternal light, a spotless mirror of the working of God, and an image of his goodness".[28] We will return to this in chapter 4.5.1.

To understand the designation of Jesus Christ as the image of God, we must take into account that the statements in this regard exist in a hymnic context. Thus, the designation is not initially a matter of theological doctrine, but of doxology. In Paul's writings the term 'glory' (δόξα), connected to the metaphorical imagery of shining and radiating, has a close semantic link to the concept of image, since 'glory' appears as the reality depicted in such an image. The glory of Christ is the glory of God or its reflection, by analogy with the *kabod* (כבוד) that was placed on Moses' face (Ex. 34:29–35). The radiance of Christ's light is intended to illuminate humans and thus give them a share in the glory of God (2 Cor. 4:6). The image of Christ is therefore not an image at rest in itself, one which makes God recognizable when it is viewed. Rather, there is a radiance, emanating from Christ himself, which affects and transforms the beholder. It attracts the gaze and draws the viewer into the depicted reality. It is not merely a matter of looking at it, but of a spiritual 'seeing' of what is revealed in Christ. The image reveals the essence of that which is depicted.

With their reference to the 'iconic difference' between the image and what it shows, theological approaches that focus on the notion of 'image' offer a starting point for representational Christology. Taking such an approach, the indication is that Jesus Christ is the image of God, who as such becomes the archetype of true humanity and thus the model for conformity to Christ (Rom. 8:29), as well as the ethical model for Christians' actions.[29] The term 'image' here means not only (the rather external) depiction of a reality which is separate from it. That would underdefine Jesus' close relationship to God. What makes him the 'image of God' is that God is present in him.

Even the photographic image of a person not only *designates* the person depicted and *refers* to them, but also *identifies* them. Like a name, the photograph on an identity card, say, stands for and identifies that person. Therefore, deference to a person's image can be perceived as vicarious deference to the person themselves—and desecration of an image concomitantly as desecration of the person.

---

28 See also Chapter 4.5.
29 In reference to Col. 3:10–13, Rom. 15:5ff., 1 Thess. 1:6, and Phil. 2:5ff., Jacob Jervell writes, "in the ethical use of the image motif, God and Christ are models for Christians to emulate" (Jervell, "Bild Gottes", 496).

THE AGENDA: 'REPRESENTATION' AS THE KEY CONCEPT OF CHRISTOLOGY 63

The theological understanding of 'icon' goes even further. An icon of Christ in an Orthodox church not only shows a picture of Christ but is like a window through which the real Christ appears and—through the eyes of faith— becomes 'visible'. Icons are not pictures to be looked *at*, but transparencies *through* which one looks *into* a reality beyond. The icon represents this reality and thereby affects the viewer. It imprints itself in the viewer's imagination, unfolding a 'power of imagination' over them; at the same time, it leads them beyond the self to Christ. There is no 'iconic difference'.

If one understands Christ himself as an icon of God, as in Col. 1:15, then it follows that Christ makes present the living, potent presence of God (or God makes present Godself in him). God is imprinted on him; he is imprinted with God's stamp, so to speak.

The concept of representation, as understood in this study, is therefore semantically close to the idea of Christ as the 'image' or 'icon' of God. However, it is also open to other fields of metaphor that go beyond the figurative and thus transcend visual metaphor, in which the indwelling of God in Jesus is expressed. Descriptions of Jesus Christ as the incarnate 'Word' of God and the subsequent acoustic imagery ('addressing', 'proclaiming', 'hearing', 'answering', etc.) find a place in this field of meaning as well as, for example, in the imagery of recognizing and understanding (e.g., in the speech of Jesus as the "exegesis of the Father" proposed by John A. T. Robinson,[30] or in the designation of Jesus as the 'human face' of God[31]).

Another term that can be assigned to this field of meaning is 'parable'. If understood as the equivalent of the German 'Gleichnis', it means not only an allegorical story but a real similitude [*gleich*]. In that sense Wolfgang Schrage designates Jesus as "the eschatological parable of God."[32] In all aspects of his existence he corresponds to God's love and call. The synonymity of 'image' (Heb.: צלמ) and 'likeness' (דמות) in Gen. 1:26 suggests this way of speaking.

According to John Dominic Crossan, "[t]he parabler becomes the parable. Jesus announced the kingdom of God in parables, but the primitive church announced Jesus as the Christ, the Parable of God."[33]

---

30   Robinson, *The Human Face of God*, 189.
31   Robinson, *The Human Face of God*, 189.
32   Translated from Schrage, *Theologie und Christologie*, 138. See also Schweizer, *Jesus, das Gleichnis Gottes*.
33   Crossan, *The Dark Interval*, 124.

3.2.7.2   Sacrament

In theology and in the Church's usage, the concept of sacrament was and is related to ritual symbolic acts with which the Church (or—theologically interpreted—Christ himself) incorporates the faithful into the covenant made by God through Christ (baptism) and strengthens them in their membership in the body of Christ (the Eucharist). In Catholic understanding, there are additional symbolic acts in and through which God's grace is conferred: confirmation, forgiveness of sins after repentance, anointing of the sick, marriage, and ordination. One of the concerns of Reformation theology was to tie sacramental theology and the Church's sacramental practice to the proclamation of Christ and to understand them as part of the process of Christ making himself present. This led to seeing Christ himself as the sacrament of God. In the eighteenth thesis to the 'Disputatio de fide infusa et acquisita,' Martin Luther wrote, "only one sacrament is known to Holy Scripture, and that is Christ the Lord Himself".[34] This view can be traced back through Augustine[35] and to the use of the term *mysterion* (μυστήριον) in Paul and in the Deutero-Pauline writings. Paul refers to the proclamation of Christ as the mystery of God (1 Cor. 2:1ff., 6–16). In Col. 2:2 Christ himself is named as "God's mystery"[36] and thus identified as the mysterious Wisdom of God that encompasses creation and consummation. Similarly, Col. 1:27 speaks of "Christ *in you*".[37] Even after the introduction of the Latin term *sacramentum* by Tertullian and the narrowing of the term's meaning to the means of salvation administered by the Church, this broad and fundamental meaning remained, leaving Luther to take it up again and for it to continue to have an effect up to the present.

Karl Barth raised the question of whether the Church had done well "when it ceased to recognise in the incarnation, in the *nativitas Jesu Christi*, in the mystery of Christmas, the one and only sacrament, fulfilled once and for all".[38] In his later work he decisively answered this question in the negative, demanding that the concept of sacrament no longer be applied to individual church

---

34   "Unum solum habent sacrae literae sacramentum, quod est ipse Christus Dominus" (WA 6, 86).

35   Ep. 187, 34 (PL 38,845): "Non est enim aliud Dei Sacramentum nisi Christus".

36   In Col. 4:3 the wording is "the mystery of Christ".

37   For more on this, see Bornkamm, "Mysterion", 825–28.

38   Barth, CD IV/2, 55. Already fifteen years earlier he had declared that, "the basic reality and substance of the sacramental reality of [God's] revelation, is the existence of the human nature of Jesus Christ" (Barth, CD II/1, 53). For more on this, see Hempelmann, *Sakrament*, 91–100.

acts but only to Christ. Eberhard Jüngel joined in and proposed the axiom that "Jesus Christ is the *one* sacrament of the Church".[39]

The majority of Protestant theologians, however, did not follow this radicalism, and in Catholic theology it was certainly inconceivable. But there, too, the accent shifted from Church to Christ in the context of the Second Vatican Council. This was reflected in talk of Christ as the 'primordial sacrament' [*Ursakrament*], which Carl Feckes in particular introduced into Catholic theology.[40] In some ecclesiological studies this concept was applied to the Church.[41] However, the Church could also be called the 'fundamental sacrament' [*Grundsakrament*], 'root sacrament' [*Wurzelsakrament*], or 'whole sacrament' [*Ganzsakrament*] in order to preserve the term 'primordial sacrament' [*Ursakrament*] for Christ, as in the work of Leo Scheffczyk[42] and Karl Rahner.

After presenting the Church as the 'primordial sacrament' [*Ursakrament*] in his earlier writings,[43] Rahner later applied this term to Christ[44] and called the Church the "fundamental sacrament [*Grundsakrament*] of the salvation of the world".[45] Synonymously with the term 'primordial sacrament' [*Ursakrament*] he also spoke of Christ as the 'real symbol' [*Realsymbol*] of God's promise of gifting Godself.[46] According to Rahner, Jesus Christ

> as the God-Man [is] the primordial sacrament par excellence, because he is the signified (God in his self-communication to humanity) and the effective, exhibitive sign of this self-communication of God and humanity's acceptance of it (in his humanity and the historical life in which that humanity occurred) in person and unity.[47]

---

39 Translated from Jüngel, *Das Sakrament*, 334–5. Reprinted in Rahner, *Was ist ein Sakrament?*, 36 (emphasis mine). See also Jüngel, *Die Kirche als Sakrament?*, 456–7.
40 Feckes, *Das Mysterium*, 93–102.
41 Especially in Semmelroth, *Die Kirche als Ursakrament*, but also Hans Urs von Balthasar, Erich Przywara, *et al.*
42 Scheffczyk, *Jesus Christus*, 9–61; *id.*, *Die Kirche*, 63–120.
43 Such as in Rahner, *Kirche und Sakramente*.
44 Translated from Karl Rahner, "Anonymes Christentum und Missionsauftrag der Kirche" in *Schriften zur Theologie* 9, 509 and with increasing frequency thereafter (*Sämtliche Werke* 22/2, 320); *id.*, "Der eine Jesus Christus und die Universalität des Heils" in *Schriften zur Theologie* 12, 270 (*Sämtliche Werke* 22/1, 898); *id.*, "Ekklesiologische Grundlegung" in *Sämtliche Werke* 19, 63–4.
45 Translated from: "Karl Rahner, Das neue Bild der Kirche" in *Schriften zur Theologie* 8, 329–54.
46 Translated from Rahner, *Kirche und Sakramente*, 34ff.
47 Translated from Karl Rahner, "Ekklesiologische Grundlegung" in *Sämtliche Werke* 19, 63.

In Christ, then, three dimensions come together: the sacred presence of God, the human sacrament, and the act of sacramentalization, that is, the acceptance of the sacred presence of God by Jesus.

In the theological discussions on the concept of sacraments in the context of the Second Vatican Council, a gradation finally emerged: Jesus Christ as the primordial sacrament [*Ursakrament*], the Church as the fundamental or foundational sacrament [*Grundsakrament*],[48] and the individual sacraments as the fundamental ordinances of the Church.

Depicting the significance of human or ecclesial action and of the Church in general in the event of salvation has always provoked controversy between Protestant and Roman Catholic theologies. While Catholic theology holds on to the sacramentality of the Church, even if (since Vatican II) it has more strongly emphasized that this is a quality assigned to it by Christ, Protestant theology emphasizes the sole soteriological efficacy of God in Christ and denies the sacramental quality of the Church.

How should the concept of sacrament be related to the concept of 'representation'? In the history of theology, the latter played an important role, especially in the doctrine of the Eucharist. As early as Tertullian it was being used to describe the relationship between bread and the body of Christ[49]—although in that instance not in a specific or technical sense. In scholastic discussions 'representation' became a *terminus technicus* of sacramental theology.[50] It could also be applied to the Church as a representation of the body of Christ, for example in the bull 'Unam Sanctam' of Boniface VIII, which states: "she [the Church] represents [repraesentat] the one mystical body whose Head is Christ".[51] This expresses an understanding of the Church based on sacramental theology.

Calvin used the concept of representation in his doctrine of the Lord's Supper.[52] In the *process* of the Eucharist (not only in the elements), Christ makes himself present and gives us a share in the reality of God's salvation. In contrast to an (objective) understanding of the Eucharist, according to which it also works without the inner participation of the person receiving it—as it were like a medicine (*ex opere operato*)—Reformation theology emphasized that the sacraments must be received in faith. Sacraments, however, are not

---

48 *Lumen gentium* 1 speaks of the Church as *analogous* to a sacrament: she is "*like* a sacrament" (veluti sacramentum) (DH 4101).
49 "[...] the bread by which he represents [repraesentat] his own proper body" (Tertullian, *Adv. Marcionem* I, 14,3, p. 25).
50 For more on this, see Hofmann, *Repräsentation*, 65–101.
51 DH 870.
52 Calvin, *Institutes* IV, 14,5f.; 17,1; 17,10.

only communications, but also "acts of inclusion".[53] This is also true of 'representation' in the sense understood here.

Even in its broad, singular, Christ-centered sense, the concept of sacrament is close to that of representation as I define it. The conceptual content and scope of 'representation', however, is broader and more nonspecific than that of 'sacrament', which I see as an advantage. Its shoulders are not burdened by the history of the concept of sacrament; it has not been the subject of confessional disputes. Moreover, 'representation' aims more strongly than 'sacrament' does at a *process* (the process of making present) as opposed to an entity (Christ, the Church, the 'good of salvation', the means of salvation, etc.); nor is it linked to a particular ecclesiastical practice, as occurs with the diversely used concept of sacrament.

One strength of the concept of sacrament over that of representation, however, is that it accentuates the material dimension and the corporeality and historicity of the presence of God or Christ. A sacrament is always bound to a physical element—water in baptism; bread and wine in the Lord's Supper—while a representational relationship can also exist between entirely spiritual entities. This objection certainly applies to 'representation' in general, but not necessarily to representational Christology. In the latter, the term is sharpened to refer to personal and fundamentally bodily representations, to the representation of God in the person of Jesus. Christ in his corporeality is the representative of God: Docetism is thus averted.

The concept of representation also leads beyond the distinction between *exemplum* and *sacramentum*. It allows for an understanding of Christ as the (real) presence of God—and in this sense as a sacrament. As such Jesus sets an 'example' of true humanity towards which human beings in general (not only Christians) can orient themselves in the shaping of their basic relationships. The assumption of a supernatural causality and quasi-magical effect on the human being can thereby be dispensed with altogether. On the other hand, 'representation' also means far more than mere signification. Whoever recognizes in Christ the representative of God stands in relation to God, in the force field of his presence. God's presence exerts its spiritual impact by transforming those who are affected by it.

In terms of the history of theology, the concept of representation can be understood as a late response to the "crisis of the sacramental idea".[54] According to the Platonic-Augustinian understanding, the image contained the reality of what it showed; it was its 'face'. That idea was dominant until the Middle

---

53   Jüngel, *God as the Mystery of the World*, 10.
54   Translated from the subtitle of Pratzner, *Messe und Kreuzesopfer*.

Ages. The object depicted was really present in the image, and vice versa: the depiction was the hypostasis—the manifested presence—of the object. The manifestation (or the depiction) is of the same being or essence as that which it manifests or depicts: God is present as 'divine nature' in the person of Jesus Christ in a real and substantial sense. The body of Christ is present in the host in a real and substantial sense. The presence of Christ in *mysterio/sacramento/figura* is his real presence.

Even in the early Middle Ages (e.g., Ratramnus of Corbie), however, approaches were developed in which (spiritual) signs and (true) reality diverged. Accordingly, the sacrament was no longer the tangible substantialization of the risen body of Christ, but the *representation* of this reality (to be 'seen' with the eyes of faith). It lost its real content. These developments were reflected in the disputes over communion during the Reformation period, focusing on whether the body and blood of Christ were *substantially* contained in the elements of the Lord's Supper, whether it was a matter of a *spiritual* real presence of Christ, or merely a *symbolization* of union with Christ. The assumption of a physical presence of Christ in the elements had become controversial. The 'natural' unity between Jesus Christ and God (in terms of two natures of Christ) thus also became questionable.

In regard to that history, the concept of representation offers itself as an appropriate middle ground. The representation of God in Christ is *more* than a sign or an image: it makes the presence of God manifest. But the representative thereby remains distinct from the reality of God that he represents. There is no (numerical or substantial) oneness in the sense of equating one with another; but there is a personal identification, in which God identifies with Jesus and Jesus with God.

3.2.7.3 Symbol

As with both image and sacrament, symbols also connect two domains with each other: that of the entity depicted and that of the depiction, the symbolized content and the symbolizing substance. According to Karl Jaspers the 'symbol' expresses

> the presence of another in vivid fullness, in which the reference and the referent are inseparably one, the symbolized is present in the symbol itself. [...] Symbol [...] means standing in for an Other, even if this can only be there in the symbol and in no other way. In symbols we are meaningly directed to the Other, which thereby becomes object and is present in it.[55]

---

55 Translated from Jaspers, *Der philosophische Glaube*, 157–8.

However, the symbol does not only indicate this other reality, but also discloses it in a particular sense. In the symbol, a material and thus sensory 'carrier substance' is bound up with a meaning inherent in this carrier. It is thus a 'meaning-carrier', i.e., it has a meaning which points beyond itself. The carrier substance could be objects, actions, words, or images, but also people or communities. Everything can become a symbol once it is used and understood as such, i.e., once a reference function is attached to a phenomenon so that it stands for something else which reveals itself in it. Whether this meaning lies in the symbol itself and 'shows itself' directly, or whether it is attributed to it and only illuminated through an act of interpretation, depends on the understanding of the symbol and its philosophical embedding. An epistemological realist would assume the former, a nominalist the latter.

The relationship between the appearance of a symbol and its meaning can be defined in different ways: from an ontological *participation* in a reality underlying the symbol and manifested in it, to a *similarity* based on a transfer of properties, to a mere *signification* of a meaning. Ontic participation moves the symbol closer to the sacrament, while signification moves it closer to a sign.

The philosophical theories of symbols developed in and since the nineteenth century tend more in the latter direction, that is, toward the mere signification of a meaning, as we shall see in a moment with Charles Sanders Peirce. They do not presuppose that there must be a similarity in appearance between the symbol and that which it symbolizes (as in the case of a memorial stone to a person which shows the head of that person) or a substantial connection (as in the case of a golden coin which *has* the value that it indicates).

Empirical objects or issues of reference can be designated by a symbol which gets its meaning by convention (as in the case of a road sign). The symbol does not need to resemble the symbolized reality or participate substantially in it. If, however, the object designated is a reality that is beyond human cognizability, as in the case of religious 'objects' which are accessible only through symbols, then the religious traditions need to claim that the symbols are *authentic* manifestations of the divine reality. They undergird that claim by proclaiming that the symbol is instituted by this transcendent reality itself and participates in its very being. The Church invites believers to recognize the symbol as a manifestation of the divine reality. The symbol is analogous to the reality. The symbol thus comes close to the sacrament. This is the case with Karl Rahner,[56] who coined the term 'real symbol' [*Realsymbol*], as well as with Paul Tillich,[57] while Karl Barth, who strictly rejects the *analogia entis* doctrine, never uses the concept of symbol.

---

56   Karl Rahner, "Zur Theologie des Symbols" in *Sämtliche Werke* 18, 275–311.
57   Tillich, *Systematic Theology*, Vol. 1, 239–40.

Paul Tillich, who has presented a notable (but also criticized) theory of symbols in recent Protestant theology,[58] first distinguishes between signs and symbols, and second between living (i.e., genuine, true) and dead symbols.

(a) While signs merely point to a reality that is different from them, symbols participate in the reality represented by them and allow participants in the symbolic action to do the same. They make this reality accessible; and only thus does it become effective. Symbols exist in the fields of religion, poetry, and art, as well as in community life.[59] Religion is particularly dependent on symbols, because "that which is of vital concern to humans must be expressed symbolically".[60]

(b) True symbols transcend themselves in relation to the symbolized reality. They function as mediators to this reality; thus they have not only a depicting but also a mediating function. Where they no longer perform this function, but draw attention to *themselves*, where they thus become self-referential instead of negating and transcending themselves, they sink to the level of pseudo-symbols.

True *religious* symbols participate in the power and meaning of the divine reality, point away from themselves—i.e., away from their creaturely materiality—toward this reality, and thus offer a share in it. This process can also be described the other way around: as the manifestation of the divine reality in the symbol. The divine ground and power of being manifests itself in a finite entity, thus making itself accessible to the recipient and putting them in relation to itself.

Thus, these symbols are not mere presentations, but instances of present*ing* in the present tense, i.e., not only static images of meaning, but 'living', dynamic communications of divine reality, acting as transformers both from and towards it. They themselves are part of a life cycle; they are involved in a process of development, usage, and possibly also dying off. Three 'agents' are involved in that process: the symbolized divine reality, which manifests itself in the symbols; the religious authorities, which use and interpret the symbols; and the recipients, who let themselves be affected by them, but also understand their meaning in their own way.

Two kinds of usage endanger the transcendental function, and thus the truth, of the religious symbol. One is that the symbol is identified with the symbolized reality. In doing so it becomes an idol: its materiality is declared

---

58 See especially Tillich, *Systematic Theology*, Vol. 2, 88–96; 136–138; 150–165; and *id.*, *The Religious Symbol*, 3–21.
59 Tillich, *Wesen und Wandel des Glaubens*, 139–40.
60 Tillich, *Wesen und Wandel des Glaubens*, 139–40.

sacred and thus idolized. The other danger is that the symbol detaches itself from the symbolized reality and solidifies as a contingent reference to it. It becomes a metaphor and/or is only performed in lifeless routine, as the object of an externalized faith. The spirit has, so to speak, moved out of it. It has lost its power and will die off sooner or later.

Tillich connects the concept of symbol with the concept of representation: a genuine symbol reveals itself through its intrinsic power to represent the divine. The central symbol of the Christian faith is 'Christ'. This symbol refers to the person of Jesus and the historical fact of his existence. As 'Christ' Jesus is the one "who represents God to man".[61]

The 'Christ' symbol stands alongside other symbols like 'Son of David', 'Son of Man', 'Son of God', 'Kyrios', and 'Logos'. These are attached to Jesus in order to qualify him as the bearer of the 'New Being'.[62] Unlike Roger Haight, Tillich does not refer to the person of Jesus Christ as a symbol of *God*, but as a symbol of the New Being, i.e., of essential, true humanity: it is a soteriological symbol. To define the relationship of Jesus to God, Tillich uses the concept of representation.

On the one hand, Jesus represents the love of God in his self-giving love that even takes existential self-destruction upon itself.[63] In this self-sacrifice, he carries out the basic process of the (true) religious symbol, which denies its finite existence as material bearer of meaning and transcends itself in relation to the infinite reality of God. This is expressed in the symbols of both 'cross' and 'resurrection'. On the other hand, in his unity with God, Jesus represents the unbroken essential unity between God and humanity under the actual conditions of existence. "He represents to those who live under the conditions of existence what man essentially is and therefore ought to be under these conditions".[64] This is expressed in the symbol of 'incarnation'. Tillich summarizes these two dimensions in the statement that Jesus as essential man "represents not only man to man but God to man".[65] In both respects, Jesus not only *exemplifies* what he represents, but also *communicates* it by giving others a share in it.

---

61   Tillich, *Systematic Theology*, Vol. 2, 93. In contrast to the two-dimensionality of the relationship presupposed in the current representational Christological approach, however, Tillich explicitly excludes Jesus also representing (actual) humanity vis-à-vis God (*ibid.*). Jesus represents God and *true* humanity to humans.
62   See Tillich, *Rechtfertigung und Neues Sein*.
63   Tillich, *Systematic Theology*, Vol. 2, 138.
64   Tillich, *Systematic Theology*, Vol. 2, 93.
65   Tillich, *Systematic Theology*, Vol. 2, 94.

Jesus' *sharing* of the presence of God is thereby connected with the act of *receiving* on the part of his followers. Only in the act of recognition, i.e., the believing acceptance of Jesus as manifestation of the New Being, does he become the Christ for his followers.[66] There is no Christ without the community that recognizes him, i.e., without belief in and witness to Jesus *as* Christ. This believing testimony is expressed in the fact that the name of Jesus is associated with the 'Christ' title.

Here, I will not offer a general discussion of Tillich's theory of symbols; my concern is only with the relationship between (religious) symbols and representation. I refer to Tillich in what follows but go beyond him to evaluate his approach for the present account of representational Christology.

Representation is the *execution* of the symbol, the *act* of symbolizing. Only in that act is the symbol alive: *in usu*, in a process of communication. This use consists of a representation. Only where the religious symbol actually carries out this representation does it function as a symbol. Applied to the 'Christ'-symbol this means that it only proves to be true where it really communicates the New Being and does not only become the object of a doctrine about Jesus Christ. It has not only a cognitive expressive function that declares Jesus to be the Christ, but an evocative and performative function that 'presents' the New Being. When understood like this, the Christ symbol is a sacrament. It reveals the presence of the New Being in Christ Jesus and relates the recipient to it.

Of particular importance for representational Christology is the *critical* aspect of Tillich's symbol theory. Above we considered two ways in which symbols are used that undermine their transcendental function: idolatry and externalization. Idolatry in particular draws Tillich's criticism. Like every symbol, the Christ symbol is in danger of being objectified, i.e., understood literally. The distinction between symbol and symbolized reality gets lost. The sacrament becomes a magical sacramentalism; the symbol becomes an idol. What Tillich calls the prophetic protest against this tendency must also be given its due place in representational Christology. He insists on the fact that the representative must not be equated with the reality represented by him without differentiation. The reality that he represents lies beyond him. Where Jesus is known as the Christ, this means that he *represents* the universal and unconditional will of God for salvation in a definitive form for the Christian faith.

Emphasizing that this is a *definitive* representation, a claim to truth is made, but it must not be understood as an absolute claim. It is an expression

---

66 Tillich, *Systematic Theology*, Vol. 2, 99.

of Christian faith based on the communication of the New Being in Christ. Creeds are always bound to the believing person or community, even if they claim to have a universal validity.

But Tillich goes even further. He takes into account that the 'Christ-event' is bound to world history and does not want to exclude the possibility that there could be further divine manifestations in other areas and at other times in the universe.[67] In his *Systematic Theology* he does not yet relate this possibility to other religions. In his later works, however, in which he theologically processes his engagement with the phenomenology and history of religion as well as his encounters with Buddhism and Shintoism in Japan, he also considers religions as mediators of God's revelations:

> Religions are based on something that is given to man wherever he lives. He is given a revelation, a particular kind of experience which always implies saving powers. One never can separate revelation and salvation. There are revealing and saving powers in all religions. God has not left himself unwitnessed.[68]

For the Christian faith, Christ is the ultimate revelation of God. Yet this claim "does not exclude, but includes, similar claims to unique revelation made elsewhere".[69]

Let us take a step back from the consideration of Tillich's symbol theory and ask instead whether the concept of symbol can function as a guiding concept for Christology in general. That concept is exceedingly diffuse.

> If [...] symbol can mean both empty formulaic signs and very substantial images of meaning, both the material form of sign and the whole of form and content, both arbitrary and strongly motivated iconic signs, and both certain types of signs and signs in general, then one may well claim with some justification that this concept is in crisis.[70]

This accurate diagnosis by Armin Burkhardt does indeed cast considerable doubt on whether this concept should be the basis of Christology. It creates more problems than it solves. These problems do not even consist first and foremost in the wide-ranging content of the concept (with regard to the concept

---

67 Tillich, *Systematic Theology*, Vol. 2, 99.
68 Tillich, *The Significance*, 81ff. Reprinted in: *Main Works / Hauptwerke*, Vol. 6. 433.
69 Translated from Tillich, "Offenbarung", 664–5.
70 Translated from Burkhardt, *Geballte Zeichen*, 465–6.

of representation, too, possible meanings had to be eliminated in order to prepare it for Christological use), but above all in the ontological presuppositions of the respective symbol theories, which cannot easily be stripped away. Thus, Hermann Deuser rightly observes that Tillich's symbol theory depends on an ontology that separates nature and spirit, being and its meaning, in order to then assign these spheres to each other.[71]

Deuser, on the other hand, refers to the semiotics of Charles Sanders Peirce. Peirce distinguished between 'index', 'icon' and 'symbol',[72] which he called "three kinds of representations".[73]

- An 'index' is physically (mostly causally) connected to the object or state to which it refers, like the fever that indicates a disease. One can also speak of 'symptoms' or 'signals'. In addition to these natural indices, there are also intentional ones that are used deliberately in communication situations, such as wearing a uniform to represent a professional role. In linguistics, indexical expressions are those whose meaning is derived only from the context of the utterance, such as demonstrative pronouns like 'this' or 'that'.
- An 'icon' on the other hand, has a qualitative similarity to the object to which it refers, as with pictograms (for example, a stylized wheelchair indicates facilities for humans with a walking disability). In language, onomatopoeic expressions (such as 'cuckoo') belong to this type of sign.
- In contrast, the meaning of 'symbol,' according to Peirce, is based on an arbitrary convention, as in the logos of companies and institutions, road signs, and most linguistic expressions.

In all three of these types of signs, there is no presence of the object referred to in the sign itself. 'Index', 'icon', and 'symbol' are signs that do not attest to and impart the real presence of the signifier.[74] 'Representation' for Peirce denotes a reference, but not an act of making something or someone present. He decidedly does not assume an ontic participation of the signifier in the signified. There is also no relation between image and archetype. We can thus dispense here with the ontology on which Tillich bases his concept of symbol. On the other hand, this also makes it difficult to apply this concept of symbol to Christ. Christ not only *points* to God; he *makes God present*. He not only *shows* God,

---

71 Deuser, *Gott*, 16–17.
72 Peirce, *Philosophical Writings*, 104–15. In the following brief remarks, I draw on Nöth, *Handbuch der Semiotik*, 131–226.
73 Peirce, *Collected Papers*, 558.
74 See, however, Martin Vetter's interesting attempt to make Peirce's semiotics fruitful for the theology of the sacraments: Vetter, *Zeichen*, esp. § 11. Along with Peirce, Vetter emphasizes the importance of the intellectual disclosure of the relation between sign and the signified, so that the dyad of sign and signified becomes a triad that includes the interpreter.

he also allows God to speak and act through him. Tillich's symbol theory can express this more easily than Peirce's semiotics. Tillich's symbol theory, however, cannot be detached from its ontological presuppositions and, with the idea of *analogia imaginis*,[75] falls back on a conception of analogy that places the symbol in the vicinity of the sacrament.

I prefer the term 'representation' to that of 'symbol'. Not terminologically, but factually speaking, it is more compatible with biblical traditions and with traditional theological forms of expression than the concept of symbol. It can be linked with the idea of the 'incarnation of the Word', the 'indwelling of wisdom' in Jesus, and his being 'filled with the Spirit' of God. All these expressions are about the being of God in Jesus—but they involve thinking about this not so much ontologically as actually and relationally.

The term 'representation' emphasizes the status of an act in which God is made present more strongly than the concept of symbol. It refers to an interaction between God, Jesus Christ, and humanity. While 'symbol' tends to be associated more often with an object, with material symbolic matter, the concept of representation can be related more clearly to the action of a person, and to his/her 'being-there' [*Da-Sein*].

3.2.7.4 Revelation

We can make a fundamental distinction between an informational and a communicative understanding of revelation. An informational understanding involves the transmission of a message following the model of sender and receiver, whereas a communicative understanding involves a relational act in which the communicating person reveals him- or herself. According to an informational understanding, revelation consists of the disclosure and impartation of supernatural truths or instructions (declarations of will, counsels, commissions, interpretations, etc.). A communicative understanding does not exclude an informational understanding but goes beyond it and clearly speaks with a distinct accent; in this understanding, God not only reveals some*thing*, God always reveals God*self* as well. Revelation means the processes of making-oneself-present, self-disclosure, self-revelation, self-communication of God, all of which generate relationship with humanity. It means the opening up of Godself to humanity and the world and that means the constantly renewed initiation of a relationship between God and humanity. If one understands 'revelation' in this communicative sense, then the term comes close to that of 'representation'.

---

75 Tillich, *Systematic Theology*, Vol. 2, 125.

When we speak of 'revelation' as God's *self*-communication, we not only name God as the author and subject, but also as the content of the revelation. God communicates Godself. The relationality of God is not only proclaimed but actualized. Revelation is more than a giving of oneself *to be known about*. *Self*-communication is more than a proclamation: it is giving of oneself to the other. The communication says: God in Godself [*an sich*] is God 'for us'. This understanding of revelation is therefore not propositional but existential, not verbalistic but actual, not static but dynamic, not doctrinal but relational and communicative. 'To reveal' is thus used as a reflexive verb. God's essence is expressed in all forms of God's creative, salvific, and inspirational relation to the world.

In this understanding, revelation is not an 'absolute' communication, i.e., it is not independent of addressee and reception. It takes place only where it is recognized and acknowledged as such by the addressees. It becomes a revelation only when it is received. 'Revelation' thus belongs to the class of words Gilbert Ryle called 'achievement words', 'success words', or 'got it words'.[76] The same is true for 'representation'.

In Christian understanding, *Jesus Christ* is the realization of God's promise to give Godself. In him, that is, in the 'Christ-event', God's salvific self-communication takes place. This event includes Jesus' speaking, teaching, acting, suffering, and dying, as well as his being in eternal communion with God ('resurrection'), in which he encounters us as *Christus praesens*. The presence of God in Christ aims at situating its addressees in relation to God and thus at transforming them salvifically. Protestant 'Theology of the Word of God' describes this transformative participation in the acoustic metaphors of speaking and hearing, of word and answer. It is understood as a matter of a kerygmatic 'word of action' seeking to reorientate those addressed in their understanding of life.

To justify this understanding of revelation exegetically, one can refer to the character of Jesus' proclamation. At no point does he make use of the Old Testament messenger formula ('Thus says the Lord'), i.e., he does not appear as a messenger of God who, as it were, received a message from 'outside' and was commissioned to pass it on. Rather, he speaks out of an intimate relationship with God, 'out of God'. Nor do we find here the usual stylistic elements of a prophet's calling, such as the prophet's resistance to the commission given to them and then the appeal to inspirations or direct revelations to legitimize the proclamation they are executing. Additionally, however, we might refer to

---

76 Ryle, *The Concept of Mind*, 149–53.

explicit statements in which the biblical testimonies describe Jesus' relationship to God, such as Mt. 11:27 and Jn. 14:9, as part of substantiating this understanding. Jesus Christ not only makes God known but represents him.

In twentieth-century theology, Karl Barth in particular understood revelation as God's self-communication in Christ.[77] According to Barth, everything there is to say about God is to be said on the basis of God's self-revelation in Christ. The doctrine of the Trinity gives voice to this self-revelation. It presents God as the revealer [*Offenbarer*], the revelation [*Offenbarung*], and the revealedness [*Offenbarsein*]. God is the subject of revelation, a revelation accomplished once and for all in Jesus Christ and made accessible to humans in the power of the Spirit. In all three dimensions, God is the *auctor*. However, the 'self' in the term 'self-revelation' has three differently accentuated meanings here: in the first case, it refers to the originator; in the second, to the occurrence of communication; and in the third, to knowledge of the revelation. Barth identifies these three dimensions with one another:

> If we really want to understand revelation in terms of its subject, i.e., God, then the first thing we have to realize is that this subject, God, the Revealer, is identical with His act in revelation and also identical with its effect.[78]

Again, we ask how the concept of revelation relates to that of representation. The understanding of revelation as God's *self*-revelation brings it close to this concept. But even if this understanding of revelation transcends the epistemic dimension, (i.e., if it is related not only to *knowledge* of God but to God's relational action as a whole), it remains more strongly attached to the epistemic dimension than is the case with the concept of representation. In this respect the understanding of revelation as God's *self*-revelation is narrower than the concept of representation. 'Revelation', even if it is understood as a giving of oneself, primarily designates the giving of oneself to be known and the believing recognition of God's saving actions in the world. Representation, however, designates God's making present of Godself and thus making known Godself in that presence: God's 'being-there'.

The advantage of the concept of revelation over that of representation seems to consist in the fact that it is firmly anchored both biblically and in theological history. But this advantage becomes fragile when one sees the diversity of terms used to indicate a revelatory event in the New Testament tradition (the

---

77   Barth develops his doctrine of revelation most notably in *CD* I/1, §§ 8–18.
78   Barth, *CD* I/1, 296.

majority of which are not applied to Jesus Christ[79]): λέγω, γνωρίζω, δηλόω or φαίνω, and ὁράω in passive usage. With the abstract generic term 'revelation' they are all made synonymous. Markus Bockmuehl states that

> to describe the New Testament view of divine revelation is basically an anachronism. A theological question thus brought to the text is reasonable and legitimate in its own frame of reference, but obviously derives from a model of discourse that belongs to another time and place.[80]

This 'other time' does not begin until the period of medieval scholasticism, at which point the term 'revelation' is first used in the singular as *terminus technicus*. It is even later in theological history that the idea of the 'self-revelation' of God emerges. It owes its existence to the theological reception of Hegelian philosophy, within which context the term does not mean God's communication to humanity, but rather God's spirit becoming conscious of itself in the human spirit. Only through the theological transformation of this concept at the hands of Philipp Konrad Marheineke in the nineteenth century and Karl Barth in the twentieth does 'revelation' become interpretable as a relational event with a structure analogous to that of representation.

One can relate the two terms to each other in such a way that 'revelation' designates the epistemic dimension of 'representation': the giving of divine presence to be known in its representative. Representation is thus to be understood as the event which makes revelation initially possible and in which it takes place, but which also reaches beyond the idea of giving oneself to be known. The more the concept of revelation is extended beyond the intellectual dimension of 'giving oneself to be known' to the relational dimension of 'giving oneself', the closer it gets to the concept of representation.

I take up this thematic thread again in chapter 4.7 in order to shed more light on the dialectic between revelation and the hiddenness of God's presence.

3.2.7.5 Substitution

The terms discussed so far—'image', 'sacrament', 'symbol', and 'revelation'—all address different ways and dimensions of making present, but the term 'substitution' [*Stellvertretung*] is different from all of them. It aims less at the 'being' of the representative, in which the 'being' of the one they represent becomes

---

79   In this context Mt. 11:27 is of particular importance; it was in connection with this passage that patristics conveyed the idea of revelation to Christ. See Stockmeier, "Offenbarung", 48–49, 62–63, and 67ff.
80   Translated from Bockmuehl, "Offenbarung", 470.

present, and more at performing a function in the place of another. Someone steps (up) in another's place, discharges their rights and duties, and acts in their name and with their authority. In Christology, the term 'substitution' has its place in the doctrine of the 'work' of Jesus, i.e., in soteriology. According to 2 Cor. 5:21, Jesus has carried out an exchange of places or roles: he takes the place of the sinful human, takes on their sin, shoulders the responsibility of the consequences of sin, and grants them his own righteousness so as to justify them before God.

Stephan Schaede describes the semantic field covered by the term 'substitution' in view of its Latin 'antecedent terms'.[81] I summarize his delineations less out of historical, but out of systematic, interest. In doing so, I assume that the Latin precursor terms do not determine the later use of the term, but reveal important components of meaning that could be actualized in it:

(a) *Vicariatio* signifies the temporary replacement of one person by another who is subordinate to, authorized by, and refers to that person.

(b) *Substitutio* denotes the initial act of one person replacing another (where the choice to replace is mostly made by a third person/institution), but not the subsequent action of this person in the position assigned to him. In contrast with *vicariatio*, the substitution made here is not a temporary one; it is permanent and definite. The substitute person (*substitutus*) is not inferior in social rank to the one they have replaced, but either equivalent or superior to that person.

(c) *Subrogatio* means the (usually premature) removal of a person from their office and the appointment of another person in their place. The subrogating and the subrogated person are usually of equal rank. The term can also refer to the relief of a public official's workload by a person placed at their side.

(d) *Procuratio* means attentive advocacy for a person or institution through having been granted power of attorney. The procurator can conclude legally valid transactions in the name of the company owner with relative independence; the lawyer can conduct a legal dispute on behalf of a client; the guardian can act for their ward. In this context, the meaning of advocating for ('in favour of') is, more or less, combined with that of the substitutive form of representation ('in place of'). The care can be for the client (for example, in the case of a social worker), but also (as in the case of a procurator) for the person or institution giving the mandate. In many cases, however, *procuratio* means representation of *interests* rather than representation of *persons*. The procurator does not take the place of the person they represent. For example, the

---

81 See Schaede, *Stellvertretung*, 7–270.

attorney in a criminal case would certainly not take on their client's culpability or punishment.

(e) *Repraesentatio* has three possible meanings, according to Schaede. First, it refers to the mere depiction of something real that is absent and thus made to appear (as in an actress 'playing' a real person as a role), where the representation *refers to* what is represented. Second, *repraesentatio* can denote the *realization* of something hitherto merely potential or ideal (as in the financial realization of a book value), or the transition from a symbolic to a real presence (such as when the ruler appears in person: *repraesentare* here means 'to be present/to turn up'). Third, this term can mean the *replacement* of something or someone by stepping into its place; in this case, what is represented is not referred to, nor is it realized, but instead it is replaced.

(f) Terms like *lociservatura* or *locitenentia* that are composed of derivatives of *locus* and a verb (*servare* = 'to preserve' or *tenere* = 'to hold') denote forms of placeholding or replacing in different contexts. For example, in the seventeenth century, a person temporarily substituting for a judge was called *lociservator*, while *locitenentia* can mean commanding a post, holding a (military) position, or standing in for someone who is absent.

(g) *Intercessio*, in Roman law, refers to advocating for someone. A third person engages for the rights of another person. This act can take place negatively, as an objection to a decision of a legal or political authority; or positively, as an intercession for a person before an institution. The purpose of intercession is to persuade this authority to use its power of decision and action in favour of this person. The intercessor, who has a higher status than the person concerned, thus tries to protect the latter. If this person is accused, then the intercession consists of the request for forgiveness or for a more lenient punishment. In the context of Christology and soteriology, *intercessio* is understood as Christ interceding for the sinful human being before God (Rom. 8:34, Heb. 7:25, and especially Lk. 23:34).

This compilation of the Latin antecedent terms of the noun 'substitution' makes clear that in its basic meaning the term initially indicates a change of position—i.e., someone takes the place of another person. This process can be further defined, on the one hand, with regard to the constellation of relationships in which this change takes place and, on the other hand, with regard to its purpose:

- The *constellation* of relationships can involve two or three figures: three, if the person appointing the substitute is not the former (or actual) job holder, but a third person; two, if the process takes place between the former (or actual) job holder and their substitute, i.e., if the job holder allows *themself*

to be substituted. There can be either a hierarchical or an egalitarian relationship between the appointing and the appointed person.
- The *purpose* can consist in the assumption of responsibility to take a burden away from the appointing person, but also in the standing in for the former (or actual) holder of the position. Both can be combined with the purpose of acting for the benefit of those to whom this function is exercised.

Against Schaede's profound treatment of the history of the term 'substitution' one can object that the Christological meaning of this term cannot be adequately derived from the Latin precursor terms. At least as important is the Jewish understanding of being commissioned as a messenger of God as it is handed down in the Old and New Testament. According to this concept, the messenger receives a mission and the authority to carry it out: he thus becomes the representative of the sender.

In the Christological and soteriological context, the distinction between *exclusive and inclusive substitution* is important. It was introduced by Albrecht Ritschl in order to reject the notion of a vicarious satisfaction made by Christ, as Anselm had set forth in his doctrine of satisfaction. According to Ritschl, Christ's work of salvation is not to be understood in terms of exclusive substitution, according to which the substituting person acts to the exclusion ('instead of') of the one they represent. According to inclusive substitution, Jesus does not *replace* the human being, but includes them in his action. He acts in the place of the human being standing before God, whose relation to God is thereby changed. The human being can now exist before God again and find in that existence their actual selfhood.

In that inclusive understanding, substitution is connected with the granting of participation. The human being is included in the action of Jesus Christ—even, according to Paul, into the mystical body of Christ itself. It is not just a matter of standing together in solidarity, but of actively standing up *for*, that is, an act of participatory *procuratio* that aims at transforming the represented. Christof Gestrich sees this understanding of substitution as the predominant one in the Bible:

> substitution in the Bible never means replacement! On the contrary, it means enabling and empowering the one who is actually affected. The truly guilty party is enabled to atone in their own person and through this to regain their status as a child of God.[82]

---

82 Translated from Gestrich, *Die Wiederkehr*, 327–8.

Dorothee Sölle understood 'substitution' precisely in this inclusive sense and sharply distinguished it from 'replacement'. Jesus does not replace humans by his actions, as if they could and should remain passive. He is a placeholder in the sense that he keeps a place free for human beings, which they are supposed to take in order to fill it with their own actions in a responsible way.[83]

Sölle's actual thesis, however, focuses on Jesus' relationship not to humans, but to God. It consists in understanding Jesus as representative of the absent ('dead') or experienced-as-absent God, and as one who acts and suffers in his place in the world. It is precisely in this place that Christians are also to act. In an a-theistic faith they are to represent God acting in the world, especially in their commitment to those suffering under strife, injustice, and poverty (according to Mt. 25:31–46). The incarnation of God therefore takes place as God's coming to humanity. Jesus brought the God who was once enthroned in heaven into the everyday life of ordinary people. Through complete self-emptying, God depends on representation by humans to exert influence in the world:

> when the time was fulfilled, God had done something for us for long enough. He put himself at risk, made himself dependent upon us, identified himself with the non-identical. From now on it is high time for us to do something for him.[84]

Sölle emphasizes the provisional character of this process of substitution. The substitute represents the actual 'office holder' only temporarily. This is also how she wants the 'office' of Jesus to be understood: as an intermediary executing of God's role. He does not occupy God's place but keeps it free so that it can be reassumed by God at any time. But God will never return as before, as the distant God ruling over the world. God has left this heavenly realm forever and has become God-in-the-world, continuously incarnate wherever human beings act in harmony with the spirit of God—in love. Thus, the substitution of Jesus does not mean 'replacement' in relation to God either.[85] Like a human being, God cannot be replaced but can be represented. In this respect, inclusive substitution accords with the relational event of representation.

Substitution and representation are also in agreement in not ascribing to Jesus Christ a physical unity of being with God in the sense of a 'divine nature', and in preserving his distinctness from God. For Sölle, this means that incarnation would be misunderstood if it were conceived of as a complete giving of

---

83 Sölle, *Christ the Representative*. Similarly, McLeod Campbell, *The Nature of the Atonement*.
84 Sölle, *Christ the Representative*, 152. See also Graham, *Representation*, 21–80.
85 See Graham, *Representation*, 39–58.

self by God in human form. The relationship between Jesus and God is determined not ontologically, but functionally. Jesus takes the functional place of God; Sölle even goes so far as to call him an 'actor' of God.[86] To substantiate her insistence on the difference between God and Jesus, she invokes the statement of the Philippian hymn that Jesus did not claim divinity for himself: "in his being with God [he] cannot be seduced into having God".[87]

However, the question remains regarding what determines and enables him to be 'with God'. In my Christological approach I answer this question with reference to the Word, Wisdom, and Spirit of God: the presence of God in the power of the Word, Wisdom, and Spirit that is within Jesus is what makes him God's representative.

Stephan Schaede criticizes the distinction between inclusive and exclusive substitution, arguing that every substitution contains inclusive and exclusive elements. In his view, the exclusivity lies in the absence of the person who is represented, whereas in regard to the person who represents him/her it is inclusive because he is included in the representation process.[88] If the exclusive element is too strongly emphasized, substitution turns into replacement. If, on the other hand, the inclusive element is given too much weight, it becomes a cooperative partnership or an act of solidarity.[89] In both cases, the relational pattern of 'substitution' is dissolved. Applying his model to Christ yields the following: according to the model of exclusive substitution, Christ obtains reconciliation with God *instead of* humans. If, on the other hand, the inclusive substitution is overemphasized, the substitutionary suffering *for* becomes a suffering in solidarity *with*.

If one draws the concept of representation into this polarity, then it rather leans toward the inclusive side, albeit without settling there definitively. Here, however, we must not allow the concept of representation to commingle with the concept of substitution (for that would narrow its meaning), but rather ask what the relationship of the two concepts is to each other, especially in view of Christology. We can identify the following differences between, on the one hand, a substitutionary Christology and soteriology and, on the other, representational Christology:

---

86 Graham, *Representation*, 140.
87 Translated from Sölle, *Atheistisch an Gott glauben*, 19.
88 Schaede, *Stellvertretung*, 627–8.
89 Karl Rahner replaced the motif of substitution with the idea of Jesus' unconditional solidarity (Karl Rahner, "Versöhnung und Stellvertretung," in *Schriften zur Theologie* 15: 251–264 [*Sämtliche Werke* 30, 359–370]).

(a) Representation is not merely about substitution, but also about making present. Representation is *more* than the execution of a function for a certain purpose; it is the manifestation of a personal presence. Of the three meanings that Schaede recognizes in the Latin term *repraesentatio*, the second is the most likely to connect with Christology (transition from a symbolic to a real presence). But even this meaning does not really fit the concept of representation as I propose it for Christology. For in relation to Christ, representation cannot be conceived of as the realization of something potential or ideal but as the concentrated presence of God in Jesus.[90] In contrast, the first of the meanings mentioned by Schaede (representation as the depiction of something absent) falls short, and the third (representation as replacement) is quite at odds with a representational-Christological understanding. According to this representational understanding, 'representation' means the personal presence of God in the human Jesus filled with God's Word, Wisdom, and Spirit. Everything he said and did was part of this representation, as was everything that happened to him—both on the part of humans (passion, 'cross') and on the part of God ('resurrection').

Participation in the salvific presence of God granted *pro nobis* takes place in the representation itself and not only in a purpose connected with it. Anselm answered the question of why God became human ('cur Deus homo') with just such a declaration of purpose: to bring into effect reconciliation with God. In contrast to this, representational Christology thinks of divine salvific efficacy as God's salvific presence, from which, however, humans constantly close themselves off. Where God is present, there is salvation—even amid man-made disaster. To speak of a *will* for salvation is to refer to God's being.

To assume that Jesus Christ *takes the place of* humanity presupposes a Logos-Incarnation Christology 'from above'. In the act of incarnation, the Word of God divinizes the human nature. In contrast, representational Christology gives greater weight to Jesus' humanity. As Jesus of Nazareth, he does not have to *take* the place of humanity, since he *stands* there already—and thus he stands in the presence of God. As a human being, he does not *step in* for humanity, but *represents* it to God. If one frees the idea of substitution from its connotation of X-standing-in-for-Y and understands it entirely through the metaphorical sense of someone spatially standing *at* the same place as another (without occupying that place and substituting the other), then it becomes transferable to the idea of representation.

---

90 See also Schaede, *Jes 53*, 141.

(b) The term 'substitution' used in the context of Christology and soteriology refers above all to the substitution of *humanity* by Jesus. The Son of God takes the human being's place in order to carry out—according to Luther—the 'happy exchange'[91] (Christ receiving our sin, and we Christ's righteousness). The reverse direction of relationship, in which *God* is substituted, Sölle emphasizes in her Christology 'from below', but in other approaches to Christology it remains rather in the background or plays no role at all. In contrast, representational Christology encompasses both relationships equally: Jesus' relationship to God as well as his relationship to humanity.

(c) Representation means *more* than substitution—both in view of Jesus' relationship to God and in view of his relationship to humans. This can be stated even if one understands substitution not only as *acting* as a substitute, but as substituting someone's *existence*, i.e., not only as *doing* something in someone's place, but as a standing in for the *person*, including their guilt and its consequences. Representation means 'placing in front of': Jesus places the human before God and God before the human. Thus, he mediates between God and humans.

Regarding Jesus' relationship to humanity, representational Christology takes an opposite line to a substitutionary Christology that is based on the notion of atonement. It holds that Jesus is not condemned and punished in place of human beings in order to make them righteous; rather it is as a human that he suffers the consequences of his surrender to God, dies into God (so to speak), and is present in the presence of God—as *Christus praesens*. On his relationship with God, representational Christology's stance is that Jesus does not stand in place of God, but carries God's presence in himself, so that it radiates out from him.

The term 'substitution' is not helpful for representational Christology. It is also questionable from an exegetical point of view. According to James D. G. Dunn, 'substitution' does not do justice to Paul's understanding of the death of Jesus. This is instead much better revealed in the idea of sharing and participation: "it is rather that Christ's sharing *their* death makes it possible for them to share *his* death".[92] Dunn suggests that it is the concepts of 'participation' and 'representation', rather than substitution, which are central to Pauline soteriology, for these "help convey the sense of a continuing identification with Christ in, through, and beyond his death, which [...] is fundamental to Paul's soteriology".[93] Dunn, however, understands substitution in the exclusive sense.

---

91   WA 7, 25–28.
92   Dunn, *The Theology of Paul the Apostle*, 177–8.
93   Dunn, *The Theology of Paul the Apostle*, 177–8.

Even if one understands substitution as inclusive, it is doubtful that Pauline Christology can be developed in this way. Representational Christology seems better suited for this, since it expresses God's 'being in' Jesus more strongly than the functional concept of substitution can. In this perspective, God not only acts *through* Jesus, but is present *in* him and includes believers in this presence. The term 'substitution' can be used—in a metaphorical sense—to illustrate the representation using spatial imagery, and in this way to provide an aid to understanding it.

Compared with the 'related terms', my preference is for the concept of representation. In my opinion it expresses more clearly than the other concepts the presence of God in Jesus Christ while also distinguishing between the entity that represents itself (God the Father), the content of the representation (God's unconditional grace), and the figure of representation (Jesus). Jesus Christ is the embodied presence of God, but this presence reaches beyond the representation.

CHAPTER 4

Implementation: Unfolding Representational Christology

In this part of the study, I will elaborate on the representational Christology outlined in the previous chapter, turning here to how this Christology engages with biblical tradition and theological history up to the present day.

Firstly, I show how this Christological approach brings together the dual doctrines of the person and the ministry of Jesus Christ, which have often been differentiated in Christological studies (4.1). The philosophical and theological foundations of that approach are then identified in the context of the Christology of the Early Church (4.2). Like other Christologies developed in and since the nineteenth century, representational Christology replaces the paradigm of substance (which prevailed in the Alexandrian school in particular[1]) with personal, relational, and historical forms of thinking to do with 'relationship' and 'occurrence' (4.2.1). Such a personal and dynamic interpretation is more accessible to modern understanding. But it is also more closely connected to the New Testament traditions, which are influenced by Israel's history-related faith in God than by the ontological thinking of Greek philosophy (even if they are influenced by Hellenism and expressed in the light of Jewish philosophy of religion). Thus, representational Christology can define the relationships between God and Jesus, and between Jesus and humanity, in terms of a unity that preserves the distinctions between them because it is both personal and relational (4.2.2). Moreover, representational Christology makes a feature of Jesus' humanity rather than minimizing it (4.2.3).

On the basis of the two distinct relationships set out in the prologue of John's Gospel (the relationship of the Word of God to God and the relationship of the eternal Word to the incarnate Word), chapter 4.3 addresses how this unity that is sensitive to difference is already present in a New Testament text so central to Christology. While the history of theology placed greater emphasis on unity than on difference, representational Christology tries to keep both in balance.

---

1 Recent studies of the history of Early Church theology problematize the idea of two relatively homogeneous "schools"—the Alexandrian and the Antiochian. Nevertheless, this paradigm still seems to me to make sense as distinguishing two ways of Christological thinking that exhibit within themselves a certain diversity.

Chapters 4.3, 4.4, and 4.5 deal with the question of what it is that makes Jesus the representative of God. The answer arrived at goes back to, and transcends, the Christology of the early church councils, namely: the presence of God in him, as expressed in terms of the 'Word' (4.3), the 'Spirit' (4.4) and the 'Wisdom' (4.5) of God. In chapter 4.6, I take stock of the reflections offered in the preceding three chapters.

Chapter 4.7 discusses how the self-communication of God takes place in the tension between revelation and hiddenness. As has already been identified in chapter 3.2.7.4, self-communication goes beyond 'revelation' as making oneself to be known: it is a giving of the self. But the epistemic dimension is always connected with it: for dedicating oneself to the other implies making oneself known. Self-revelation which is connected with the self-communication in the 'Word', the 'Spirit', and the 'Wisdom', however, does not constitute a transition from being hidden to being revealed. Revelation is marked by a continuing hiddenness. In this sense, Jesus is the representation of God revealing Godself in his hiddenness.

Chapter 4.8 then turns to the question of Jesus' ministry and impact, i.e., to soteriology. The discussion here focusses especially on interpretations of his death on the cross and 'resurrection'. To what extent is this an event which brings salvation? How does this event affect those it is addressing?

At the end of this part, I return, in chapter 4.9, to the distinction between the person and mission of Jesus introduced in 2.4 and place it in the broader context of distinguishing between 'Christ-event' and 'Christ-content'. While some Christological studies of the last two centuries emphatically reject this distinction, others make use of it, and my approach for representational Christology follows suit.

4.1 Person and 'Work' of Jesus Christ

Since Thomas Aquinas, Christologies were mostly grounded on the distinction between the person and the 'work' (*opus*) of Jesus Christ.[2] The doctrine of the

---

2 In his *Summa Theologica* (STh), Thomas first presents the ontological status of Jesus' person, i.e. the human and divine nature (STh III, qq 1–26). He then demonstrates the salvific significance of Jesus Christ in view of his conception (qq 27–34) and virgin birth (qq 35–37), his baptism (qq 38f.), the evidence of divine authority in his life (qq 40–45), his suffering (qq 46–49) and death (qq 50–52), his resurrection (qq 53–56), and exaltation (qq 57–59). In the Prooemium to STh III, these sections are combined into two parts: "Concerning [the Saviour], a double consideration occurs: the first, about the mystery of the Incarnation itself, whereby God was made man for our salvation; the second, about such things as were done

person (Christology in the narrower sense) was concerned with Jesus' human and divine status, while the doctrine of the 'work' was concerned with his revelatory and salvific significance (soteriology). The question of Jesus' divinity was usually answered with the two-natures doctrine. Since Calvin, the question of the mode of mediation of salvation has mostly been answered with the doctrine of the threefold 'office':[3] the prophetic, the priestly, and the kingly offices, with the priestly office being the most central.

Luther linked Christology and soteriology closely. The notion of there being two natures in the person of Jesus Christ served to substantiate his salvific significance. To this end, Luther preferred the expression 'office' (*munus, officium*) to that of Christ's 'work' (*opus*). '*Munus*' has not only the meaning of 'commission' and 'service', but also of 'grace' and 'gift'.[4] This grace applies to the person, whereas the term 'work' distinguishes between doing and being in the person of Jesus Christ.

Dogmatic accounts of Protestant orthodoxy divided this doctrine into three: the doctrines of the person (in his two 'natures'), the 'states' (the state of humiliation and the state of exaltation), and the threefold 'office' of Jesus Christ.

When describing Jesus' soteriological significance, the term 'office' is just as antiquated and misleading as the term 'work'. It creates the impression that Jesus acted as a mere 'functionary' of God and that his function included suffering and dying. This suffering and dying is thus understood as the 'official' exercise of a divinely ordained plan of salvation, part of a wider framework of a history of salvation aimed at overcoming the condemnation of humankind's sin. This explicitly states (or at least implicitly suggests) that God willed and decreed this death, which casts a dark shadow over our understanding of God. Chapter 4.8 of this volume proposes a different view.

The term 'work' (*opus*) is more open compared to that of 'office' because it does not present Jesus' deeds as the performance of a divinely ordered service. But even this term is misleading: it places too much emphasis on active conduct and payment rendered according to one's merit.

In contrast, I prefer the expression 'ministry and impact', by which I mean the transforming power radiating from Jesus' speaking, doing, and behaving; from his life, suffering, and dying-into-God; and from his abiding spiritual

---

and suffered by our Saviour—i.e. God incarnate". This is the basis of the distinction between the "person" and "work" of Jesus Christ.
3 Calvin's doctrine of the threefold "office" of Jesus was included in the Geneva Catechism and was then adopted by Lutheran theology. In Johann Gerhard's "Loci theologici," a separate doctrine of "officium Christi triplex" appears for the first time (Gerhard, Loc IV, chapter XV, Th.2, 321–324).
4 See the lemma "munus", in *Oxford Latin Dictionary*, 1146.

presence. I intend 'impact' to be understood not in the sense of objective effective causality nor in the sense of the implementation of a plan of salvation. Instead, I intend it to mean a personal and relational influence on humans, who let themselves be seized, touched, affected by it, and thereby positioned in a new relationship to God. It constitutes influence through spiritual radiance. This is the basis of the significance and meaning which Jesus has for those humans affected by him. This effect is not achieved *before* its reception, but *in* it. Jesus' salvific significance does not lie in the fact that he acquired from God a 'treasury of salvation' that he could then bestow on others, but in the fact that through him God exerts a salvific influence on human beings' basic relationships, especially on their relationship to God.

There can be no separation between how we understand the person of Jesus and his salvific significance. Twentieth-century Christologies emphasized this interrelatedness repeatedly. Christology simply does not, cannot, exist in a narrower sense pertaining *only* to the person of Jesus (as 'Jesusology'), separately from his ministry and its effects. Christology is always soteriology; the difference is merely one of perspective. The order of knowledge prioritizes the experience of salvific transformation; the order of being prioritizes the presence of God in Jesus' person as the precondition for such an experience taking place. In the order of knowledge, the presence of God in Jesus' person became apparent because the people who encountered him experienced this as an encounter with God. In the order of being, encounters with him could be experienced as an encounter with God because he was God's representative. One can enter this circle on either side. Reformation theology, however, tended to focus on Christology by approaching it from a soteriological direction.

Melanchthon expresses this in his well-known dictum: "This is to know Christ [...] to know his benefits and not as [scholastic theologians] teach, to perceive his natures and the mode of his incarnation".[5] Calvin followed suit on this matter, and, according to Karl Barth, Jesus Christ exists "in the totality of His work".[6] Paul Tillich considers the doctrine of the person of Jesus to be a function of soteriology.[7]

Wolfhart Pannenberg reverses this definition and adheres to the priority of the person.[8] His critical question about a Christology that takes soteriology as its starting point is:

---

5   Melanchthon, *Loci communes* 1521, 68.
6   Barth, *CD* IV/1, 124.
7   Tillich, *Systematic Theology*, Vol. 2, 150.
8   Pannenberg, *Grundzüge der Christologie*, 32–44; id., *Systematische Theologie*, Vol. 2, 441–2.

Is it still Jesus himself who is being spoken of? Is it not rather a matter of projections onto Jesus' figure of the human desire for salvation and deification, of human striving after similarity to God [...]. Along this line also lies the distinction between the Christ *principle* and its application to the historical *person* Jesus, from A. E. Biedermann to P. Tillich.[9]

Representational Christology understands the distinction between the person and the impact of Jesus Christ merely as two differently accented viewpoints, two aspects of Christology, two directions of expression in which the significance of Jesus Christ is addressed:
- with regard to his *person*, that he is the representative of God toward humanity and the representative of humanity toward God;
- with regard to his *ministry* and *impact*, that he represents God's salvific presence to humanity in all its separation from God and desire for salvation, and that he represents to God the conditions and experiences of the human existence.

These two aspects—the presence of God in the person of Jesus and his soteriological significance—can be summarized in the expression 'Christ-*reality*'. That term unites the dimensions of being and of doing. 'Doing' in this context includes more than just making things happen; it includes acts of communicating and of demonstrating, exerting a soterial impact even by means of inaction, and the radiance of pure presence.[10] Moreover, it includes the effect that these actions have on those affected by them and the transformation evoked in them; even their own actions belong to this reality, insofar as they are inspired by it.

The concept of representation binds the two aspects of Christology together: how we perceive Jesus Christ's person, and how we perceive his ministry and impact. It overcomes too strong a distinction between the person and the 'work'.

Representation is an act tied to a particular position, and in order to occupy that position the representative must stand in a relational framework. In the case of Jesus Christ, this is the position between God and humanity: not an empty space in-between them, but wholly with God and wholly with humanity. Jesus' Christhood consists of being placed into this position. His ministry and his impact are rooted in facing up to the 'role' connected with that position and exercising it, both actively and passively. Ministry and impact belong inseparably together in this matter and cannot be divided into two separate doctrines.

---

9 Translated from: Pannenberg, *Grundzüge der Christologie*, 41–2.
10 See chapter 3.2.4.

- With regard to the person of Jesus, the term 'representation' covers those semantic fields in which the divinity of this person has traditionally been expressed. These include terms such as 'incarnation of God', 'sonship of God', 'revelation of God', 'image of God' (Col. 1:15: εἰκὼν τοῦ θεοῦ), being 'in the form of God' (Phil. 2:6: ἐν μορφῇ θεοῦ), etc.
- With regard to Jesus' ministry and impact, 'representation' allows us to express his soteriological significance. Here the term indicates the fundamental process of God's salvific self-communication in Jesus Christ, which in traditional soteriological thinking has been denoted in different ways using diverse metaphors such as 'justification', 'reconciliation', 'redemption', 'mediation of salvation', etc. These terms can all be understood as illustrating what is meant by the representation of God's salvific presence *pro nobis*.

The doctrine of the person of Jesus is thus transformed into an explication of the fact that Jesus represents God's salvific presence to humanity and represents humanity to God. The doctrine of the 'work' refers to the '*pro*' aspect of this representation, to its beneficial effect for humans. It is done 'for us',[11] 'for many',[12] 'for all',[13] 'for the ungodly',[14] and 'for others'.[15]

4.2 Revisions of Logos-Incarnation-Nature Christology

In the following chapter I condense the predominant stream of Christology in the history of theology (which took shape in the councils of the Early Church, flowed through the Middle Ages and the Reformation, and has been in turmoil since the Enlightenment) into the term 'Logos-Incarnation-Nature Christology'. This term hugely condenses down the complexity of that interpretation of Jesus Christ, but what matters to me is not individual expressions so much as the fundamental features in relation to which I will define representational Christology.

The three critiques highlighted in the next three chapters are not specific to representational Christology but are found widely in modern Christological approaches of various kinds. These are, firstly, a critique of the substance-based

---

11 Lk. 22:19.20b, Rom. 5:8; 1 Cor. 15:3, 1 Thess. 5:10, Gal. 3:13, 2 Cor. 5:21, and elsewhere.
12 Mt. 26:28; Mk. 14:24; Mk. 10:45 and elsewhere. The Greek πολλοί ('many') is largely synonymous with πάντες ('all').
13 2 Cor. 5:14ff.; 1 Tim. 2:6; Tit. 2:11; 1 Jn. 2:2 and elsewhere.
14 Rom. 5:6.
15 In "Resistance and Submission: Draft of a Work" (DBWE 8, 556–561) Dietrich Bonhoeffer spoke of Jesus as "the man for others" and as him being "only there for others". Thus the *pro nobis* is replaced by a *pro aliis*.

definition of the relationship between Jesus and God; secondly, a critique of the overemphasis on Jesus' unity with God at the expense of the distinction between them; and thirdly—and closely related to the second point—a critique of the lack of emphasis of Jesus' humanity. This has resulted in revisions of the classical Logos-Incarnation-Nature Christology.

4.2.1   Relationship Instead of Unity of Two Natures

The Council of Chalcedon attempted to resolve earlier Christological disputes with the formula that the person of Jesus consists of the divine and the human nature, without thereby assuming a duality in his person.[16] In this way a twofold definition of relationship was established:

(a) With regard to the *person* of Jesus, the concept of consubstantiality (ὁμοουσία) defined his two relationships—to God on the one hand and to human nature on the other. In an ontological sense they were thus conceived in terms of unity of essence. God is 'physically', ontologically, substantially (as divine nature) present in Jesus Christ.

(b) With regard to the relationship between the divine and human *natures*, the Council developed a fourfold negative definition: 'without confusion' (ἀσυγχύτως) / 'without change' (ἀτρέπτως) and 'without division' (ἀδιαιρέτως) / 'without separation' (ἀχωρίστως).[17] In this line of thinking the two natures are neither combined with one another nor made to complement one another; neither are they partially present in this person, but in both cases wholly present. Thus, one can speak of a consubstantiation of the two natures in Jesus Christ. However, the four negative definitions mean that the two-natures doctrine only describes which ways of thinking do *not* apply; the doctrine does not offer a plausible or illuminating and positive way of conceiving the connection of the divine and the human in Jesus Christ. It wants to unite what is incompatible, but in doing so it only indicates that the two natures can be neither united nor separated.

4.2.1.1   Turning Away from the Concept of Substance

The Early Church doctrines of the Trinity and the two natures in the person of Jesus Christ skillfully based their definitions of Jesus' relationships with both God and humanity on Hellenistic ontological thinking (especially Middle Platonism). The Alexandrian school of Logos-Incarnation-Nature Christology is based on the distinction between the 'nature' (i.e., the What) of humanity in general on the one hand and the concrete humanity of the particular person

---

16   DH 301.
17   DH 302.

(i.e., the Who), in this case Jesus, on the other. The person is the concrete realization of the human nature that ontologically preceded it. The hypostasis of the Logos unites with the human nature to form a 'hypostatic union' in the *one* human being Jesus. This 'one' is thus not split into two, as would have been the case if, for example, Jesus had had a divine spirit and a human body, or if he had had two consciousnesses and/or two wills in himself.

The substance-focused, ontological way of thinking which lies behind the concepts of 'natures' and their 'hypostases' is bound to its historical context, i.e., to Hellenistic metaphysics. It is as far removed from the biblical traditions as it is from the plausibilities of the present. If one repeats it without translating it into modern day forms of thought, it generates misunderstandings that leave faith open to the suspicion of irrationality. The Platonic prioritizing of 'what' before 'who' has lost its power to illuminate. Even if 'nature' is not understood as a static 'what', this ontology is nevertheless very different from our present-day understanding of reality as a dynamic and relational network of historical processes. The traditions of the OT and NT, too, are better understood in terms of the categories of act, event, occurrence, and relationship rather than those of being and substance.

Such forms of thought are even more pertinent when dealing with *personal* realities, as with the person of Jesus Christ. Persons are constituted by relationships. The question of 'who' can only be answered in terms of relationships and relational *acts* and *events*. Above all, thinking in terms of relationship, act, and event, rather than substantiality, is more appropriate when it comes to the reality of God. Emmanuel Lévinas identifies why: "the intelligibility of transcendence is not ontological. The transcendence of God can neither be thought of nor phrased in the terminology of 'being' [...]".[18] We must instead think of God's transcendence in dynamic and relational categories—as relational events.

Like Heinz-Günther Schöttler (and many others), I think we need to "free Christology from its ancient ontological prison of thought and language".[19] It seems to me that representational Christology offers a suitable way to do this. In what follows, I first describe its relational theological underpinnings in order then to clarify how it further defines the Christological relational structure through the idea of representation.

---

18 Lévinas, *Gott*, 121.
19 Translated from Schöttler, *Mose und Jesus*, 397.

4.2.1.2   'Relationship', 'Act', and 'Event' as Guiding Categories

The guiding categories of representational Christology are 'relationship', 'act', and, 'event', but they are not specific to it; to a greater or lesser extent it has this approach in common with most Christologies since Schleiermacher. The divinity of Jesus is not defined statically, ontologically, on the basis of substance metaphysics; but rather personally, relationally, and historically—as something that happens.

In ancient Syria (especially in Antioch) Christological reflections were already being established which were closer to the Hebrew and Aramaic way of thinking—as it shaped even the Hellenistic-influenced biblical tradition—than to Alexandrian ontology. What was of interest was less the *nature* of God and Jesus Christ and more his *relationship* to God and the relations made possible by him. It was not so much the very being of Jesus Christ's person that mattered, but rather the fact that God had chosen him, poured out the Spirit upon him, and empowered him for his saving work. In the present debate, Christological approaches developed in this way can help to take Jewish and Muslim concerns seriously and lead to a comprehensible understanding of Christ among Christians. Roger Haight, for example, draws on Antiochian theology.

The Reformers adopted the two-natures doctrine but developed it not so much along ontological lines of argument as—even if only rudimentarily—in personal, relational terms, as an event.[20] They understood the person and 'work' of Jesus Christ less in terms of existential manifestation of the divine essence and more in terms of the presence of the speaking and acting God. With the development of a historical paradigm in the Western intellectual culture since the end of the eighteenth century, the need to situate the contents of the Christian faith in a historical frame of reference became increasingly obvious.

With this Christology based on a relational ontology, the Early Church doctrine of two natures in the person of Jesus Christ is transformed into a doctrine of two relationships which constitute his person. Namely: the relationship of Jesus to God and God's salvation, and the relationship of Jesus to the humanity to which he belongs; that is, to the human condition of existence.

4.2.1.3   Representation as a Pattern of Relationships

Representational Christology is based on an 'ontology' of the person, their relationship(s) as well as their function within the framework of a dynamic understanding of reality as processes. However, what is specific to it as a

---

20   See, e.g. Joest, *Ontologie*.

Christological approach is not the relational ontology itself, but the application of the concept of representation to the two relationships that are constitutive for the person of Jesus. These are defined in the sense of a 'making-present', so as to exclude thinking in terms of 'substance'. Jesus is the representative of God and God's salvific self-communication towards humanity and the representative of humanity towards God. Jesus' divine humanity, his Christhood, consists in carrying out these representations. The *vere Deus* thus becomes the expression of Jesus' unique *relationship* with God. The predicate of divinity does not concern a divine 'nature' in him, but the intense relationship within which he is united with God. What makes him, or his relationship with God, special is his unique intimacy with God. In that sense we can state: God is *in* him. This in-dwelling is a relational act.

This must be emphasized: an act! It is not a question of static relations, but of movement, which the term 'relational *ontology*' could obscure. The concept of representation, on the other hand, emphasizes a dynamic. Christology is about the interaction or communication of God towards humanity and humanity towards God, focused on the person of Jesus.

Jesus represents *God*'s relationality and thus makes this a reality that can be experienced. In Jesus, God's commitment to community is proved. The fact that in his self-understanding and in the whole of his life Jesus is grasped and permeated by the presence of God makes him the representative of true humanity (*verus homo*). Thus, it is not because he has a superhuman nature that Jesus is divine, but because God indwells his human existence.

As the representative of God, Jesus 'embodies' how God defines Godself as well as defining true humanity. In this way, he also becomes the source of the *understanding* of God and of humanity. In terms of understanding *humanity* this means that along with the revelation of God's purpose for human beings (true humanity) their deviation from this purpose (i.e., humanity as it actually is) also becomes clear. In terms of understanding *God* it means that in Jesus we see God's commitment to the intended purposes laid out for 'his people', for all the nations of the world, and for all cosmic reality. Through the 'lens of Christ' the eye of faith can discern these purposes and their final realization. The story of Jesus opens up the story of God to the world and to humanity: Jesus is the one who interprets or exegetes God.[21] And vice versa: the story of God opens up the story of Jesus.

The model of hypostatic union that underlies and defines Alexandrian Christology can only be interpreted as exclusivist: the Word of God, which is

---

21 See also Jn. 1:18: μονογενὴς θεὸς ὁ ὢν εἰς τὸν κόλπον τοῦ πατρὸς ἐκεῖνος ἐξηγήσατο.

consubstantial with God, has united itself with human nature in Jesus (and only in Jesus). In contrast, the model of representation enables us to make the double distinction between that *which* represents itself and the act of representation, between the symbolized content and the symbol, between the 'Christ-*content*' and the 'Christ-*event*'. I take up this thread again in chapter 4.9.

4.2.2 Unity and Difference

The grammar of the Christian doctrine of God and Christology generally operates with a dialectical definition of the relationship between unity and difference (which radiates out into other theological doctrines, e.g., that of the Lord's Supper). In the theology of the Trinity, the unity of God's being is conceived together with the difference of the three 'persons'; in the Christology of two natures, the unity of the person of Jesus Christ is conceived together with the difference of two natures. This dialectic is demarcated (especially clearly in the Chalcedonian Definition) on one side over against an overemphasis on difference and separation, and on the other side over against an overemphasis on unity, on blending or merging.

Representational Christology seems to me better capable of bringing this grammar to fruition than Logos-Incarnation-Nature-Christology. With the concept of *homoousios* (ὁμοούσιος), the latter emphasizes the essential *unity* of the person of Jesus Christ with God as well as with humans, while the representational model allows unity and difference to be held in balance. The element of difference is reinforced by the transformation of the two-natures doctrine into a two-relations doctrine: representational Christology not only *connects* Jesus Christ with God, whom he represents, but also *distinguishes* him from God's divinity. It not only *connects* him to humanity, but also *distinguishes* him from it. And it not only *connects* the two representations with each other, but also *distinguishes* them from each other.

The distinctiveness of the two natures was preserved even in the Chalcedonian doctrine of *unio hypostatica*. The presence of divinity within humanity does not make the human Jesus into God and God into a human being. 'Unity', then, cannot be understood in terms of an undifferentiated sameness. It is not a 'unity' of the two natures resulting from a transformation of one into the other, or the blending of the two into a new third (a God-man or man-god). 'Unity' is not to be understood as synthesis in the sense of physical fusion, but in the sense of consubstantiality. The Chalcedonian 'without confusion' and 'without change' preserves the distinctiveness of the two natures. It also preserves the distinct features of both divine and human nature. Moreover, the *homoousios* (ὁμοούσιος) allows us to conceive of a difference—albeit a very slight one—between the nature (οὐσία) of God and the hypostasis of this nature in the person (πρόσωπον) of Jesus. This differentiation does not concern the substance of being, but the material form, the manifestation of this nature. Chalcedon, after all, was sensitive to differences.

A key concern prompting the making of that distinction in Christological approaches throughout history is to preserve the unity and oneness of God. What must be ensured is that Jesus' divinity does not challenge monotheism.[22] Therefore, 'consubstantiality' and 'unity of essence' cannot mean complete identity. Even unity of substance does not equal undifferentiated sameness.

Representational Christology, which operates on a relational basis, makes a clearer distinction between God and Jesus than the two-natures-approach allowed it. It defines Jesus' double relationship to God and to human beings in terms of a *unity in difference*. If the relationship between two entities/subjects is understood relationally, i.e., according to the pattern of the 'relationship' rather than of the 'unity of nature', then the element of difference is already intrinsic to this definition. Relationships always exist between distinct subjects.

With the concept of representation Jesus can, on the one hand, be put into the closest conceivable relation to God, and in this relational and representational sense he can have divinity attributed to him and he can even be said to 'be God'. On the other hand, the concept of representation rejects the idea of a unity of substance with God. The unity between Jesus and God does not exist on the physical plane, but nor does it exist only on the mental plane. As will become clearer later on, it is a *spiritual* unity: a communicative oneness sustained by the Spirit of God. 'Unity' in this personal sense of a relational unity represents a communion of diversities that cannot be without each other. It is in this sense that God's 'in-dwelling' in Jesus is to be understood.

- For Jesus' relationship with God, this dialectic of unity and distinctness means that Jesus lives in the most intimate relationship with God and yet is a human being distinct from God.
- For Jesus' relationship with humanity and the world, this dialectic of oneness and distinctness means that he is fully human and yet not 'of the world' (Jn. 17:14–16: ἐγὼ οὐκ εἰμὶ ἐκ τοῦ κόσμου). He overcame the world (Jn. 16:33: ἐγὼ νενίκηκα τὸν κόσμον). His distinctiveness from humanity has traditionally been expressed by the theologoumenon of his sinlessness (Heb. 4:15: χωρὶς ἁμαρτίας).

This dialectic as it applies to both relationships we can further define as follows:

(a) Jesus' *unity with human beings and with human existence* (this is the way I translate the notion of 'human nature') has its basis in the fact that he

---

22   See Bernhardt, "Monotheism."

was human and experienced human existence right to the very extremes of dehumanization—betrayal, accusation, public shaming, torture, and being put to death. His life did not play out like a metaphysical drama of salvation in which the Son of God, who came from heaven, was only *apparently* exposed to despair, the fear of death, and the experience of God-forsakenness. He really suffered these conditions, and thus also carries within himself all that caused them: the guilt of the human beings who transgressed against him. His stigmata represent a humanity falling short of its divine destiny: a sinful humanity. He represents that as a victim.

But his humanity also includes his physical needs, his spiritual development (Lk. 2:52), and the limitations of his horizons resulting from the embedding of his thought, life, and work in a certain historical context. The fact that he was mistaken about the imminent coming of the Son of Man and the dawning of the end times it would bring about (Mk. 13:30; Mt. 10:23) also proves him to be an actual human being (*vere homo*).

(b) The *distinction of Jesus from humanity and from human existence* appeared when the human world in which he lived hardened itself against God and his creatures. Jesus set himself apart from it in his speech and actions. This applies to all manifestations of social, ethnic, and religious discrimination and to all conditions that do not correspond to God's saving presence. He also sharply criticized religion in this context, earning himself the enmity of the Jewish authorities.

(c) *The unity in the relationship between Jesus and God* has its basis in the supreme intensity of Jesus' indwelling of God's salvific presence. This fundamentally shaped his entire personhood and ministry, so much so that his followers experienced God's presence in their encounters with him and could speak of him as 'their God' (Jn. 20:28: ὁ θεός μου).

(d) But this is contrasted with the *distinction from God* which Jesus himself made, and which Paul and even the Gospel of John maintained, in which the unity of Jesus with God is most strongly emphasized (Jn. 10:30: ἐγὼ καὶ ὁ πατὴρ ἕν ἐσμεν). For all that Jesus claimed authority for himself, he also always clearly *distinguished* his person and mission from God as the initiator of this mission. He did not declare himself the center of his proclamation and practice but proclaimed the dawn of God's reign (and fulfilled his own proclamation). As a devout Jew, he was theocentrically oriented.

This is expressed in the Synoptic Gospels, for example in Mk. 10:18 and 13:32, in Mt. 7:21 and 20:23 and other similar passages, the first three appeals made in the Lord's Prayer, and Jesus' cry of being forsaken by God (Mk. 15:34). He pointed away from himself to God and the dawning Kingdom of God. In Jesus, as in early Christianity, we thus observe the coming together of Messianism with the monotheism resulting from the *Shma Israel* (Mk. 12:29).

The announcement that Christ submits his work to God and hands it over to him in the end (1 Cor. 15:28) accompanies Paul's declaration of the supreme immediacy of Jesus Christ, according to which God acts *in* and *through* him. In several statements, Paul clearly marks the difference between Jesus and God, such as 1 Cor. 3:23 and 11:3 but most clearly in 1 Tim. 2:5:

> for there is one God; there is also one mediator between God and humankind, Christ Jesus, himself human (εἷς γὰρ θεός, εἷς καὶ μεσίτης θεοῦ καὶ ἀνθρώπων, ἄνθρωπος Χριστὸς Ἰησοῦς).[23]

At no point, however, does Paul refer to Jesus as God: in Rom. 1:8 and 7:25 he gives thanks to God *through* Jesus Christ, while the direct thanks to Jesus in 1 Tim. 1:12 should not be understood in the sense of a prayer, but as an expression of gratitude. Paul sees the Son of God as subordinate to God.[24] Even where he speaks of the 'Lord' as having equality with God, Paul emphasizes that Jesus relinquished this. The Philippian hymn testifies to Jesus Christ's self-abasement, and that he did not hold on to this equality with God like a trophy but laid it aside (Phil. 2:5–11). The worship of the exalted Lord referred to in Phil. 2:10 is not to be equated with praying to God. It is done for the glory of *God* (Phil. 2:11: εἰς δόξαν θεοῦ πατρός).[25]

Christ acts in God's name and God acts through Christ. By his obedience to God, in his belonging to God, he relates humans to God. James D. G. Dunn summarizes thus: Paul

> sees Jesus not as a pre-existent divine being, but as a man, a Jew, whose God is the one God, and yet who so embodied God's creative power and saving wisdom (particularity in his death and resurrection) that he can be identified as 'the power of God and the wisdom of God'.[26]

In John's Gospel, the difference between Father and Son (as the incarnate Word/Logos of God) is articulated through the motif of mission and return. There is an intimate unity between God the Father and the 'Son', but at the same time there is a difference in relation to mission. God sends out the Word, which embodies itself in Jesus and returns to God as Christ. For his part Jesus does not call himself the 'Word of God' at any point.

---

23 See also: 1 Cor. 8:6.
24 See also: 1 Cor. 15:24–28.
25 See also: Rom. 15:7 and 2 Cor. 4:15.
26 Dunn, *Christology*, 211.

The Johannine Christ emphasizes that he does not act on his own authority, but on behalf of God (Jn. 4:34; 5:30 and elsewhere); he has come in the name of God (Jn. 5:43: ἐγὼ ἐλήλυθα ἐν τῷ ὀνόματι τοῦ πατρός μου); he knows himself to be dependent on God (Jn. 5:19ff.; 10:29; 14:24b, 28; 17:1–3). On the one hand, he insists that relationship to God is determined by relationship to himself (Jn. 8:51); on the other hand, as mediator to God, he seeks not his own glory but the glory of the one who sent him and to whom alone all glory is due (Jn. 8:49ff.). He explicitly confesses the 'only God' as commanded by the *Shma Israel* (Deut. 6:4f.) (Jn. 5:44; 17:3). On the one hand, there is an emphasis on the unity between Jesus Christ and the Father (Jn. 10:30, 12:45, 14:9); on the other, the Johannine Christ confesses that "the Father is greater than I" (Jn. 14:28: ὁ πατὴρ μείζων μού ἐστιν). Despite the essential unity, there thus remains a theocentric subordination.

These definitions of 'difference' are understood against the background of the Jewish accusations that Jesus had equated himself with God (Jn. 5:18; 10:33, 19:7) and thus disregarded God's uniqueness. Adam's sin consisted in claiming equality with God for himself. Jesus did not claim finality for himself, but for God and thus the dawning reign of God.

4.2.3 *The Humanity of Jesus*

The greater emphasis that Logos-Incarnation-Nature Christology tended to place on Jesus Christ's divinity resulted in the downplaying of his humanity. This was only increased by the Hellenization of the ancient world's intellectual culture.

This process begins with the Greek translation of the Hebrew Bible. In Ps. 110:1, for example, both 'Yahweh' and 'Adonai' are translated as 'Lord' (*kyrios*). However, 'Adonai' there refers to King David as God's anointed (cf. Mt. 22:41–46, Acts 2:34). In its almost two hundred other instances of usage in the Old Testament, this word refers almost exclusively to *human* lords: 'my lord' or 'my master'. Most translations into English, German, and other languages clarify the difference between God and the human lord by using capitalization: 'the LORD says to my lord'. Through the usage of *kyrios* for both meanings, and by virtue of the application of this verse to Jesus Christ in the New Testament (e.g., Mk. 12:36), the term 'Adonai' is conceptually aligned with God. Now David is no longer the '[human] lord' addressed by God, but the speaker who assigns to Jesus as 'Lord' the place at the right hand of God. "[A]s such he shares the throne with him"[27] and is God's earthly representative. Paul, who also quotes

---

27 von Rad, *Old Testament Theology*, Vol. II, 219.

Ps. 110:1 in 1 Cor. 15:25, distinguished much more clearly between God and Christ.[28] With his turning away from Christ "according to the flesh" (κατὰ σάρκα, 2 Cor. 5:16)[29] and his assumption of a pre-existence of the Son of God, however, he prepared the way for the subsequent lack of emphasis on Jesus' humanity.

Early Church discussions of Jesus Christ's divine *nature* led to a divinization of his person that was problematic for Jewish thinking about God, with its emphasis on God's unity and uniqueness. The *predicate* of the sonship of God became an *essential attribute*, and a functional depiction became ontological. The theocentrism which was fundamental for Jewish thinking about God and oriented to the first commandment became combined with a Christocentrism. The *mediator* of God's saving work could thereby be declared its *subject*.

Christological approaches influenced by Alexandrian theology tended to see Jesus Christ as wholly constituted by divine nature, as taught, for example, by Cyril of Alexandria. Thus, human nature was seen as not only formed by this divine nature but remolded by it. Human nature is declared to be a dependent bearer of the divine.

In contrast, the Council of Chalcedon espoused the doctrine of *two* natures in the one person of Jesus Christ. The two-natures doctrine rejects any overemphasis on Jesus' divinity at the expense of his humanity. It thus corrects the tendency, evident in parts of Alexandrian theology, to grant Jesus' divine nature something of a monopoly. Instead, both natures are held in balance. The Council Fathers did not accept Apollinaris of Laodicea's view that the Logos of God had replaced the human mind of Jesus and merely joined itself to his body—thus denying Jesus full humanity. Instead they insisted that the Logos had united itself in Jesus with his entire humanity: body, soul, and spirit.

At the Council of Constantinople in 533 AD, however, the doctrine of *anhypostasia* denied the independence of Jesus' human nature. It states that Jesus' human nature does not have its own basis of being, and so also has no personal independence. His divine nature is what forms his person; it is the 'bearer' of his human nature. This doctrine sought to avoid giving the impression of two centers of subjectivity in the person of Jesus, thus eliminating one of the fundamental problems of the two-natures doctrine. The cost this incurred was the subordination of human nature to divine nature.

Luther followed this line. Not entirely unfairly, his Christology has been described as leaning towards Monophysitism. He maintained that the humanity of Jesus has no essential meaning for Christ's saving work. God uses this humanity as a kind of tool to bring forth salvation. His human obedience and suffering do not represent a 'meritorious work': it is God alone who acts. What

---

28 See chapter 4.2.2.
29 See Bernhardt, *Zur theologischen Bedeutung*, 355–75, esp. 366–71.

is decisive is the victory over the power of sin achieved by the divinity of Jesus Christ. The role his humanity played in this was, instead, functional—a means to an end.

Apollinaris took to its logical conclusion his insight that two natures in one human being are incompatible with each other. He thus showed that if it is to make any kind of sense, the two-natures doctrine leads inevitably to the disempowerment of Christ's human nature. Consubstantiality in the unity of one human being is inconceivable, since a unity cannot be formed by two natures which are both complete in and of themselves. They can only exist independently.[30] Baruch de Spinoza struck the same note. The assumption of a hypostatic union seemed to him as irrational as the statement "that a circle had taken upon itself the nature of a square".[31]

On the other hand, it is logically possible to conceive of two different relationships, roles, and functions together in one person without problematizing or endangering the unity of this person. Unlike the two *natures*, the two *relationships* with which relational, representational Christology deals are not only compatible, but also directed towards each other.

The assumption that Jesus' relationship with God constitutes the core of his humanity does not so much minimize that humanity. It rather indicates that the determination of humankind is realized in him. He is in a unique way taken up and embraced by God's Spirit, to the point that this Spirit completely defines his personhood. He lives entirely in and from being filled with the Word and Spirit of God. This presence constitutes his person, as expressed in Luther's formula that "fides facit personam" (faith constitutes the person) when it comes to the believer.[32] Such a conception allows Jesus to be truly understood as a human being, equal in everything to other human beings except in the quality of his being personally related to God. But this Word and this Spirit did not come over him through eliminating his personhood and using him like a mere tool or instrument. In his humanity he is attuned of his own free will to this urging of the Spirit; he is ready to be completely open to and to be filled by the Spirit.

4.3 Defining Relationships with Sensitivity to Difference

Chapter 4.2 defined representational Christology in relation to the Logos-Incarnation-Nature Christology of the Early Church. I now go back even

---

30 PG 26, 1096B.
31 73. Letter XXI to Heinrich Oldenburg.
32 WA 39/I, 283.

further to examine the main reference point of Logos-Incarnation Christology in the biblical tradition: the prologue to the Gospel of John, especially Jn. 1:1ff. and 1:14. This prologue deals with two relationships, one between God (or God the Father) and the Logos (or Word of God) (Jn. 1:1ff.), and the other between the eternal and the incarnated Logos (λόγος ἄσαρκος / ἔνσαρκος) (Jn. 1:14). Here I define both relationships as unity *in difference*.

The first indicates difference by the phrase "the Word was *with* God" (or directed toward God[33]) and, in later interpretations, by the idea of the emergence ('begetting') of the Word from God the Father. It is also reflected in the doctrine of the Trinity.

The second expresses difference in the motif of the 'incarnation' of the Word, which is reflected in debates about Christology.

Both definitions of relationship place stress not on difference, but on unity. But this unity is not a unity without difference, an undifferentiated sameness. The unity is not to be defined in the sense of a 'oneness' (*idem*), but in the sense of a *personal and relational* identity (*ipse*).

In this sense, Jesus Christ can be closely 'identified' with God in a personal and relational way, but neither as the self-same entity nor in the sense of a unity of substance. He is not God, and neither is he of divine substance. Rather, he is the human manifestation of the Word, the Spirit, and the Wisdom of God: the representative and as such the 'revelation' of God. This does not mean that he is merely the messenger of a message distinct from himself. That he is the *embodiment* of this message is part of the message itself. This message identifies him as the one who reveals it.

It bears repeating once more that distinguishing does not mean separating! This should be kept in mind as it applies to the drawing of the following distinctions. Between the two sides being distinguished there is an indissoluble connection, but not an undifferentiated identity. The goal here is not to establish a Christology that separates the Logos from God and the eternal from the incarnated Logos or in general Jesus from God. Rather, it is to define a personal, relational identity that is sensitive to difference. On the one hand, this allows us to state the identity between the *repraesentandum* (*that which* is to be represented: the salvific presence of God and thus God as the *Who* of the representation) and the representative (Jesus Christ). On the other hand, it also opens up the possibility of thinking about the *repraesentandum* as more encompassing than the *repraesentans* (the representative). Even if one dares

---

33   See chapter 4.3.1.1.

to make the supreme doxological declaration that 'Jesus is God', this does not go so far as to say that God *is* Jesus.

The two distinctions within these relationships identified above were always part of the Logos-Incarnation Christology of the ancient world. Alexandrian theology, however, tended to minimize them, as shown in 4.2.2. The soteriological interest in Jesus' true divinity, which guaranteed real salvation, was particularly prominent.

In the following chapters I consider these two relationships in more detail. In 4.3.1, I turn to the relationship, and thus also the difference, between God and the Logos (Word) of God. Thus, 4.3.2 deals with the relationship, and thus also the difference, between the eternal Logos and its incarnational form in the person of Jesus. I also incorporate into 4.3.1 the intellectual and historical contexts of Johannine theology, such as the Jewish philosophy of religion of Philo of Alexandria, while in 4.3.2 I trace the lines of thought set out in John's prologue through the history of theology up to the present.

It is undoubtedly not part of the intended message of John's Gospel that other forms or occurrences of the Logos of God in the history of religion be assumed. That message is completely focused on the one and only such form (as the Gospel understands it), namely Jesus Christ. But it seems possible to extrapolate such an assumption from an interpretation, developed from the Gospel of John, of the relationships between God the Father, the Logos of God, and the incarnation of the Logos, focusing on the theme of a unity in difference.

Further elaboration on the element of *difference* in these two relationships, between God and the Logos as well as between the eternal and the incarnate Logos, will illustrate how representational Christology is compatible with the witness of the New Testament to Christ.

4.3.1   *The Difference between God and the Logos or Word of God*
4.3.1.1   The Logos of God in the Prologue of John

John's Gospel begins with a multivalent definition of the relationship between God and the Word of God, which I will cite from the NRSV: "In the beginning was the Word, and the Word was with God, and the Word was God. He was in the beginning with God". Was the Logos *with* God, and thus explicitly distinct from him, or was he God, and thus identical to him? Exegetical endeavours to clarify this multivalence fill entire volumes.

A dialectic permeates the witness to Christ of John's Gospel. On the one hand, it can be read in the sense of a prophetic, messenger Christology: one could invoke all those passages in which the Johannine Christ claims to be the messenger of God and thus submits to God as subordinate (e.g., Jn. 5:19; 5:30; 7:16–18; 12:44, 49; 14:28; 16:5a; 17:3b, 18a, 21b, 25; 20:17). On the other hand, it can also be read as Christology 'from above', which emphasizes the unity of the Logos-made-flesh with the eternal Logos and the unity of the eternal Logos with God the Father (notably at Jn. 10:30). In the first case, the Logos-Christ is made subordinate to the Father; in the second, their unity is affirmed. The history of interpretation of John's Gospel oscillates between these two basic options and continues in the debate between West-Syrian-Antiochian Christology and Alexandrian Christology.

The representational Christology advocated here is closer to the prophetic, messenger Christology and the Antiochian school, without losing sight of the presumption of unity. In accordance with Michael Theobald, this approach assumes that it is precisely the radical subordination of the Son to the Father which "is the condition for the fact that the one sovereign God himself has, in him, completely gained voice".[34]

Let me make a preliminary hermeneutical remark here: The interpretation of John's prologue, like interpretation of the Bible in general, cannot allow itself to be tied down to the intellectual framework of the Councils of the Early Church. It must turn again and again to the biblical sources and consider the Jewish and Hellenistic intellectual background of the terms used there. This also affects interpretations of 'Word of God' and 'Son of God'. In this sense, Theobald calls for

> the summoning up of courage to spell out anew what is meant in John 1—in responsible language which is not readily available but must instead emerge out of the patient struggle for the meaning of the text in an unaffected way, so to speak, within dialogue with the faith community.[35]

On the subject of Jn. 1:1ff., I have pointed out in a previous publication that the Greek preposition *pros* (πρός), when followed by the accusative, should not be translated as 'with'. Instead, it indicates an orientation toward something, which could yield the following possible translations: 'the Word was toward God / turned toward God / directed toward God / in relation to God'. But if the πρός in John 1:1ff. expresses not a 'being with' but being directed toward something, then by πρὸς τὸν θεόν we should understand the relationship between God and the Logos not in terms of a static constellation but as indicating an act and a movement—as an active, relational *occurrence*.

The Logos is from God and toward God; he is not God himself, but the self-*communication* of God. He is God in the mode of utterance or revelation.

---

34   Translated from Theobald, *Die Fleischwerdung*, 303.
35   Translated from Theobald, *Studien*, 13–14.

He expresses the self-identification of God. The essence of God's self-revelation is love, and so the Logos is God's self-giving love.

One way of putting it is that the Logos is himself God, but not God himself. This wordplay is based on the exact wording of Jn. 1:1ff. Where θεός refers to the Logos, it is without the definite article; where it refers to God, it is with the definite article (ὁ θεός). Thus, the Logos is referred to as 'God' but it is not equated with 'the God'. Craig S. Keener expresses that unity-in-difference between God-the-Father and the Logos by the formula: "fully deity but not the Father".[36]

In Jn. 1:6, 12, 13, 18a, however, θεός without a definite article is also used for 'the God', but the Son of God is not referred to as θεός with a definite article. In these verses, too, the begotten Son is not equated with God, but is placed in the closest proximity to God. The New International Version translates Jn. 1:18: "No one has ever seen God, but the one and only Son, who is himself God and is *in closest relationship* with the Father, has made him known".

Let us now consider two particular verses from John's Gospel which are repeatedly cited as evidence of the unity of the Christ-Logos with God: 10:30 and 20:28.

In Jn. 10:30 (ἐγὼ καὶ ὁ πατὴρ ἕν ἐσμεν; most often translated as "the Father and I are one"), the ἕν is neuter, so the exact wording would be "I and the Father, we are *as one*" (in Latin: 'unum', in German: 'eines'). That means: they share the same concern or cause. It is a unity of the will. The 'Son' lives and works in perfect harmony with the 'Father' and the 'cause of God'.[37] As the context of this verse shows, it is not the *person* of Jesus Christ being discussed here, but his God-empowered *ministry*.

Thomas' confession of Christ at Jn. 20:28 ('my Lord and my God'—ὁ κύριός μου καὶ ὁ θεός μου) probably contains an ironic allusion to Domitian's imperial moniker and expresses Thomas' personal relationship with (or worship of) Christ. He addresses Jesus as 'his' God with the form of address common in the ancient Near East. In no way does this imply an identification of Jesus Christ with *the* God: Christ is revered as God's embodied presence, but not identified with God.

Returning to John's prologue, we read in Jn. 1:3 that the Logos shares in God's eternity before all creation. In his preexistence, his closeness to God is even more immediate than either Torah or Wisdom. While Wisdom is called the

---

36 Keener, *The Gospel of John*, 374.
37 See chapter 2.3.

first of God's creatures (in Prov. 8),[38] the Gospel of John attributes divinity to the Logos without equating him with God.

In the Gospel of John, however, 'logos' is not to be understood ontologically, but as a *nomen actionis*, a word of action. It is God's creative Word of Power spoken at the beginning, which calls everything into being and continues in God's speaking throughout history (especially, but not exclusively, through the Torah and the prophets), before becoming 'flesh' (σάρξ) in Jesus Christ (Jn. 1:14). The Logos is God's act of self-communication, and the content of this self-communication.

4.3.1.2 The Philosophical and Religious Context: Philo of Alexandria

The philosophy of religion of Philo of Alexandria is of great importance for understanding Johannine and early Christian Logos-Christology. Under the influence of middle Platonism, both Hellenistic Judaism and consequently Philo strongly emphasized the transcendence and immutability of God. This raises the question of how God's immanence (God's activity in creating, preserving, and governing the cosmos) can be reconciled with his transcendence. The idea of 'hypostases' of God, which was then introduced into the Christian doctrine of the Trinity and Christology, offers one possible answer to this question.

In the 'hypostasis' the nature (οὐσία) of an underlying reality is realized in a concrete individual being. The 'higher', divine reality subsists or 'exists in' the hypostasis, but also transcends it. The hypostasis manifests its being. As an embodiment of this nature (i.e., in its form of existence), the hypostasis has a certain independence, but it essentially exists in the reality through which it is constituted. A hypostasis is therefore a derived reality. Plotinus gives an example of this: heat has its very essence in fire. Fire underlies it and is in it at the same time.[39]

The hypostases of God are not intermediate beings between God and human; they belong entirely on the side of God. They are manifested expressions of being, self-communications of God, whose function consists in mediation between the utterly transcendent God and the material world. But the more their person-like embodiment is emphasized (as in the case of Wisdom playing before God), the more inevitable becomes the question of how they relate to the divinity of God.

---

38 See also Col. 1:15, where Christ is called "the firstborn of all creation" (πρωτότοκος πάσης κτίσεως).

39 Plotinus, *Enneads* V 1:3; 4:2.

Philo finds numerous such hypostases in the Hebrew Bible, especially the Word, Wisdom, and Spirit of God; it is the Logos that is his special interest.

(a) Philo speaks of the *Logos* with different emphases:

- The Logos is *in God*, as the divine reason of God that spiritually conceives the work of creation.[40] He is the blueprint of creation, so to speak, and the archetype of all created things.
- The Logos is the divine power *in the cosmos* that permeates and sustains it.[41] In this understanding, which touches on the Logos-philosophy of the Stoa, the Logos is almost synonymous with Wisdom.
- The Logos is a "second God"[42] *next to* God. He is divine, but his divinity does not touch and certainly does not usurp the Godhood of "the highest One, Father of the universe".[43] He is preexistent, of divine nature, image of God, firstborn son.[44] As a divine being, he belongs at God's side without taking God's place. He is so close to God that there is no distance between him and God.[45] He is the hypostasis of God,

> the firstborn of God, the Logos, the eldest of his angels, the archangel who rules over them; he has many names: 'ἀρχή', 'name of God', 'word [λόγος] of God', 'human being in the image of God [εἰκών]'.[46]

The Logos mediates ontologically and epistemically between creator and creation.[47] Ontologically, he accomplishes this mediation by bringing forth the cosmos and suffusing it with the creative power of God. Epistemically, he bridges the gap by making accessible an understanding of God that would otherwise exceed the capacities of the human mind.

(b) *Wisdom* is the shining glory of God as the eternal light. The relation of the Logos to the Wisdom of God Philo defines in various ways. In part, he identifies the two with each other;[48] in part, he confines Wisdom entirely to the transcendent world of salvation and regards it as the source of the Logos which governs the cosmos.[49]

---

40 "De opificio mundi", LCL 226, 19–20.; "Legum allegoriae" III, LCL 226, 96.
41 E.g., in: "De fuga et invention", LCL 275, 112; "De plantation", LCL 247, 8–10.
42 "Quaestiones Genesis" II, LCL 380, 62.
43 "Quaestiones Genesis" II, LCL 380, 62.
44 "De agricultura", LCL 247, 51; "De somniis", LCL 275, 215.
45 E.g., in: "De fuga et invention", LCL 275, 101. See also "Legum allegoriae" II, LCL 226, 86.
46 "De confusione linguarum", LCL 261, 146–47.
47 "Quis rerum divinarum heres sit", LCL 261, 205–206.
48 "Legum allegoriae" I, LCL 226, 65; "Quod deterius potiori insidiari soleat", LCL 227, 115–118; "De fuga et invention", LCL 275, 109.
49 "De virtutibus", LCL 341, 62.

(c) Philo virtually equates the *Spirit* with the Wisdom of God. It is a real and incorporeal being, a kind of world-soul. He relates it more strongly than Wisdom to the endowment of reason in human beings.

The biblical motifs of God's creative Wisdom, his revealing Word, and his illuminating and sanctifying Spirit lent themselves to being bridge concepts between Greek philosophy and biblical tradition. In the context of early Jewish thinking about God, they could be interpreted as being anchored in God and therefore consubstantial with God, but simultaneously possessing a relative independence from God as forms of expression. Through them God works *ad extra* and thus makes Godself present in creation. In particular, a theology of creation based on Wisdom offered itself as a cornerstone for this bridge-building. The idea of the powerful Word of the Creator, Wisdom, and the Spirit as modes of God's activity played a central role in this theology. Philo understood these modes of action as expressions of God's *one* act of creating, preserving, and governing; for him, therefore, the terms 'Logos', 'Wisdom', and 'Spirit' are almost interchangeable.

Philo teaches that the hypostases continue to 'hypostasize' or manifest themselves: the cosmos is the material manifestation of the Logos, while angels are incorporeal manifestations of the Spirit who act as mediators of God's revelation. He even refers to figures such as the patriarchs and Moses as manifestations of the Logos or Wisdom or Spirit. The necessary distinction between hypostasis and personification must not be made too sharply. Personification is a form of hypostasis in Philo.

The prologue to John's Gospel goes beyond Philo only insofar as it recognizes in *Jesus* the unique and universally significant manifestation of the Logos and calls this the Incarnation.

4.3.1.3 Divine Beings besides God?

The idea of divine beings emanating from and relating to God, which was widespread among Jewish thinkers in the Hellenistic context, explains why 'high' Christologies were formed relatively early in Christianity's history. ('High' here denotes Christologies which emphasize the divinity of Jesus Christ). This can still be understood within the context of intra-Jewish debates and is not only the result of later Hellenization.

Such divine figures appear in the late writings of the Hebrew Bible and in extra-biblical pseudepigraphical writings: the personified Wisdom in Wisdom literature (Prov. 8); the Son of Man in the vision of Daniel (Dan. 7); the Messianic Son of Man in the fourth Book of Ezra; the raptured Enoch transformed into an angel, referred to as 'Little Yahweh' in §15 of the Hebrew Enoch Book; and so on. As in Philo, when these other sources speak of such beings, they do not question the unity and uniqueness of God; on the contrary, they reinforce these qualities.[50] For these beings are not equal to the one and only God; rather, they are set apart from God, put into service by God. They are manifestations of his presence. To speak of a 'binitarianism'[51] is therefore at least ambiguous if not outright misleading. Monotheism was never called into question by the notion of divine beings.

James D. G. Dunn argues against understanding the Word, Spirit, and Wisdom of God as 'intermediary figures':

> They all remain in the literature of our period (Philo included) ways of speaking of God's powerful interaction with his world and his people, God's experienced immanence through nature and revelation, in Torah, prophet and saving act, which yet did not infringe his transcendence. Their pre-existence is the pre-existence of God, of God's purpose to create and redeem. However much the language used of them may depict them as independent entities, it never rises above the vivid metaphors and poetic imagery of Hebrew thought.[52]

John 1:1 goes beyond this, however. As Hans Conzelmann has already remarked on this verse,

> the Logos is with God, and he is God. Is there ditheism here? The Jewish wisdom is the first creature and is thus removed from God. The Johannine Logos, on the other hand, is not created. In fact, the idea of two gods breaks through.[53]

It was to ward off this suspicion that the doctrine of the Trinity was developed.

However, in considering early Christian Logos-Incarnation Christology, one must keep in mind that its terminology does not consist of pinpoint-accurate concepts drawn from theoretical language. Rather, they are confessional statements formed in the context of the "poetic imagery of Hebrew thought"[54] (Dunn), to be understood in a doxological and always metaphorical register.

---

50   This is also true of Exod. 7:1, where God says to Moses, "Behold, I have set you as God (elohim/אלהים) for Pharaoh".
51   On more recent discussion of early Jewish "binitarianism", see Hurtado, *One God*; Boyarin, *The Gospel of Memra*, 243–84; Schäfer, *Zwei Götter*.
52   Dunn, *Christology*, 252ff.
53   Conzelmann, *Outline*, 335.
54   See footnote 52.

The following quotation from Justin's 'Dialogue with Trypho' illustrates how open the idea of the emergence of the Logos from God still was in Christian theology of the mid-second century:

> God has begotten as a Beginning before all His creatures a kind of Reasonable Power (δύναμις λογική) from Himself, who is also called by the Holy Spirit the Glory (δόξα) of the Lord, and sometimes Son (υἱός), and sometimes Wisdom (σοφία), and sometimes Angel (ἄγγελος), and sometimes God (θεός), and sometimes Lord (κύριος) and Word (λόγος). Sometimes He also speaks of Himself as Chief Commander (ἀρχιστράτηγος), when He appeared in the form of a man to Joshua the son of Nun. For He can have all these names, from the fact that He ministers to the Father's purpose, and has been born (γεγενῆσθαι) of the Father of His own will.[55]

It is clear to Justin that the 'reasonable power' of God is one that is named 'by the Holy Spirit' with various designations. It has come forth from God but is distinct from God. As such, it may itself be called 'God' (without the definite article).

The *Logos* as hypostasis was brought to the fore in the course of further Trinitarian and Christological debates. Especially in the dispute with Arius, Alexandrian theologians emphasized the unity of essence between the incarnate Logos and God. But even here the difference remained. For unity of essence does not mean undifferentiated sameness.

We must continually recall the openness of biblical tradition and early Christian theology, in contrast to the conceptual definitions of the Early Church councils. Christology can only be unfolded with a plurality of key concepts each with their different emphases. If one of them is foregrounded—like the Logos concept in ancient Christology—then it must prove itself by its ability to integrate the intended meaning of other concepts. Ultimately, the three forms of God's self-communication in the Word, in the Spirit, and in Wisdom are in essence *a single entity*, to which different effects are attributed and which are experienced and designated differently. This is also asserted in the Trinitarian principle: *opera trinitatis ad extra indivisa sunt* ("the operations of God in the world are undivided").

Christianity took the modes of God's self-communication to his creatures, as they were delineated by Hellenistic Judaism, into the being of God and interpreted them by means of Greek philosophy. Islam, on the other

---

55 Justin Martyr, *Dialogue with Trypho* 61:1, pp. 126–7.

hand, followed the tradition of rabbinic Judaism, apocalypticism, and Jewish Hekhalot mysticism more closely, so that it consistently distinguished God's self-communications from God. For that purpose, for example, God sends revelatory and mediatory angels. In contrast to Christianity, Islam thus pursues the "program of an anti-Trinitarian Reformation".[56]

4.3.2 The Difference between the Logos and His Personification
4.3.2.1 'Incarnation of God'?

The theologoumenon of the Incarnation is often abbreviated in theological presentations and generally in the language of the Church as 'Incarnation of God', narratively visualized in the story of the birth of Jesus and celebrated at Christmas. However, the expression 'Incarnation of God' is highly misleading. Using the term 'incarnation' [Mensch*werdung*, becoming-human] implies that God has undergone a transmutation into a human, who would then exist as a God-being. Understood literally, this indicates a transformation of essence: the Logos not only adopts the 'flesh' but *becomes* 'flesh'. This indicates that in Jesus we see God descended from heaven. But this would mean the infinite God becoming finite. It would mean the self-relativization of the absolute, which would then no longer be absolute. We cannot entertain the idea that God is at the same time infinite and finite, at the same time absolute and not absolute. Talking about the 'incarnation of God' in this way is as self-contradictory as Spinoza's statement that a circle is a square.[57]

The decisive biblical reference point for Logos-Incarnation Christology—Jn. 1:14—does not speak of an 'incarnation of God', however, but of the 'incarnation' of the 'Logos'. But even 'incarnation' in the sense of 'becoming flesh' appears problematic if understood in a literal sense. Incarnation is mostly understood as a singular act constituting the beginning of Jesus' life (whether the miraculous virgin conception or the birth of Jesus).

Against such problematic interpretations, we should note the following: (a) Incarnation is not to be understood as a singular event at the beginning of Jesus' life, but as the fundamental signature of his entire existence:

> The union of the Logos with this human life continued *throughout the whole of the earthly history of Jesus* as the eternal Son of God took shape in him through the relation to the Father.[58]

---

56 Translated from Feldtkeller, *Religionswissenschaftliche Perspektiven*, 235.
57 See chapter 4.2.3.
58 Pannenberg, *Systematic Theology*, Vol. 2, 383 (my emphasis).

This is expressed in the second part of Jn. 1:14, which says that the Word of God *took up residence among us*. The ingressive, aorist verb ἐσκήνωσεν asks to be translated as an act ('took up his dwelling' / 'pitched his tent'), rather than as a state ('dwelt'). Moreover, ἐν ἡμῖν could also be translated as '*in* [i.e., not 'among'] us': 'the Word took up residence in us'.

(b) The expression 'incarnation' is to be understood as a term of contrast. It helps to guard against a spiritualized understanding of God's self-communication in his 'Word'. Instead, the expression emphasizes the corporeality of this presence in a real human being (or, put more precisely, in this human being's fullness of existence). 'Incarnation' describes the relationship between the eternal Logos, i.e., God's self-communication, and the manifestation of the Logos in the human Jesus of Nazareth, between the λόγος ἄσαρκος and the λόγος ἔνσαρκος.

(c) The phrase 'incarnation of God (or of the Word of God)' is not to be understood as a transformation in which God (or the Logos) gives up God's original state of being and passes into a new one. The Council of Chalcedon explicitly rejected this notion ('without change'). The difference between the humanity of Jesus and the divinity of God is not abolished in this act. The Christ-event consists precisely in the fact that God's divinity is present in a human being without being absorbed in it and without dissolving it into divinity. Both aspects persist—on the one hand divinity, the 'divine nature', and the Word of God, and on the other the humanity of Jesus. There is no mixing and no transformation. But this position cannot be maintained if both divine and human nature are thought of as substances.

Given the risk of misinterpretation inherent in using the term 'incarnation', it is advisable to approach the term with caution, provide guidelines for understanding it, and place it alongside other interpretations of the mystery of Christ. 'Incarnation' is a powerful image that illustrates the fundamental conviction of God's presence in Jesus. But it is not a kind of theory with explanatory power. It does not indicate the reason for Jesus' dignity as Christ but is a confessional expression by which this dignity is ascribed to him.

4.3.2.2 Foundation in the New Testament

It could fairly be asked whether the enormous impact of the incarnation motif in the history of Christology is in inverse proportion to its biblical attestation. It is for this reason that Jürgen Becker goes so far as to demand that

> it would be best to abandon the interpretive model of 'incarnation' as a matrix for Johannine Christology. For only very marginally does the

Evangelist make use of this keyword, and then with a meaning that, after Irenaeus, theologians of the incarnation no longer share.[59]

James D. G. Dunn, however, sees the primary root of later incarnational Christology not in Jn. 1:14, but in the reception of Wisdom theology already visible in the later Pauline epistles and in Colossians and Ephesians. The attribution of pre-existence to Wisdom was transferred to Christ. This conception was connected to 'Adam-Christology', according to which Christ was only appointed the Son of God with the 'resurrection'. Dunn writes that a "backward extension of the Son of God language"[60] can be observed in the Gospels. This unfolds from the 'resurrection' back to the beginning of Jesus' public activity (baptism in the Jordan), to birth and conception, and from there on to timeless eternity (especially in the Gospel of John, where Christ is presented as the eternal Word of God made human).

How do we explain the difference between Becker and Dunn in interpreting the incarnation motif? Becker starts from the *one* verse which explicitly deals with the 'incarnation' of the Logos: Jn. 1:14. Dunn, on the other hand, suggests that this motif can also be invoked indirectly and implicitly, through the attribution of pre-existence and creation mediatorship. This attribution is also found in Paul (Phil. 2:6–9; 1 Cor. 8:6), in the Deutero-Pauline writings (Col. 1:15–20), and in Heb. 1:2ff. In contrast to Becker, Dunn speaks of 'incarnation' in a broader sense, with greater reference to Wisdom theology. He indicates that hints of the incarnational concept can also be seen in the motif of mission (Christ as the Lord [κύριος] sent by God, coming from the glory [δόξα] of God) and in Pauline and Deutero-Pauline image Christology (Christ as the true image of God).

Speaking of the incarnation of the Logos in Jn. 1:14 should arguably be understood as an effort to supersede a Spirit Christology which was advocated in the Johannine community and can be reconstructed in outlines from their writings.[61] The First Epistle of John rejects a Spirit Christological view which assumes that the Spirit was given to Jesus at his baptism, empowering him for his ministry, but that the Spirit left him again before his death (for which those in favour could cite Lk. 23:46, in which the dying Jesus 'commends his spirit' into God's hands). Michael Theobald argues that the author of the

---

59   Translated from Becker, *Johanneisches Christentum*, 131.
60   Dunn, *Christology*, 256.
61   See Theobald, *Studien zum Corpus Iohanneum*, 13–32, esp. 20–32.

Gospel of John, in contrast to this "separation Christology",[62] emphasizes Jesus' divine dignity which already existed *before* the descent of the Spirit (Jn. 1:30), and stresses the *permanent* indwelling of the Spirit (Jn. 1:32f.).[63] In this way, Theobald ranks Logos-Incarnation Christology above Spirit Christology.

This, however, creates a tension between the motifs of the gift of the Spirit and the incarnation of the Logos. How can Jesus be the Logos in the flesh even before receiving the gift of the Spirit? Having interpreted the "polarity between incarnational and baptismal Christology as possibly decisive for determining the pragmatics of the prologue",[64] Theobald sees the allusion to Jesus' baptism as a "scene of recognition or revelation (Jn. 1:31) of the incarnated Logos, but not as a foundational Christological event".[65] Lastly, he writes, "what happened at the Jordan was not Jesus' elevation to 'Son of God' but his 'revelation' to 'Israel' (v. 31) as the 'Son of God' from eternity (v. 34)".[66]

Accordingly, the idea of the incarnation aims to anchor Jesus Christ more radically in God than Spirit or baptismal Christology was able to do. It wanted him to be understood as the personification of God's eternal, creative Word.

In Luke's and Matthew's Gospels, this anchoring is carried out in a Spirit-Christological way; but it does not follow the Adoptionist idea that Jesus was gifted with the Spirit of God at a certain point in his life (baptism) and that this Spirit left him again at his death. Rather, the Spirit of God is in Jesus from the beginning of his life and is poured out on all flesh after his death, at Pentecost (Acts 2:17). Thus, the concern of the Johannine conception of the incarnation is addressed in Spirit-Christological terms.

There were two possible interpretations that could be developed in connection with John 1:14a ("and the Word [the Logos] became flesh and lived among us"). Antiochian theology took up the *indwelling* of the Logos in Jesus and preferred the idea of '*assumptio carnis*' ('assumption of the flesh') to that of 'incarnation'. The distinction between the Logos and Jesus was thus more clearly accentuated than in the Alexandrian school, which read the text as speaking not only of the Logos *dwelling* in the flesh, but that he had *become* flesh. The literal translation of the verse reads, "and the Word [the Logos] became flesh and *camped* among us". Using the verb 'to camp' alludes to the Jewish concept of God's indwelling among the Jewish people, itself referring to the tradition of the Tent of Meeting at Sinai (Exod. 19ff.; 33:7–34, 35; 40:34–38). In rabbinic

---

62 Theobald, *Studien zum Corpus Iohanneum*, 21–22, 598.
63 Theobald, *Studien zum Corpus Iohanneum*, 25.
64 Theobald, *Studien zum Corpus Iohanneum*, 14.
65 Theobald, *Studien zum Corpus Iohanneum*, 16.
66 Theobald, *Studien zum Corpus Iohanneum*, 25.

theology, the indwelling of God was expressed by the motif of the *Shechina*. According to Jürgen Moltmann, this encompasses three considerations:

> the present *indwelling* of the Lord in Israel, the form assumed by the *condescension* of the Eternal One, and the *anticipations* of the glory of the One who is to come.[67]

At the heart of the Christian faith is the conviction of God's presence in Jesus of Nazareth, not only in his person, his speech and actions, but also and especially in the brutal destruction of this life and mission, in his suffering and death. In this is revealed that God is present even in the deepest suffering. In the bodily reality of Jesus, God resorts to living through the absolute lowest point of human existence: the trauma of a cruel death by torture, the complete dehumanization, in which the one thus maltreated feels abandoned even by God. Jesus dying on the cross and crying out that he has been abandoned by God (Mk. 15:34) is the epitome of God's self-communication in God's deepest *kenosis* (κένωσις).

4.3.2.3 Christ as *totus Deus* but not as *totum Dei*

This chapter broadly surveys the history of Christology with a special focus on Reformed theology and its so-called 'Extra Calvinisticum'. Along the way, I touch on Calvin, the Heidelberg Catechism, Karl Barth, Christian Link, John Hick, and Perry Schmidt-Leukel. The question is how these various approaches define the *distinction* between the eternal Word of God and its personal manifestation in Jesus. I first consider those Christological approaches that see the Logos of God as being present also 'outside the flesh' (*extra carnem*) of Jesus, then those that extend this line further by assuming that God's salvific self-communication is also made independently of Jesus Christ (*extra Christum*). To close, I offer reflections on the relationship between the name 'Jesus' and the title 'Christ'.

4.3.2.3.1 Extra carnem

Reformed theology places more emphasis than Lutheran theology on the difference between the Logos of God and the person of Jesus Christ, or between the two natures in Christ. Lutheran theology taught that there is an exchange of properties (*communicatio idiomatum*) between the two natures. In other words, Jesus in his humanity has divine properties (such as omnipotence,

---

67 Moltmann, *The Trinity*, 28.

omniscience, omnipresence) and in his divinity has human properties (such as the misery of the birth in the manger or the suffering on the cross). Calvin, on the other hand, highlighted the distinctness of natures (as taught by Antiochian theology). In his eyes, there is an 'extra-incarnational' Word of God— not only *before* Jesus' birth, but also *during* his life and *after* his death. This is not to say that the eternal and the incarnate Word are two distinct Words to be separated: they are one and the same. What it does say, however, is that the eternal Logos of God is not fully absorbed into his manifestation in Jesus Christ; he reaches beyond it. He transcends both the personal form in which he is manifested and the earthly acts of this person. The incorporeal, non-fleshly Logos (λόγος ἄ-σαρκος) is 'greater' than the Logos manifested in the flesh (λόγος ἔν-σαρκος), who is now in heaven after his exaltation. He 'dwells' in the body of Christ, but is not limited to this indwelling; rather, he is universally present and effective throughout the entire cosmos.[68]

Christian Link sees Calvin's view as a further development of understanding the mediating role of the Logos in relation to creation already advocated in the Early Church, following Ps. 33:6, Heb. 1, and Col. 1:16.[69] The 'Extra Calvinisticum' connects Christ with creation, Christology with the doctrine of creation, the second article of the Creed with the first; once the pneumatology that was so important for Calvin is added, the doctrine of the Trinity starts to evolve.

Yet we must not equate the 'Extra Calvinisticum'[70] (as Lutherans referred to it polemically, starting with Theodor Thumm) with the motto 'finitum non capax infiniti'. This phrase is an objection the Reformed side voiced toward Lutherans which was subsequently passed off as an axiom of Reformed theology. The axiom states that the finite (i.e., physical human existence) is not able to completely encompass the infinite (i.e., the divine). Heiko A. Oberman writes that Calvin did not hold the (negative) view that the finite cannot host the infinite (*finitum non capax infiniti*), but rather the inverse positive framing that the infinite can enter into the finite (*infinitum capax finiti*) without being absorbed into it.[71] There are also statements leaning in this direction in Lutheran theology and indeed in that of Luther himself, especially those in which he speaks of the 'hidden God'. However, Luther unequivocally rejects the idea of the divine nature being present in a way which is detached from the human nature of Jesus Christ.[72]

---

68 Calvin, *Institutes* II, 13,4; IV 17,30.
69 Link, *Schöpfung*, Vol. 1, 174–5.
70 For the history of this term, see Willis, *Calvin's Catholic Christology*, 8–25.
71 Oberman, *Die 'Extra'-Dimension*, 253–82.
72 WA 26, 333.

The idea that the Logos is also present beyond his incarnation in Jesus (*extra carnem*) has consequences for the doctrine of the Lord's Supper and for theological epistemology. The Logos' omnipresence throughout the whole world opens up the possibility that we can "with experience as our guide ... find God just as he declares himself in his Word".[73] This is the basis of achieving knowledge of God by experiencing God's works of creature (natural theology), which need not interest us here. What is important, however, is Calvin's application of this Christological approach to the doctrine of the Lord's Supper, according to which Christ cannot be bodily present in the Lord's Supper (or in the elements of bread and wine). As Calvin puts it:

> therefore, since the whole Christ is everywhere, our Mediator is ever present with his own people, and in the Supper reveals himself in a special way, yet in such a way that the whole (*totus*) Christ is present, but not in his wholeness (*totum*).[74]

Christ is *wholly* present without the *whole* Christ being present. Here, the *totus* designates qualitative or essential wholeness, which can be present even without wholeness in the quantitative sense (*totum*).

Calvin took the distinction between 'Christus *totus*' and 'Christus as *totum*' from Peter Lombard's Books of Sentences;[75] he wanted to answer the much-discussed contemporary question of whether Christ remained human between his death and 'resurrection'. The answer runs that, in terms of his *person/ hypostasis*, Christ was *wholly* in death (in the tomb and in the underworld); but in terms of his *natures*, it was not the *whole* (of) Christ that was dead, only his human nature. The eternal Son of God is wholly united with the flesh, but also exists beyond it.

Calvin found numerous other references in the history of theology for his view of the eternal Logos having a 'surplus' not contained with the incarnate Logos. Such links reach back to the Fathers[76]—indeed, one of Lombard's main sources was John of Damascus. Thomas Aquinas, too, declared that Christ had descended from heaven, but that his divine nature had not ceased to be in heaven.[77] Luther, on the other hand, held that in Jesus Christ God "has

---

73   Calvin, *Institutes* I, 10, 2, p. 98.
74   Calvin, *Institutes* IV, 17,30, p. 1403.
75   Petrus Lombardus, *Sententiae* III, 22,3 (PL 192, 804). This is also quoted in the *Institutes* IV at 17 and 30.
76   Willis, *Calvin's Catholic Christology*, 34–60.
77   STh III, qu.5, art. 2c, ad 1. See also STh III, qu.3, art.7b; STh III qu.10, art.1b.

completely poured forth Himself and withheld nothing from us that He has not given us".[78]

The 'Extra Calvinisticum' had a broad impact, not least through its inclusion in the Heidelberg Catechism. It is presented in the answers to questions 47 and 48, where it states that Christ's divine nature "is not limited with the human nature".[79] Here, however, the 'Extra Calvinisticum' does not refer to the incarnation and the Lord's Supper as in Calvin, but to the ascension of Jesus. The emphasis is thus not on the fulfillment of the cosmos by the divine Logos, but on the fact that Jesus Christ is 'with us' until the end of the world.

Despite expressly declaring his support for the 'Extra Calvinisticum' in his earlier writings,[80] in 1947 Karl Barth described the Heidelberg Catechism's statement on this topic as an "industrial accident ["Betriebsunfall"] for theology"[81] and as a "statement of unbelief".[82] His objection was to the unity of the divine-human person being called into question; but Calvin had already countered this objection and the Heidelberg Catechism had itself explicitly and decidedly rejected it too. For Barth, incarnation meant that the eternal and the incarnate Logos are indistinguishable. The Christus *totus* must also be the Christus as *totum*.[83]

On the other hand, Barth also upheld the heritage of the Reformed tradition and wanted to preserve the distinctiveness of the eternal Word of God from its incarnation in Jesus. Summarizing Barth's interpretation of the incarnation in CD I/2 in 1938, Eberhard Busch writes:

> the central Christological sentence 'the Word became flesh' was [according to Barth] not to be understood as if the flesh were now itself the divine Word, but rather as meaning that the Word in his becoming flesh does not cease to be the Word, the *subject* who speaks, acts, reveals and reconciles and thus comes to us who are in the 'flesh'.[84]

In the sentence 'the Word of God became human/flesh', Barth emphasized 'became'. By highlighting the Incarnation as an event (of *becoming* human), Christian theology breaks through static Greek thought. Attributing "concreteness, contingency, historical uniqueness" to the Logos means the total collapse

---

78 Luther, *The Large Catechism*, 2nd part, 2nd article.
79 Heidelberg Catechism. Answer to Question 48.
80 E.g., in Barth, *Unterricht*, 196.
81 Translated from Barth, *Die christliche Lehre*, 70.
82 Barth, *Die christliche Lehre*, 71.
83 See also Sumner, *Karl Barth and the Incarnation*, esp. 198–203.
84 Translated from Busch, *Barth*, 57.

of Platonist ontology.⁸⁵ Barth accentuated the process of *implementation* of divine-human unity in Jesus Christ as the definitive word of God.

In his 'Lichterlehre' (doctrine of lights), Barth explained that the universal Word of God is also able to produce true words *extra muros ecclesiam*.⁸⁶ It is not the case that truth is the exclusive preserve of the one Word of God;⁸⁷ even outside this context there can be found "words, truths, even 'revelations'"⁸⁸ capable of yielding "illumination".⁸⁹ For this doctrine, however, he did not make recourse to the 'Extra Calvinisticum', instead emphasizing that the 'lights' are reflections of the light of Christ. Thus, the potential for universality that lies in the 'Extra Calvinisticum' remains unexplored.

But it is precisely this potential that is of considerable importance for representational Christology. It opens up the possibility of distinguishing between the eternal and the incarnate Logos without separating the two. From the *extra carnem* there arises an *extra ecclesiam*. With reference to Calvin, Christian Link indicated the consequence of God's spiritual omnipresence in his Word, namely that in those spheres untouched by Christ's proclamation God can make Godself known beyond (albeit always in relation to) the revelation in Christ. In this way, God also exerts a claim over these spheres. Conversely, moreover, there is

> a secularism, it may even be a distinctly atheistic humanism, which seems to testify to the truth entrusted to the Church at least as clearly and firmly as the Church does, and sometimes even better and more consistently.⁹⁰

According to Link, the 'extra' is especially relevant for defining the relationship of the Logos to the Israel of the Old Testament.⁹¹ But it does not only apply 'backwards': the Logos dwells outside the body of Christ in the present and the future as well. If a consistently historical Christology emerges from the 'Extra Calvinisticum' ("far beyond Calvin's own inklings"⁹²), then the history that takes place *after* the Incarnation of the divine Logos is also filled with this Logos—both *world* history and history of *religion*s. Even Calvin opposed those

---

85 Barth, *Erklärung*, 107.
86 See also Barth, CD IV/3, 112, 127, 137, in the context of CD IV/3, 41–167.
87 See also Barth, CD IV/3, 98–9.
88 See also Barth, CD IV/3, 138.
89 See also Barth, CD IV/3, 143.
90 Link, *Das sogenannte Extra-Calvinisticum*, 97–119, reprinted in: Link, *Prädestination* (I am quoting from that edition), 148.
91 Link, *Das sogenannte Extra-Calvinisticum*, 165.
92 Link, *Das sogenannte Extra-Calvinisticum*, 165.

who asked, "What have the impious, who are utterly estranged from God, to do with his Spirit?"[93] This Spirit-Christological universalism, however, cannot be thought of without Logos-Christological universalism.

In his reflections on Barth's doctrine of the lights ('Lichterlehre'), Link suggests we also take other religions into consideration. Drawing on this doctrine he concluded "that non-Christian religions can also become representations of revelation".[94] But here, too, he left no doubt that this is to be interpreted in terms of a *Christocentric* universalism. The λόγος ἄσαρκος must not be understood as an anonymous self-communication of God. It is the Christ Logos! *Extra carnem* does not mean *extra Christum*. The *extra* of divine nature cannot be detached from its *intra* in human nature. If one applies this doctrine to other religions' sources of revelation and streams of tradition, they can indeed be put into a positive relationship to God's acts of revelation and even of salvation, in the sense of an 'inclusivism' in the context of the theology of religions. They are appreciated as expressions of the universal reality of Christ—but not in the way they understand themselves.

4.3.2.3.2 Extra Christum

John Hick, who likewise stands in the Reformed tradition derived from Calvin, takes a significant step beyond Link's interpretation. He, too, makes use of the 'Extra Calvinisticum' and the distinction between *Christus totus est* and *Christus totum est*, but he does so in order to arrive at a theological recognition of other religions' sources and streams of tradition that is no more centered on Christ. He does not merely see the Logos or love of God as being at work *extra carnem*, but also *extra Christum*.

In the following I refer first to an essay from 1966 in which Hick explores how the Chalcedonian *vere Deus—vere homo* can be made plausible within a modern understanding.[95] In later works on Christology, he revised this position; however, his earlier reflections offer valuable insights into how the *totus-totum* distinction might be used.

The premise of Hick's argument is that we understand God's nature as love—an understanding in which love is not a quality but an activity. The 'consubstantiality' between Jesus and God consists in the shared identity of the love practiced by Jesus and the divine love that fundamentally determines God's actions. Hick therefore suggests speaking of *homoagapé* rather than

---

93   Calvin, *Institutes* II, 2,16, p. 275.
94   Translated from Link, *Das menschliche Gesicht der Offenbarung*, 295.
95   Hick, *Christology at the Crossroads*, 137–66. He included this essay as Chapter 11 ("Christ and Incarnation") in his essay collection "God and the Universe of Faiths". It was reprinted in 1975.

homoousia.⁹⁶ He emphasizes that Jesus not only *showed* God's love, and that his love was not merely *like* God's love, but that it was "actually and literally [...] God's Agapé"⁹⁷.

For Hick, the 'is' in the phrase 'Jesus is God's love' is a term of identification. Identity, however, can be asserted either qualitatively or quantitatively.⁹⁸ A statement of *qualitative* identity is akin to an analogy of proportion, e.g., that the love woman A and woman B feel for their respective children is qualitatively identical.⁹⁹ Applied to Jesus, this leads to a gradual understanding of the Incarnation, meaning that God's love is realized in Jesus to a greater degree than in other human beings. Hick seeks to go beyond this to bring out the uniqueness of the Incarnation of God's love in Jesus. Therefore, he advocates understanding the phrase 'Jesus is the love of God' in terms of a *quantitative* (or numerical) identity. Accordingly, Jesus' love not only possesses the same quality *as* God's love, not only *resembles* that love, but exists in it. Jesus' love *is* (wholly) the love of God. But it is not *the whole of* God's love: *totus*, but not *totum*. It does not have the same quantitative scale as the latter. In terms of set theory: the 'set' of Jesus' love has the same members or elements as the 'set' of God's love but is smaller than it. They are not congruent.

The love of Jesus is thus positioned in relation to the love of God according to the part-whole mathematical model. It *is* the love of God, but not the whole of the love of God. The difference lies in the extent, the range of the action. The enactment of God's love is *infinite*, whereas the enactment of Jesus' love is *finite*. The latter is practiced by a finite human who lived in a specific historical context. Like all historical phenomena, it is thus particular. The universal scope of God's love goes beyond the love embodied in, and practiced by, Jesus. God's love and consequently God's nature is therefore *wholly* present in Christ (*totus deus*), without *the whole* of this love or the whole of God (*totum Dei*) being exhausted in him.

> Jesus [...] was *totus deus*, 'wholly God', in the sense that his *agape* was genuinely the *Agapé* of God at work on earth, but not that he was *totum dei*, 'the whole of God', in the sense that the divine *Agapé* was expressed without remainder in each or even in the sum of his actions.¹⁰⁰

---

96   Hick, *Christology at the Crossroads*, 164.
97   Hick, *Christology at the Crossroads*, 154.
98   Hick, *Christology at the Crossroads*, 156ff.
99   Hick, *Christology at the Crossroads*, 156.
100 Hick, *Christology at the Crossroads*, 159 (emphases in original).

One aspect of this approach that is questionable is the way in which the distinction between 'quantitative' and 'qualitative' is drawn. 'Qualitative' merely signifies similarity or sameness, with 'quantitative' being used here for a numerical identity, whereby the one entity has a greater extent than the other. But then it is no longer an exact *numerical* identity; one cannot distinguish between 'quantitative' and 'numerical'. In his critique of Hick, Ingolf Dalferth draws attention to the fact that, in a Leibnizian sense, numerical identity between two objects only exists if one possesses all the properties of the other (and to the same extent), which applies neither to Jesus and God nor to the love of Jesus and the love of God.[101] If it did apply, Jesus would not only be *totus Deus*, but also *totum Dei*; but this runs counter to Hick's objective to distinguish between the two terms.

In his later work on Christology,[102] Hick moved away from asserting numerical identity and toward a representational Christology. At this juncture he became receptive to the Spirit Christological approaches of Donald M. Baillie[103] and Geoffrey W. H. Lampe,[104] which he had criticized prior to his turn towards a pluralistic theology of religion in the early 1970s. He became increasingly hostile to the claim of Jesus Christ's uniqueness, and he 'pluralized' this claim by assuming that other religions' central figures and contents are just as unique in their own ways. The question that needs asking is whether and to what extent religions reveal the love of God; having established that, they each deserve the appropriate degree of recognition.

Hick now emphasized, even more clearly than before, that 'Incarnation' is a metaphorical term. He no longer attempted to make the Chalcedonian doctrine of two natures plausible but instead regarded it as 'incurably' aporetic. Moreover, to him it seemed to lead inevitably to a soteriological exclusivism:

> if Jesus was literally God incarnate, and if it is by his death alone that men can be saved, and by their response to him alone that they can appropriate that salvation, then the only doorway to eternal life is Christian faith. It would follow from this that the large majority of the human race so far have not been saved. But is it credible that the loving God and Father of all men has decreed that only those born within one particular thread of human history shall be saved?[105]

---

101 Dalferth, *Der Mythos*, 333.
102 Esp. in: Hick, *The Metaphor*; id., *An Inspiration Christology*, 5–22.
103 Baillie, *God was in Christ*.
104 Lampe, *God as Spirit*.
105 Hick, *The Myth of God Incarnate*, 180.

Perry Schmidt-Leukel seeks to avoid this exclusivist consequence of Logos-Incarnation-Nature Christology. Relying on Karl Rahner's statement that Jesus is the "unique, supreme case of the total actualization of human reality",[106] he assumes a plurality of 'incarnations' of God.[107] Alongside Jesus there are other embodiments of absolute reality, such as the Buddha.[108] Ultimately, according to Schmidt-Leukel, *every* human is designed to embody the presence of God. In support of this position, one could point to the Greek Church Fathers who saw the goal of salvation in the *theosis* (θέωσις) of human beings (as images of God). But they assumed that this goal could only be reached by following the path of Christ.[109]

Schmidt-Leukel understands both 'incarnation' and the two-natures doctrine in a broader sense. He interprets incarnation as an expression of revelation: God reveals Godself in the work of Jesus, and so is inherent in this event. Yet not only here, but wherever the divine is made present in a finite medium, 'two natures' are revealed. On the one hand, the revealed divine should be distinguished from the finite medium, but on the other hand it is so tangibly effective in and through the medium that revealer and revelation are perceived in unity.[110]

4.3.2.3.3 *Jesus as Christ*

If one distinguishes in this way between the eternal Word of God and its taking on personhood in Jesus, then the phrase 'Jesus is the Word of God' cannot

---

106 See Rahner, *Foundations of Christian Faith*, 218.
107 It was precisely the Incarnation, however, in which Rahner saw the reason for the "absoluteness" of Christianity: "Christianity understands itself as the absolute religion intended for all humans, which cannot recognize any other as having equal rights beside itself [...], because it is based on the incarnation, the death and the resurrection of the one Word of God made flesh" (Translated from: Karl Rahner. "Das Christentum und die nichtchristlichen Religionen". In *Schriften zur Theologie* 5, 139. [*Sämtliche Werke* 10, 559]).
108 Schmidt-Leukel, *Buddha and Christ*, 151–75; *id. Buddha und Christus*, 202–19; *id.*, *Gott ohne Grenzen*, 283–96.
109 See also Catherine Keller's statement (*On the Mystery*, 151): "Within the Christian narrative, the incarnation in Jesus of that divine *Logos*, that world-creative Wisdom, is portrayed as a distinctive event. Indeed, it may be considered unique in this strong sense: only this person, as far as we know, has so *realized* the divine lure as to become 'at one' with it. That intimate union or 'sonship' is not a metaphysical given, but an event of becoming [...]. But does this make the incarnation an exclusive revelation of God in the final or competitive sense usually meant by identifying Jesus as the 'only Son of God'? To the contrary: the whole point of the unique incarnation is to open up a new intimacy with the infinite. [...] In other words, to embrace this *logos is to become a son or a daughter of God*" (emphases in original).
110 Schmidt-Leukel, *Grundkurs Fundamentaltheologie*, 218.

be inverted as 'the Word of God is Jesus'. Raimon Panikkar expressed the same thought in his famous formulation: "Jesus is Christ, but Christ is not (only) Jesus".[111] He, too, distinguished between the timeless, supra-historical, cosmic Christ and the historical Jesus of Nazareth without separating the two. For Panikkar, the Christ-reality needed to be de-historicized, i.e., freed from the limitations of historical particularity, and related to the entire cosmic-divine-human reality in the sense of an *incarnatio continua*. He does not see this as meaning "to deny [the Christ-reality's] historical factuality, but simply not to equate its historicity with its reality".[112] Reality is 'more' than just a sequence of historical events; the Christ-reality reaches far beyond Jesus' life manifested in history and the historical manifestation of his 'resurrected' body in the formation of the Christian Church.

According to Panikkar, it is only through this distinction between the historical person of Jesus and the Christ-reality that the universal dimension of the 'Christ' can be asserted. In order to unfold its transforming power, the event of the cosmic Christ-reality needs to occur again and again in different cultural and religious contexts. Historical concreteness and universality are by no means mutually exclusive; rather, they are conditional upon one another. The restriction of the Christ-reality to its incarnational form, on the other hand, reduces this universality.

However, Panikkar's Christological reflections can occasionally give the impression of overemphasizing the dimension of the cosmic Christ-reality over against the particularity of Jesus' life (including its Jewish context). The passion and death of Jesus also take a back seat. In terms of the classical three offices doctrine, this means that the kingly office is foregrounded, while the priestly loses importance. Representational Christology, on the other hand, allows the historically concrete to be weighted just as strongly as the supra-historical universal.

4.3.2.4 Emphasis on the Unity between the Eternal and the Incarnate Logos

Christological approaches that emphasize the distinction between the eternal Word of God and his human form invoke the Chalcedonian formulae 'without change' and 'without confusion'. Those who stress the unity between the two will point to 'without division' and 'without separation'. Unity here does not mean conflation and distinction does not mean separation.

In this brief section I will show how a distinction between the eternal Logos of God and his 'incarnation' in Jesus was rejected, especially in Catholic

---

111 Panikkar, *The Unknown Christ of Hinduism*.
112 Translated from Panikkar, *Trinität*, 13.

theology, as being too far-reaching in the eyes of the Magisterium. Among the Christological approaches rejected in this manner were those of the Catholic theologians Jacques Dupuis and Roger Haight.

Dupuis took pains to maintain conformity with Roman Catholic Church doctrine and he remained within the framework of Christocentric universalism.[113] Nevertheless, his approach became the object not only of theological criticism but also of magisterial condemnation, principally because he had applied the above distinction within the theology of religions. According to him, too, "the Christ-event, however inclusively present, does not exhaust the power of the Word of God, who became flesh in Jesus Christ".[114]

This led to Dupuis receiving an official warning in 2001 from the Vatican Congregation for the Doctrine of the Faith.[115] He was accused of separating the saving work of the *logos asarkos* from that of the Word incarnate (*ensarkos*). Arguing against such a separation, the Congregation objected to the idea that there were two orders of salvation, one of which extended beyond the Church. But Dupuis had never claimed that. Rather, he had always insisted on distinguishing between the two modes of the one Logos' being and working, without separating them.[116]

The Vatican's position ran counter to Dupuis' distinction between *logos asarkos* and *ensarkos*. It is perhaps most notably expressed in the encyclical 'Redemptoris missio':

> To introduce any sort of separation between the Word and Jesus Christ is contrary to the Christian faith. [...] Jesus is the Incarnate Word—a single and indivisible person. [...] Christ is none other than Jesus of Nazareth: he is the Word of God made man for the salvation of all. [...] In the process of discovering and appreciating the manifold gifts—especially the spiritual treasures—that God has bestowed on every people, we cannot separate those gifts from Jesus Christ, who is at the center of God's plan of salvation.[117]

This passage is quoted in the declaration 'Dominus Iesus', forming the basis for the conclusion:

---

113   Dupuis, *Toward a Christian Theology*. See also: *id.*, *Christianity and the Religions*.
114   Dupuis, *Toward a Christian Theology*, 319.
115   The statement made by the Congregation, on 24th January 2001, can be found as Appendix 1 to *Toward a Christian Theology*, 434–8.
116   Dupuis, *Toward a Christian Theology*, 299.
117   Pope John Paul II. "Redemptoris missio", § 6.

therefore, the theory which would attribute, after the incarnation as well, a salvific activity to the Logos as such in his divinity, exercised 'in addition to' or 'beyond' the humanity of Christ, is not compatible with the Catholic faith.[118]

The decree of this doctrinal condemnation formed the basis for similar condemnations of the books *Toward a Christian Theology of Religious Pluralism* by Jacques Dupuis, *Jesus Symbol of God* by Roger Haight, and others.

The concern behind such an emphasis on the unity between the eternal and the incarnate Word of God is expressed in the subtitle of 'Dominus Iesus'—namely, that it consists in securing "the unicity and salvific universality of Jesus Christ and the Church".[119] This declaration seeks to guard against theological recognition of non-Christian religions becoming too far-reaching, which it sees as an expression of relativism.

Even outside of the context of debates within the theology of religions, however, theologians may feel compelled to assert the distinctive core of the Christian faith by minimizing or eliminating the difference between the eternal and the incarnate Word of God. Mainly for soteriological reasons, they replace the idea of participating with that of identification: Jesus *is* the Logos, the second person of the Trinity, and the Logos *is* Jesus. This puts a stop to representational Christology.

4.3.2.5 'Incarnation' as a Metaphorical *modus loquendi* for 'Representation'

Instead of the 'Incarnation' of the Word of God, representational Christology speaks of the 'representation' of God's presence. It thus avoids any connotations of either God or the heavenly Son being transformed into a human. For representational Christology, 'Incarnation' or 'God becoming man/flesh' are metaphorical expressions for God's presence in the person of Jesus—in his speech and actions, suffering, and death. 'Incarnation' illustrates the human Jesus' intimate relational oneness with God. The term means that Jesus participates in the divinity of God and that this power radiates out from him.

The use of metaphorical language should not be viewed, here or more generally, as deficient in relation to literal speech. Often it is the only way of conveying certain meanings which can add a hugely enhancing significance to the merely factual world. The figurative word 'incarnation' indicates

---

118   Congregation for the Doctrine of the Faith, Declaration, "Dominus Iesus", § 10.
119   Congregation for the Doctrine of the Faith, Declaration, "Dominus Iesus".

that this human being is completely permeated by the power of God's self-communication, which has become, as it were, his 'nature'.

Of course, the application of the term 'representation' to Christology can also be read as a metaphorical one. There are different levels of metaphor; 'incarnation' is metaphorical to a higher degree than 'representation', with a greater pictorial, figurative quality, and therefore it can illustrate what is meant by 'representation'. Conversely, 'representation' helps to interpret and to clarify the term 'incarnation', but above all to prevent it from being misunderstood. As I have shown, the term allows the distinction between Jesus and God to be clearly made and for Jesus' divinity to be expressed in a way that is biblically responsible and comprehensible within the framework of contemporary plausibilities. Representational Christology does not attempt to reconcile incompatible concepts through negative formulations but offers an intelligible model for how the divine and the human can be united in one person. It can point to analogies for this in various areas of life.

Moreover, representational Christology allows us to go beyond the term 'incarnation' and use other *modi loquendi* for the meaning it aims to convey. A good starting point for this is a specific formulation in the proem of 1 John—a statement that is semantically very close to that of Jn. 1:14 but speaks neither of the Incarnation nor of the Word of God. Note that 1 Jn. 1:2a says, with reference to Jesus Christ, that "the life was revealed" (καὶ ἡ ζωὴ ἐφανερώθη). In place of a theology of the Word, here we find a theology of Life. The idea of the 'Incarnation of God' is thereby placed in a broader horizon of meaning, within which it signifies God placing Godself in relation to the world, opening Godself for it, and making Godself present in it.

In addition to 'Word' and 'Life', there are three predicates with which God's nature and action are directly described in the New Testament (using the copula 'is'), and these can also be used as *modi loquendi*: God is Love, Spirit, and Light. With each of these three terms, firstly God's nature and action are given voice, secondly God's eternal self-communication is qualified, and thirdly the 'Incarnation' of this self-communication in a concrete historical place is indicated in a personal representative. The definition of relationship between these three entities is analogous to the three *modi loquendi*: unity in twofold difference.

- According to 1 Jn. 4:8–16, God is *Love* (ἀγάπη). The eternal Love radiating from God suffuses the human Jesus, who thereby becomes its representative.
- According to Jn. 4:24, God is *Spirit* (πνεῦμα). The power of the Spirit emanating from God since all eternity makes its 'dwelling' in the human Jesus, who was chosen for this purpose and who through God's Spirit becomes the 'Anointed One'/the Messiah/Christ.

- According to 1 Jn. 1:5, God is *Light* (φῶς). The eternal light radiating from this source unfolds its brilliance in and through Jesus. As the one illuminated by this light, he becomes the 'light of the world' (Jn. 8:12: φῶς τοῦ κόσμου). But it is the light of *God*, who dwells in the inaccessible light (1 Tim. 6:16) of his glory (δόξα), a light which arose with creation itself (Gen. 1:3ff). John 1:9 speaks of this light "enlightening every human being who comes into the world".

Patristic theology made extensive use of this metaphor, as did Oecolampadius in particular among the Reformers. 'Light' is the metaphorical expression for the Spirit of God. In the brilliance of this light, God's self-communication becomes recognizable through its incarnational form in Jesus Christ.

Representational Christology, however, suggests that this need not mean that God's self-communication exists *only* in this form or is exhausted in it. It is precisely in Christ that the 'extra' dimension of the Word and Spirit of God is revealed: the universality and unconditionality of God's grace, which cannot be limited to the sphere of influence of the proclamation of Christ. In the power of God's Spirit, it can bring forth "manifestations of grace"[120] wherever and whenever it wants. There is no *extra* and *intra* for it.

Another *modus loquendi* for representation is to speak of the 'in-historicization' of God or the Word of God. But this term is misleading, since it insinuates that God's spiritual presence is unhistorical. This is not the case. God's spiritual presence does not first have to enter into history; it is already present in it, even when not yet manifest in Jesus. Where the divine *logos asarkos* manifests itself historically, it is no longer *a-sarkos*. It takes on historical 'flesh'.

In Jesus one can encounter the spiritual presence, the Word, and the Wisdom of God in the form of a single person. These can also manifest themselves in other forms, however. The Old Testament scriptures indicate that the Word of God does not become reality in a person but in the Torah and prophetic proclamations; as well as in other forms. It is the same Logos that manifests itself here. Where the Logos manifests itself in Jesus, it makes him the 'Christ'.

But the Logos of God precedes this Incarnation and transcends it in the future. He encompasses all times, all cultural and religious 'spaces'—and is equally close to them all. This is the core of what is meant by talking about the 'pre-existence' of the Word of God, a concept which stems from Wisdom theology and can be traced back to the Spirit of God. This motif allows us to express

---

120 Translated from Tillich, *Protestantische Gestaltung*, 57–61.

the idea that God's salvific presence and salvific will have existed and will exist throughout eternity.

What Nicholas of Cusa said about human beings applies to Christ in a more pointed form: namely, that he is "Deus datus",[121] 'the bestowed God', '[the] gift in which God gives Godself'. But if God is an *immoderate* giver of this gift of Godself or of the Spirit (Jn. 3:34), then it cannot be limited to a *single* historical event. It is precisely the universality of the divine grace, proclaimed by and realized in Jesus, that gives rise to the expectation that this gift will also be bestowed outside of faith in Jesus Christ.

4.3.2.6   Fullness as Wholeness

To conclude this current chapter, which has focused on how the Logos/Word of God relates to the humanity of Jesus, I will summarize my understanding of this relationship. I have spoken of the Word of God having a 'surplus' beyond its incarnation in Jesus: he is the Word of God personified, but the Word of God is 'more' than Jesus. But the reverse is also true: Jesus is 'more' than the Word of God. What does this 'more' mean?

– In the first statement ('the Word of God is more than Jesus'), 'more' refers to the cosmic vastness and universality of the Logos of God encompassing and permeating all of history. The incarnation of the Word of God in Jesus, on the other hand, is bound to a particular historical place and time. Thus, we are dealing here with the polarity of universality (or catholicity) and particularity (or contextuality). The 'more' refers to the sphere of activity and of influence.

– In the second statement ('Jesus is more' than the Word of God'), 'more' refers to the unique concentration present in the embodiment of the spiritual Word in space and time. It associates itself with a name and a face (*prosopon*—πρόσωπον), and it reveals itself in a life story, a path of suffering, and in the history of the Christian faith that emerged from this origin.

In both statements, each coming from their opposite direction, the 'more' conveys the same thing: that the spiritual presence of God is represented in its fullness in a person but is not limited to it.

'More' can therefore be defined neither qualitatively (in terms of having superior properties) nor quantitatively (in terms of existing in greater quantity). The relationship between Jesus and God (and/or God's Spirit, love, presence) should rather be defined in terms of a *fullness*. 'Fullness' can be understood as 'wholeness' or as 'completeness'. Completeness leaves no space beyond itself.

---

121   Nicholas of Cusa, *De dato Patris luminum / On the Gift of the Father of Lights*, II, § 97.

It therefore leads to a claim of exclusivity. But if fullness is understood as wholeness, then it follows that something or someone can be wholly represented without being completely exhausted in or depleted by this representation. In other words, other forms of 'full' representation can coexist alongside it. In this understanding of 'fullness' the above distinction of *totus Deus* and *totum Dei* can be transcended; it allows us to conclude that Jesus represents God or the presence of God not only in the sense that Jesus represents God *wholly*, but also in the sense that he represents *the whole of God*. In him dwells the whole fullness of God (Col. 1:19: πᾶν τὸ πλήρωμα), which, however, infinitely exceeds this finite 'dwelling place'. In Jesus, the Word of God is tangibly present in all its fullness—this is what makes his ministry and suffering the Christ-event— without this whole fullness being limited to this event.

Understanding 'fullness' as wholeness enables us to see the creative and redeeming presence of God in Jesus represented in its wholeness while not claiming that there can be no self-communication of God *extra Christum*. This understanding also prevents the meaning of Jesus Christ from being reduced to individual 'salvation facts' ('Heilstatsachen'), like focusing on the crucifixion; it is concerned much more with the *totus Christus* as representative of the 'whole God'. Furthermore, it makes it possible to think of this 'fullness' as being made present in a particular form in a particular historical context. The idea of God's presence in Jesus being complete and thus exclusive would equate him with God; it would de-historicize and decontextualize him. He would be God walking on earth.

Where the Absolute appears in a historically contingent form, this form can be completely permeated by him and represent the whole of the Absolute. It embodies his identity but is not numerically identical with him. Jesus Christ is the conditional figure of the unconditional, the finite representation of the infinite, the concrete realization of God's universal presence, the event of God's presence. Thus, it is not the case that the two realities of God and the human Jesus coalesce as a synthesis, such that there is no longer any difference between them. They remain different: "to conceive of the togetherness of God and human being as representation in Jesus Christ prevents [...] the cramped attempts (Biblicist, fundamentalist) to demand, as it were, magical identities".[122]

Jesus *is* the word of God insofar as he represents it in his person. The 'is' is not to be understood in the sense of a substance-based identification but as a personal, relational one. It is an identification which asserts that God's powerful

---

122 Translated from Deuser, *Gottesinstinkt*, 166.

self-communication and thus God's creative will for relationship and salvation is made present in Jesus. Whoever lives 'in' this presence of God is in the community of God, i.e., in communion with God and with those, living and dead, who also belong to this community. The 'is' indicates a 'representative identity'. Identity here does not mean sameness but denotes the unity of different realities: the reality of God and the reality of Jesus the human being. The two realities do not stand side by side, in need of mediation between them, but in a relationship of being *in* each other. Jesus represents the self-communication of God not as something external to him, but as his purpose, the center of who he is as a person. He not only represents this self-communication but brings it about. The Word of God manifests itself in him and through him.

In chapters 4.3.1 and 4.3.2 I have focused on the relationship between God and the Logos or Word of God, as well as the relationship between the eternal and the incarnate Logos. Doing so has illustrated that, for all the emphasis on unity in these relationships, a difference always remains and must always remain. In this context, representational Christology emphasizes that element of difference.

These reflections relate back to Logos-Incarnation-Nature Christology, the main strand of Christological doctrinal formation in theological history. Now the field of vision will be broadened. Attention must also be paid to Spirit Christology and Wisdom Christology, because in my view they also can shine substantial light on the presence of God in Jesus. 'Word', 'Spirit' and 'Wisdom' of God are not to be contrasted with each other as distinct concepts; they overlap both semantically and in terms of the historical tradition.

4.4 Spirit Christology

A Spirit-Christology approach applies to Jesus Christ not the concept of the incarnation of the Logos but rather that of the inspiration by the Spirit. In the history of theology, Spirit-Christological approaches have typically been integrated into incarnational Christology, marginalized by it, or suppressed altogether. More recently, in contrast, Spirit Christology has been pitted against the theology of the Word. Logos-Incarnation Christology has either been positioned within the broader horizon of Spirit Christology or been replaced by it.[123] However, I argue against the necessity of integrating one approach into

---

123   E.g., by Lampe, *God as Spirit*.

the other or replacing one approach with the other. We should not be following models of inclusion or exclusion. Rather, the two approaches should stand side by side and complement each other.[124]

The phrase 'Incarnation of the Word of God' seems to go beyond the idea of Jesus' 'inspiration by the Spirit' in that it does not merely say 'the Word of God is *in* Jesus' but 'Jesus *is* the Word of God'. In contrast, however, chapter 4.3 pointed out how the associations in John's prologue between God, the Word of God, and Jesus can be categorized in a way that is sensitive to difference. 'Incarnation' does not even remotely mean an identification without difference; rather, it can be understood as an (metaphorical) expression of a relational identity.

The same question about what exactly is meant by 'is' also arises in Spirit Christology. Paul seems to make a clear identification with the statement, in 2 Cor. 3:17, that "the Lord is the Spirit" (ὁ δὲ κύριος τὸ πνεῦμά ἐστιν). Immediately afterwards, however, he indicates that this statement is to be understood in the sense of a genitive compound: "Spirit of the Lord". Jesus is imbued with this Spirit, but not to the extent that we can identify him substantially with the Spirit, so that we can say he *is* the Spirit. Taking this into account, one can also speak (in a metaphorical sense) of Jesus as the 'Incarnation of the Spirit', as Hans-Joachim Kraus does in his interpretation of 1 Cor. 15:45: "the one anointed by the Spirit appears here as the incarnation of the Spirit".[125]

This chapter, then, begins by rejecting the repeated complaint that Spirit Christology minimizes Jesus Christ's divinity. It does bring this divinity to bear in a different way from Logos-Incarnation Christology, and certainly in a different way than interpretations based on substance thinking and ontology. But this does not mean that our certainty of salvation is either minimized or lost. Criticisms along these lines reduce Spirit Christology to a form of Arianism or Adoptionism which sees in Jesus only one of God's creatures that happens to have received the gift of the Spirit; and then they accuse this simplified version of being reductive. In this way, however, the fact of God's in-dwelling in Jesus is underemphasized from the outset.

---

124 Cf. The position of Clark H. Pinnock: "My point is that Spirit Christology and Logos Christology are complementary, not antithetical. One complements without replacing the other. Logos Christology is ontologically focused, while a Spirit Christology is functionally focused, but the two work together. Generally speaking, Logos addresses the Person of Jesus while Spirit addresses his work. [...] [Spirit Christology] enriches Logos Christology by doing greater justice to the role of Spirit in Christ. It gives better recognition to the missions of both the Son and the Spirit." (Pinnock, *Flame of Love*, 91ff).

125 Translated from Kraus, *Eine Christologie des Heiligen Geistes*, 43. See also: *id.*, *Systematische Theologie*, 337–446.

4.4.1 *Biblical Starting Points and Contemporary Approaches*

According to the Bible, 'Spirit' can be understood as the power of God's presence, the "power from on high" (Lk. 24:49: ἐξ ὕψους δύναμις). The power of God's spiritual 'presence' suffuses Jesus in the wholeness encompassing both body and soul. It thus fills not only his psyche or his consciousness, but his humanity in all its dimensions. This is symbolized in the narrative of the virgin birth (Mt. 1:18–25; Lk. 1:26–35), which we should not understand as a report on a historical event so much as a narrative expression of theological meaning. Firstly, this narrative says that Jesus was filled with the Spirit of God from the beginning of his life rather than only being gifted with it from a certain point in time onwards. Secondly, it says that the Spirit of God not only permeates Jesus' *spirit* but that it defines his life in its entirety, both body and soul. The presence of God in the power of the Spirit of God fully 'occupies' the whole person of Jesus. He lives in the 'atmosphere' of this presence and in this way embodies it.

The Christ title itself also points to Spirit Christology. As a Greek translation of the Hebrew *maschiah* (משיח = Messiah), it identifies Jesus as the one anointed with God's Spirit. God and the Spirit are present in and through Jesus (Rom. 1:3ff). In contrast to Adam, the 'earthly being', Christ is "life-giving spirit" (1 Cor. 15:45: πνεῦμα ζωοποιοῦν). The key Gospel motifs of 'election', 'sonship', 'commission', and 'mission' all point to one who is Spirit-filled; they characterize Jesus as wholly defined by the Spirit of God. On the basis of Logos-Incarnation Christology, the Alexandrian school expressed this theme by speaking of 'divine nature'. But this expression cannot claim to state a matter of fact. Rather, it is one possible interpretation of Jesus' status and relevance—which can also be expressed by other interpretations.

Pneumatological motifs play an important role in relation to Jesus, especially in the Lucan writings (Lk. and Acts). Jesus' sonship with God is attributed to the work of the Spirit (Lk. 1:35). According to Lk. 3:21f and parallel passages at his baptism, Jesus was gifted with the Spirit of God. John the Baptist announced that Jesus would not baptize with water but with the Holy Spirit (Lk. 3:16). Luke 4:18 records that it was the Spirit that sent Jesus. Jesus' entire ministry depends on his being suffused with the Spirit (Lk. 4:1, 14, 18; 10:21; Acts 10:38)[126] until he then places this Spirit in the hands of God with his last word on the cross (Lk. 23:46).

Matthew 12:28 tells of Jesus casting out demons by the Spirit of God and thus bringing about the dawn of God's reign. In Mt. 10:20 he promises the disciples that the Spirit will help them find the right words to say when they are

---

126 Luke 4:1 and 14 frame the temptation narrative, which is told in Lk. 4:2–13 (cf. Mk. 1:12; Mt. 4:1).

persecuted and must defend themselves in court. However, New Testament Spirit Christology is not only based on the pre-Easter Jesus, but also on the risen *Christus praesens*. Especially in the Pauline and Johannine writings, Christ no longer appears primarily as the one who receives or is endowed with the Spirit of God, but as the one who sends or pours it out. In Paul, moreover, the *eschatological* character of the New Testament understanding of the Spirit of God emerges particularly clearly. The Spirit is regarded as an eschatological gift. Paul understands it as the power of God that raised Jesus and that will also bring about the general 'resurrection' of the dead (Rom. 8:11).[127] Pneumatology is therefore closely connected with soteriology. According to Jn. 14:26, Christ promises the Spirit to his disciples, while in Jn. 3:34 we learn that he gives it "without measure" (οὐκ ἐκ μέτρου).

When the first Christian congregations dissociated themselves from the Judaism of the synagogue, they appealed to the charismatic authority of the exalted Lord in opposition to the official authority of synagogue rulers and scribes. This is particularly evident in the Gospel of John. The omnipresence of the Spirit of God can also, however, be recognized "in the Pauline and Lucan traditions as the normative original experience of Christianity".[128]

Otto Hermann Pesch rightly states that

> soon after Jn. 1:14 the remaining Christology found in the New Testament disappears into the shadows and our verse [i.e., Jn. 1:14] becomes primarily the biblical starting point of further dogmatic development.[129]

The 'Johannism' which "was previously only one of many Christological possibilities"[130] became the normative interpretation of the Christ kerygma. An important reason for this lies in the mediation that the notion of the Logos allowed between Greek philosophy and the Old Testament wisdom of the creative Word of God. Taking Jn. 1:14 as a starting point, Logos-Incarnation Christology could be developed in the ancient history of theology alongside Middle and Late Platonic thought and the Logos philosophy of the Stoics. Emphasizing that line of interpretation led to a marginalization of the early Jewish[131] Spirit-Christological approach to interpreting Jesus' person and work. This

---

127 See also 2 Cor. 13:4.
128 Translated from Ganoczy, *Trinität*, 116.
129 Translated from Pesch, *Katholische Dogmatik*, 384.
130 Translated from Schillebeeckx, *Jesus*, 387.
131 Frankemölle, *Das jüdische Neue Testament*, 192–96.

latter approach, which was greatly influenced by the Old Testament,[132] had had a formative impact on the Synoptic Gospels; Paul also referred to it and it was articulated in the dynamic Monarchianism of the second and third centuries. However, it largely receded in popularity and became integrated into Logos-Incarnation Christologies as they became increasingly normative.

This process was also connected with a reshaping of the understanding of 'Spirit': for Tertullian, Irenaeus, and Apollinaris, for example, it no longer meant the biblical *pneuma*/πνεῦμα (or the *ruah*/רוח), but the νοῦς (reason, intellect) in opposition to corporeality.[133] This shift led to a Platonizing 'spiritualization' of the Spirit of God, and to understanding the 'spirit' of Jesus as his spirituality in contrast to his corporeality. But if only the *spirit* of Jesus is assumed by God, then redemption cannot be understood as an event that concerns the body too. The language of Logos-Incarnation Christology seemed better suited to expressing holistic redemption, and so Spirit Christology became discredited.

In the recent past, however, significant arguments in favour of a Spirit-Christology have been presented by Donald M. Baillie,[134] Geoffrey W. H. Lampe,[135] Hendrikus Berkhof,[136] Piet Schoonenberg,[137] Ralph del Colle[138] and Hans-Joachim Kraus.[139] In a broader sense, the work of Paul Tillich[140] and Jürgen Moltmann[141] can also be included among these.

Such arguments are often associated with a theology that grounds Jesus in his Jewish context and is primarily founded on the Synoptic Gospels. This is very clear in the work of Hans-Joachim Kraus, who develops a Messianic Christology rooted in the Old Testament. In Kraus' approach, this is accompanied by a critique of the Hellenization of Christian theology which led to both the doctrine of two natures and the answering of the question of the person and meaning of Jesus Christ within a supernatural framework. This supernaturalism, said Kraus, was indebted not to Hebrew and Old Testament thinking but to Greek philosophy; it divided the cosmos into two spheres—a natural and a supernatural one, the one physical and the other metaphysical or

---

132 See e.g., the remarks on the gift of the Spirit being bestowed on the Servant of the Lord in Deutero- and Trito-Isaiah (Isa 42:1; 61:1).
133 See Grillmeier, *Jesus der Christus*, 198–201, 581–2.
134 Baillie, *God was in Christ*.
135 Lampe, *God as Spirit*.
136 Berkhof, *Theologie des Heiligen Geistes*.
137 Schoonenberg, *Der Geist*. See also O'Keeffe, *The Spirit Christology*, 116–40.
138 del Colle, *Christ and the Spirit*.
139 Kraus, *Eine Christologie des Heiligen Geistes*, 37–46.
140 Tillich, *Systematic Theology*, Vol. 3, 144–49.
141 Moltmann, *The Way of Jesus Christ*, esp. 73–94.

spiritual. But there have always been those who returned to a Spirit Christology that follows the biblical tradition, people like Ignatius of Antioch or Calvin. John Owen should also be mentioned.[142]

The anchoring of "Pneumatological Christology" in "Israel's messianic history of promise" is also clear in Moltmann's work.[143] He seeks to develop Christology from "the Jewish contours of the messianic promise"[144] and refers to Hans-Joachim Kraus' "Systematic Theology in the Context of Biblical History and Eschatology".[145] But let us bear in mind that the concept of the Messiah in early Judaism was not the starting point for the development of Christology. Jakob J. Petuchowski and Clemens Thoma state:

> if we seek ideas in Judaism that are structurally similar to Christology, we will not find any corresponding Jewish conceptions of the Messiah—only traditions that speak of God's condescension, which in Judaism are both numerous and central.[146]

Spirit Christology can find common ground (albeit more from the perspective of systematic than of historical theology) with Jewish scholars' recent approaches to Jesus,[147] and with the Islamic and Qur'anic understanding of Jesus as a prophet sent by God. The 'Messiah' title ('the one anointed with God's Spirit') is also applied to Jesus in the Qu'ran (Q. 3:45), which indicates that this bestowal of the Spirit existed from the beginning of Jesus' life. The story of the virgin birth in which this is symbolized (cf. Mt. 1:18 and Lk. 1:35) is also found in the Qur'an (Q. 19:17–21), which maintains that Jesus was begotten by the Spirit of God. This certainly does not exhaust everything there is to say about Jesus Christ from a Christian perspective, but it does bring up an important aspect, namely Jesus' 'prophetic ministry', as it was called in theological tradition.

---

142 John Owen connects the Chalcedonian two-natures doctrine with Pneumatology. Alan Spence summarizes his position thus: "the Holy Spirit formed, sanctified and energized the human nature which the eternal Son had assumed into personal subsistence with himself." (Spence, Incarnation and Inspiration, 63). A critique of Owen's approach can be found in Crisp, *John Owen on Spirit Christology*, 5–25.
143 Moltmann, *The Way of Jesus Christ*, 73. The quotations taken from this page are partly in italics.
144 Moltmann, *The Way of Jesus Christ*, 74.
145 Kraus, *Systematische Theologie*, § 146.
146 Translated from Petuchowski and Thoma, *Lexikon*, 34.
147 See Homolka, *Jesus von Nazareth*; Homolka and Striet, *Christologie auf dem Prüfstand*; and Homolka, *Der Jude Jesus*.

But even putting to one side such interreligious echoes, Spirit Christology enables us to understand the person and meaning of Jesus Christ in a way that satisfies the criteria both of identity and of relevance.

4.4.2 Avoiding the Minimization of Jesus' Humanity

There is no danger of Spirit Christology minimizing Jesus' humanity if it is developed in harmony with the Old Testament understanding of the Spirit of God and in view of the New Testament statements about Jesus receiving the gift of the Spirit. Such a Spirit Christology, however, must distance itself from a docetic spirituality that understands Jesus as the divine Spirit who came down from heaven and was clothed in a human body on Earth. Similarly, and much as in Logos-Incarnation Christology, the idea of a transformation of the Spirit into a human body is to be rejected.

In contrast to Logos-Incarnation-Nature Christology, Spirit Christology is better able to preserve the categorical difference between the human Jesus and God and thus to place the right degree of emphasis on his humanity. Where humanity and divinity are placed under the common denominator of 'nature', competition between human and divine natures inevitably ensues, even if it is claimed that each is fully contained in Jesus. Spirit Christology presents the relationship between the divine Spirit and the human Jesus not as the union of two natures, but as the endowment of the human with the power of God's presence: the Spirit of God so defined Jesus that Jesus could be experienced and understood as the embodiment of that Spirit. In this sense, Jesus was completely absorbed by God. The Spirit of God shaped his person, initiated his Messianic mission, and empowered him to carry it out. Jesus was so utterly flooded with the Spirit of God that he could and can be considered not only a channel of the Spirit's power, but also a representative of the *source* of this power. In the person of Jesus, the Spirit of God was manifested in a human being who was absolutely open to that Spirit.

Between Jesus and God there is not so much a common essence as a perfect communion of spirit. The unity of Christ with God has less to do with his being and more to do with his 'attitude' (his 'mind', as expressed by the verb φρονέω at Pp. 2:5f) and his actions. Geoffrey W. H. Lampe has suggested replacing the 'substantival' interpretation (Jesus is God) and the 'adjectival' one (Jesus is divine) with an 'adverbial' one.[148] An adverbial understanding of the unity of Jesus with God sees this unity in the will, speech, and actions of the human Jesus who is completely suffused with the Spirit of God. Hans Küng

---

148 Lampe, *The Holy Spirit*, 124.

has similarly spoken of a "unity of the 'throne', the knowledge, the will, and the action of Jesus with God".[149]

Such an interpretation fits well with the New Testament's descriptions of God as 'Love', 'Spirit', and 'Light',[150] which characterize primarily the *action* of God. The biblical writings show little interest in God's essence. One can therefore speak of a functional rather than an ontological identification of Jesus with God.

The problems with Lampe's proposed adverbial definition of Jesus' unity with God are, firstly, that God's in-dwelling in Jesus remains underemphasized in the idea that Jesus acts in harmony with God. Secondly, and relatedly, this definition primarily concerns Jesus' activity, which minimizes the presence of God in his suffering. Thirdly, and again relatedly, the definition focuses on the pre-Easter Jesus, losing sight of the *Christus praesens* and thus coming close to Adoptionism.

The Spirit Christology proposed here is different from both Adoptionism and classical Logos-Incarnation Christology. The latter defined the relationship between the human Jesus and God (or the Word of God) unidirectionally, as consisting of God becoming incarnate in a human being. Spirit Christology instead assumes an interaction between the inspiring and guiding influence of God on the one hand and the trusting devotion of the human Jesus on the other. 'Guiding influence' does not mean predetermination. Rather, Jesus' relationship with God is one of perfect, freely-willed harmony. In determining and defining the human Jesus completely, God's Spirit does not take away his freedom but instead *fulfills* it.

Attempts to develop a Spirit Christology based on the two-natures doctrine (as undertaken by John Owen, for example,[151]) lead to the idea that the 'spiritualization' of Jesus (i.e. his endowment with the Spirit) applied only to Jesus' *human* nature, while the divine nature which forms Jesus' person is regarded as the actual agent. Here, the Spirit is merely granted a supporting function. Such attempts still place too little emphasis on Jesus' humanity.

In contrast, a Spirit Christology that is not subordinated to the doctrine of two natures can assert Jesus' humanity without any restrictions. But it also avoids falling into the other extreme of regarding Jesus as merely a human being who was adopted by God. Instead it alludes to the testimonies of Mt. and Lk., according to which the inspiration of Jesus did not take place from a specific point in his life onwards but from the very beginning of his life. That is

---

149   Translated from Küng, *Credo*, 87.
150   See chapter 4.3.2.5.
151   See footnote 142.

why the Spirit of God is mentioned not just in the third article of the Apostles' Creed, but also in the second: Jesus is 'conceived by the Holy Spirit'. He works in the power of the Spirit as well as out of, or on the basis of, that power, which resides within him. "In the first chapters of the synoptic gospels especially, the Spirit is presented as the divine determining subject of the way Jesus took".[152] This avoids Adoptionism's two problematic assumptions:
- that (following the two-phase model) Jesus was merely a human being for the first period of his life, and then (as per Mk. 1:10ff.) he was accorded the status of sonship at his baptism;[153]
- that his adoption is grounded in his human perfection, which leads to his election by God. The relationship with God is thereby understood in an ethical sense, i.e., seen as grounded in the will of Jesus.

The position taken by Adoptionism starts 'from below' with the human being and understands his divine sonship as the result of his exaltation by God. It thus fundamentally assumes a movement of ascension. Spirit Christology, on the other hand, can also be understood as Christology 'from above'. Here the movement starts from the 'descent' of the Spirit of God.

This latter approach would suggest we understand the uniqueness of Jesus Christ in qualitative, not merely quantitative, terms. Jesus is different from the prophets, as he is from other humans in general, and not only by degree. There is a qualitative difference between (a) the functional gift of the Spirit received by prophets, kings, and priests; and (b) the determination of Jesus' existence by the Spirit of God. But his uniqueness is not an exclusive one in the long term; Paul testifies to him as the firstborn among many brothers (Rom. 8:29; cf. Heb. 2:17). If he were completely distinct from the rest of humanity, this would not be compatible with being genuinely human.

4.4.3 *Compatibility with Contemporary Forms of Thought and Language*

Spirit Christology is not bound to the intellectual background of Platonic philosophy and its reception in Alexandria. This makes it more compatible with, and freer to connect to, other intellectual and historical contexts. It can also be expressed using forms of language drawn from our own cultural context. I try to do this with formulations which may sound 'esoteric' but which I consider

---

152   Moltmann, *The Way of Jesus Christ*, 92.
153   Yet Mark 1:10ff. (with its reference back to the ritual for the enthronement of the king alluded to in Ps. 2:7), does not have to be interpreted in such a way that Jesus is "made" the Son of God in baptism. It can also be interpreted in the sense of a confirmation or revelation of the existing sonship of God. For an example of this interpretation, see Karrer, *Jesus Christus*, 196.

appropriate and meaningful. For example: Jesus lived in the energy field of God's immediate presence, concentrated this energy, compacted the field into his sphere of activity, and generated a spiritual radiation that continued to work through the presence of his spirit. The spiritual presence of God dwelling in him and radiating out from him takes hold of human beings, opens them up to God, and so transforms their personal nuclei and their basic relationships.

In contrast to the imagery of 'acting', the activity of the Spirit is described in biblical tradition using the imagery of pouring, flowing, and radiating. Expressions such as those used in Charismatic theologies can be connected to this, e.g., talking of 'power' and 'empowerment', of 'spiritual energy', 'inspiration', 'flow of power', 'influence', 'radiation', 'being filled with', etc. Within Spirit Christology, such images are to be used with caution, as a means of expression. They should not and must not shift the axes of Christology in an unhealthily spiritualizing direction.

In the world of human experience there have been (and still are) various analogies for being filled with transpersonal power, such as the experience of being seized by the power of love. In English, we can say that a person is 'in love', that is, in the energy field of love. In a similar way, Paul spoke of the believer being 'in Christ'. Applied to Spirit Christology, we can rework this as Jesus Christ being 'in the Spirit of God'; whoever is 'in Christ' is thus in the power of God's Spirit and God's Spirit is in them. But this cannot be reversed. Being in the power of God's Spirit does not automatically mean being 'in Christ'—because this power reaches beyond Christ.

4.4.4   *'Before Him, in Him, through Him, and beyond Him'*

The universal power of the Spirit reaches further than that power's personal manifestation at a single point in history and that manifestation's subsequent effects. Jesus is the bearer of the Spirit of God ('pneumatophore'/πνευματοφόρος), who is *within* his person and cannot be distinguished *from* that person, but who also reaches *beyond* it. Jesus lives and acts entirely in the power of the Spirit of God, and in this way becomes the center of this radiance. But the power of the Spirit transcends the radius of the one who is radiating it. It works before him, in him, through him, and beyond him. It is in Jesus and yet not identical with Jesus' spirit without any distinction. This is evident, for example, when Jesus wrestles with God (Mk. 14:36 and parallel passages) or despairs of him (Mk. 15:34). 'Being filled with' does not mean identity in the sense of abolishing any difference. 'Perfect harmony' in terms of a close relationship does not mean total conflation. The definition of the relationship between God, the Word of God, and Jesus as the Word-of-God-in-person, as proposed in chapter 4.3, applies in the same way to the relationship between

God, the Spirit of God, and the Spirit-bearer Jesus. We can also speak of the Spirit having both a pre-existence and a continuing existence afterwards. That Christ sent the Spirit does not mean that after Pentecost this Spirit proceeds exclusively from him. It is the same Spirit that filled him, but this Spirit is not bound to the embodiment in the person of Jesus. The idea expressed with the 'Extra Calvinisticum' can also be applied to Spirit Christology. The universality of the Spirit's activity beyond the Spirit-bearer can be more easily justified than can the universality of the Logos with reference to Jn. 1, because according to Acts 2:17 the promise of Joel 3:1 was fulfilled. Namely, the Spirit of God has been poured out on *all* flesh, including the 'Gentiles' (Acts 10:45).

The categorical difference between the divine and the human Spirit has been expressed throughout the history of theology by speaking of the 'personhood' of God's Spirit. However, the application of the concept of person to the Spirit of God is misleading and should be understood solely in functional terms. When the Spirit is spoken of as a 'person', this constitutes a warning against the appropriation of the Spirit of God by human spirituality. Even where resonances between the divine and the human spirit occur, the human spirit nevertheless always follows its own aspirations and tends thus to immunize itself against the Spirit of God. 'Redemption' in this context also means breaking out of these strategies of immunization against God's Spirit.

A soteriology that takes a Spirit-Christological approach does not interpret redemption primarily in terms of incarnational theology, that is, as God's adoption of human nature. Nor does it interpret redemption in terms of the theology of the Cross, i.e., as Jesus Christ's victory over the powers of corruption or as an atoning sacrifice. Rather, it sees redemption as the breaking down of barriers in individual and collective attitudes of mind; as the 'influx' of vital energy and strength to address crises; as the bursting forth of new hope in situations that seem hopeless; etc. This is not to be understood in terms of substance, but as an infusion of what Paul Tillich called the 'courage to be'. An inspirational soteriology of this sort assumes that the Spirit of God works universally in the whole of creation, and that it opens human beings to God's self-communication in order to bring about the renewal of their relationships with God, with themselves, with fellow human beings, with nature, and with the things of this world. This 'reconciliation' is symbolized in the 'covenant' renewed in Jesus Christ.

Soteriology and all its facets are certainly not exhausted by such a Spirit-Christological interpretation. But it nonetheless brings up an important dimension which tends to be left underexplored by soteriological approaches based on incarnational theology and the theology of the Cross. One of the advantages of Spirit Christology is that it can connect soteriology more directly with Christology than an incarnational approach can. Unlike the Spirit that Jesus received and that proceeds from him, the Logos cannot be said to come forth from Jesus and take hold of humans. Soteriology depends on the 'work' of the incarnate Logos; thus, it follows from Christology. Spirit Christology, on the other hand, anchors Christology in soteriology. In Jesus Christ is represented in a concentrated form the "one great, all-encompassing 'movement' from God to the world and to human beings".[154]

At this juncture it is worth addressing three critical questions regarding Spirit Christology:

- Can the presence of the Spirit of God in Jesus be sufficiently distinguished from its presence in Christians, in humanity or the world as a whole? We might answer that it is the same Spirit that is present in both Jesus and in humans, but that in the latter it is confronted with mental attitudes that lose their bearings elsewhere, while Jesus' whole person is exclusively defined by *this* Spirit. What sets the Spirit of Jesus apart is its perfect openness to God, which does not need redemption but itself sets redemption in motion.
- Would it be fair to say that Spirit Christology is based on an overly optimistic view of humanity and of the world, one which does not sufficiently account for the power of dispositions, actions, and structures that are contrary to God? The biblical traditions themselves contradict this view, in that the Spirit of God in Jesus confronts 'unclean' spirits and Jesus casts out demons in the power of this Spirit (Mt. 12:28 and more). Spirit Christology knows about the necessity of redemption. The Spirit is the power of 'resurrection' from death.
- Does Spirit Christology overemphasize the immanence of the Spirit and pay too little attention to its transcendence, hiddenness, and withdrawal? To this question the answer could be made that the Spirit being 'omnipresent' does not mean that it can immediately be recognizable or experienceable. As an eschatological gift, it is always also the object of a promise which is yet to be fulfilled—and therefore we must continuously renew our requests for the coming of the Spirit.

4.4.5 On the 'filioque'

We have yet to consider the consequence of this approach for discussions about the '*filioque*'.[155] The insertion of this word into the Constantinopolitanum declared that the Spirit proceeds from the Father "and the Son". This interpretation is related to the immanent Trinity (i.e., to the eternal 'begetting' of

---

154 Translated from Veenhof, *Pneumachristologie*, 324.
155 See Siecienski, *The Filioque*.

the Son and the 'spiration' of the Spirit), but equally concerns the sending out of the Son and the Spirit into the world. This explains why the mission of the Son is (not chronologically, but materially) prioritized over the mission of the Spirit,[156] so that the latter can then come forth from Father and Son. Thus the 'procession' of the Spirit of God was bound to that of the Son, and thus the Spirit of God working in the world was bound to the Word and the proclamation of God's Word; the Spirit was domesticated in both a Christocentric and an ecclesiocentric way. The function assigned to it was to enable the Word of God revealed in Jesus Christ to reach his addressees. This reduced it to a 'functionary' of Christ making his work present.

A new interpretation of the *filioque* following Jn. 15:26 would be significant not only for ecumenical relations with the Eastern churches, but also for a Christology in the context of theology of religions. It could and should communicate that it is not primarily the risen Christ, but *God*, who is the subject of the eternal and temporal outpouring of the Spirit; and that it was this Spirit who filled Jesus and whom Jesus sent forth. The Spirit sent forth by him is the Spirit of the Father, imparted through the Son. But the Spirit of God reaches further than this mediation. We must thus distinguish between the Spirit's specific content and its mode of being. With regard to its specific content or substance, there is no difference between the Spirit of God, the Spirit of Jesus, and the Spirit proceeding from Christ: it is all the same Spirit of God. In terms of its mode of being, however, there are forms of God's presence in the Spirit that have not been enacted through Christ.

Spirit Christology's fundamental statement—that the Spirit of God works before Jesus, in him, through him, and beyond him—is in tension with the assumption that Jesus Christ has priority over the Spirit. It places both in a dialectical relationship to each other: the Spirit represents God's universal, powerful presence, which is historically and personally represented through Jesus Christ. If he were not filled by the Spirit, he would not be the Christ, and without Jesus the Christ, the Spirit would be an anonymous power and God would be the unknown God (Acts 17:23: ἄγνωστος θεός, *agnostos theos*). In line with biblical tradition, a pneumatologically grounded Christology sees the Spirit as preceding the Word (i.e., Christ and the proclamation of Christ) and going beyond the Word. It is in the Word that this sending out of the Spirit finds its crystallization and its essential criterion; it is here that it becomes expressed. The criterion for examining and discerning the 'spirits' encountered

---

156 E.g., in: Thomas Aquinas, *STh* III q.7, a. 13. Thomas speaks of the grace of union, with God proceeding from Christ and the grace of sanctification proceeding from the Spirit.

in Christianity and other religions is whether the unconditional and universal grace of God comes to the fore.

The Spirit precedes Jesus, makes him the Christ, and thus is the driving force of the Christ-event. The Spirit unfolds in this event and works outwards from it without being exclusively bound to it. The powerful presence of God, which transpires in the power of the Spirit, is creation's breath of life leading that creation to perfection. It encompasses the person and mission of Jesus Christ and is represented in him. Jesus

> is the keystone in the arch of Spiritual manifestations in history. [...] The event 'Jesus as the Christ' is unique, but not isolated: [...] It is the qualitative center in a process which proceeds from an indefinite past into an indefinite future.[157]

Jesus guarantees that this process takes place according to God's unconditional and universal grace.

In his relationship with God the Father, the 'Son' himself is the recipient of the Spirit proceeding from God alone. In his relationship with humanity, on the other hand, he is the dispenser of God's spiritual power. The Spirit comes forth from God *through* Jesus Christ. Following this interpretation, it is in some sense possible to retain the *'filioque'*. The Spirit of God coming forth from Jesus, the Spirit-bearer of God, is the Spirit received from God. Jesus did not receive the Spirit for himself, but in order to inspire others with it: "from his fullness we have all received grace upon grace" (Jn. 1:16, cf. Jn. 20:22). Understood pneumatologically, receiving God's grace means being endowed with God's Spirit. For those filled with God's Spirit, it is true to say: "it is not I, but the grace of God that works in me" (1 Cor. 15:10).

Applying the preposition 'through' to the relationship between the Spirit of God and the spirit of Jesus speaks against both an identification between them on the one hand and a separation between them on the other. An undifferentiated identification would mean a Christocentric narrowing of the universality of the Spirit of God. A complete separation would lead to the assumption that Jesus in his spirit (i.e., his human consciousness) orients himself to the Spirit of God by an act of his own will—which would erode Spirit Christology. In contrast, representational Christology draws on Pneumatology to understand Jesus as God's Spirit-bearer, who is the representative of God's saving presence.

A debate about revising the *'filioque'* clause arose within ecumenical dialogues with the Eastern Orthodox Churches; from 1978 onwards, the Klingenthal

---

157   Tillich, *Systematic Theology*, Vol. 3, 147.

Conferences hosted discussions about how best to approach this.[158] The reports on these conferences propose a reformulation of the *'filioque'*, one that precisely expresses the concern of a pneumatologically-based representational Christology: "the Spirit proceeds from the Father and shines through the Son".[159] This formulation can be interpreted as meaning that God's 'Light' (i.e., his universal saving presence) is omnipresent even when obscured. It is precisely where humans "walk in darkness" (Isa. 9:1) that it shines. Jesus Christ was filled with this Light, and it shone through him. Even where he thought himself abandoned in the 'eclipse of God', the Light was not absent, as the disciples realized retrospectively in view of the Easter event. Thus, he was directly (through his work) and indirectly (through his suffering) the source of Light for those who allowed themselves to be enlightened by it. But the original and actual source of the Light was and is God (1 Jn. 1:5). The Light radiating from God shines even where the message of Christ does not reach. In this understanding, Spirit Christology asserts the universality of the Spirit's presence to its full extent.

For the definition of the relationship between the Word and the Spirit of God, the proposed modification of the *'filioque'* means that God's self-communication takes place *in* the Spirit. God reveals himself *through* the Word *in* the Spirit. Making the Spirit independent of the Word would lead to free-floating spiritual claims. In contrast, the Spirit reveals the message of Christ, the message of God's unconditional, universal saving purposes. In this role, the Spirit of God is not restricted to working through Christianity: the Spirit "blows where [he] chooses" (Jn. 3:8: τὸ πνεῦμα ὅπου θέλει πνεῖ), and "has filled the world" (Wis. 1:7). But where it 'blows', God is always salvifically present. Crucially, these considerations do not lead to a separation between the two 'missions' of God the Father—that of the Son and that of the Spirit.

Irenaeus of Lyon described the Son and the Spirit as the two hands of God.[160] Spirit-Christological approaches often take up this distinction. Different 'works' are then assigned to the two missions: for the Son's part, the bringing about of salvation; for the Spirit's, the fulfilment of creation, the sanctification of human beings, the communication of the knowledge of faith, and so on. This distinction is sometimes applied in the field of theology of religions.[161]

---

158 See the reports on the Klingenthal Conferences beginning in 1978 in Vischer, ed., *Geist Gottes*.
159 Translated from *Bericht: Das Filioque aus ökumenischer Sicht*, 20.
160 Irenaeus of Lyon, *Against Heresies* IV, 38, 3; V, 1,3.
161 For example, in a lecture that the Greek Orthodox metropolitan Georges Khodre from Lebanon delivered at a Conference of the WCC in Baar, Switzerland, in January 1990 (Khodre, *An Orthodox Perspective*, 25–31). See also Paul F. Knitter's statement: "The Reign of God, as it may be taking shape under the breath of the Spirit, can be seen as [...] an

I regard this distinction with skepticism because it threatens to split the unity of God's powerful presence. It seems to make sense as a differentiation between two aspects, but not as one between two truly distinct modes of God's activity or even as two orders of salvation. The two aspects are two sides of the *single* act of God's self-communication. They can be described with different emphases as self-communication in his Word or as radiation of his power in his Spirit. Both, however, are about the revelatory event of God's universal and unconditional saving presence within the framework of God's universal plan of salvation. In Jesus Christ the turning of God to the world is represented in God's Word and Spirit, and thus God's very self is represented. Jesus is the human face of God.

4.5 Wisdom Christology

The notion of the 'Wisdom' of God rooted in the Old Testament can and should be made more fertile ground for Christology than it has been in the past. It interprets the presence of God in Jesus not as an incarnation of the Logos or as an inspiration of the Spirit, but as an in-dwelling of the Wisdom of God.

The motif of 'in-dwelling' is found widely in Wisdom literature (Wis. 7:27; Sir. 24:7–12; Gospel of the Hebrews, Fragment 2; see also Isa. 11:2). This motif was transferred to the *Logos* as it took the place of Sophia in John's Gospel, e.g., Jn. 1:14b. Philo of Alexandria made little distinction between 'Logos' and 'Wisdom'. He referred to the Logos as the source of Wisdom and to Wisdom as the source of the Logos; but he also equated the two.[162] The New Testament

---

economy of grace genuinely different from the one made known through the Word incarnate in Jesus" (Knitter, *Jesus and the Other Names*, 113).—The declaration "Dominus Iesus" rejects this distinction: "There are also those who propose the hypothesis of an economy of the Holy Spirit with a more universal breadth than that of the Incarnate Word, crucified and risen. This position also is contrary to the Catholic faith, which, on the contrary, considers the salvific incarnation of the Word as a trinitarian event. [...]. In the New Testament, the mystery of Jesus, the Incarnate Word, constitutes the place of the Holy Spirit's presence as well as the principle of the Spirit's effusion on humanity, not only in messianic times [...], but also prior to his coming in history." (Congregation for the Doctrine of the Faith, Declaration, "Dominus Iesus", § 12.).—Amos Yong, the American charismatic theologian who originates from Malaysia, also applied the distinction between the two "economies" of the Word and the Spirit to the theology of religions (Yong, *Discerning the Spirit*[s]), but also considered its problems (Yong, *The Spirit Poured Out on All Flesh*, 111 footnote 81).

162   See chapter 4.3.1.2. In part, Wisdom seems to be a synonym of Logos ("Legum allegoriae" I, LCL 226, 65; "Quod deterius potiori insidiari soleat", LCL 227, 115–18; "De fuga et invention",

also speaks of the in-dwelling of the *Spirit* (Rom. 8:9–11; 2 Cor. 12:9). Michael Beintker states,

> where Wisdom is among humans, there is the Spirit of the Lord—this is then the conclusion in Wisdom literature. (cf., for example, Job 32:8; Prov. 1:23; SapSal. [Wis.] 7:22ff.; Sir. 39:6ff.)[163]

Jürgen Moltmann also draws attention to the close connection between the two: "Spirit Christology is also Wisdom Christology".[164]

This shows how closely discourse around the Word, the Spirit, and the Wisdom of God touch, overlap, and interpenetrate. In all three cases this discourse comes down to the presence of God in Israel, in the temple, in Jesus and in believers.[165]

4.5.1 Biblical Approaches

According to Old Testament Wisdom literature, divine Wisdom was created by God or born of God even before the creation of the world (Prov. 8:22–25). In the Septuagint, the word ἔκτισεν (meaning God 'created' her) is used in Prov. 8:22, while v. 23 uses ἐθεμελίωσεν (God 'laid her foundation') and v. 25 uses γεννᾷ (God 'begat' or 'begets' her). In Prov. 8:22–31 she is personified as a master craftsperson and as a beloved child of God, "daily his delight, rejoicing before him always". Philo called her the "daughter of God".[166] She is simultaneously with God and with human beings. As a creative, caring, guiding, and illuminating force, she radiates from God, but also possesses relative autonomy in relation to God. As a pre-existent mediator of creation, she forms the order of creation and makes it accessible to human knowledge (see also Ps. 19). She wants not only to be recognized as containing within herself all knowledge of the world and of God, but also to be followed in the active practice of righteousness and justice. Thus, she becomes the source of life and the right conduct guiding life toward its true fullness. Proverbs 8:35 has Wisdom say, "whoever finds me finds life and obtains favour from the Lord".

LCL 275, 109). In part, Wisdom is older than Logos and preexistent to it ("De somniis", LCL 275, 245–46, "De virtutibus", LCL 31, 62). See Miletto, "Philo of Alexandria".

163 Translated from Beintker, *Creator Spiritus*, 12–26, citation from 18.
164 Moltmann, *The Way of Jesus Christ*, 74.
165 See also Exod. 29:45f.; Lev. 26:11f.; Zech. 2:14f., 8:3; 2 Cor. 6:16; Col. 2:9; Rev. 21:3. Likewise, Mt. 18:20 can also be referred to in this context.
166 Philo, "De fuga et invention", LCL 275, 50–52 (S. 37). See also: Hölscher and Kampling, eds., *Die Tochter Gottes*.

Wisdom is described as a prophetess, teacher, friend, hostess, and mother[167] who fills human beings and makes them "friends of God and prophets" (Wis. 7:27). Elizabeth A. Johnson calls her "God's gracious [...] presence in the world".[168] Wisdom is a gift of God in which the giver always gives themself.

According to Sir. 24:3–9, Wisdom stretches her tent over all creation and is spread "over all the earth, and over every people and nation" (Sir. 24:6). Wisdom literature emphasizes her universality: Sir. 24:7ff. refer to her finding her ancestral home in Israel, but little reference is made to Israel's specific salvation history. The ideas of 'covenant', of Israel's 'election', and of the 'promise' associated with them play a marginal role at best. Wisdom is conceived cosmically rather than historically, and she is generally associated with revelation in creation, not specific revelation in history. Therefore, in principle she is also accessible to every rational human being.

Within Wisdom theology we can recognize different currents, which overlap and interpenetrate each other. If one examines the crucial aspect of the relationship between Wisdom and the world, two contrasting currents emerge. The first sees the world positively, because Wisdom dwells in it, constitutes and structures it, and gives it order and orientation (as in, e.g., Sir. 24). The other is more apocalyptically influenced, stemming from the anti-Hellenistic piety movement of the Maccabean period; it regards Wisdom as a prophetess sent by God, but rejected by humans (Enoch 42). Here, Wisdom has not found a dwelling place in the world, and this entails threats of judgment. In the first case, Wisdom is associated with creation and the created order, with the Torah, and with guidance on how to act in everyday life in light of God's justice. In the second, Wisdom is critical of the world, and thus of 'worldly wisdom'. Personification can be used as another distinguishing criterion. In the writings from early Hellenistic times (Job, Prov.) Wisdom appears as a hypostasized figure; under the influence of apocalyptic literature (e.g., Dan.), she appears as an eschatological revelation.

In the New Testament, the Wisdom of God is related to Christ, whose significance is thus cosmically universalized. He is declared Lord over Heaven and Earth, standing not merely as an eschatological bringer of salvation at their end of all things, but also as mediator of creation at their very beginning.

In the sayings of Jesus, as they are collected in Q, there is yet no 'Wisdom Christology'. However, many of the statements in it that are attributed to Jesus

---

167   Philo of Alexandria, for example, refers to the Wisdom of God (following Plato) as the "mother" of cosmic reality ("Quod deterius potiori insidiari soleat" I, LCL 227, 115–16; "Legum allegoriae" II, LCL 226, 49).

168   Translated from Johnson, *Die Weisheit*, 148. See also *id.*, *Ich bin, die ich bin*.

come from the apocalyptically influenced Wisdom tradition with its threatening words (Mt. 11:25–27; 12:38–42; 23:34–36, 37–39; and parallel passages). Jesus is not yet identified with Wisdom, but appears as her "last messenger, wooing, and urging".[169]

In the Gospel of Matthew there are hints that Jesus was already understood as the personification of Wisdom, especially in his sapiential characterization in Mt. 11–13. This appears most clearly in three passages: Mt. 11:19c (Wisdom is shown in Jesus' 'works'), 11:28f. (a Wisdom-inflected phrase), and 23:34 (here Jesus is said to do what has traditionally been attributed to Wisdom, i.e., sending prophets, wise men, and scribes). No wonder that M. Jack Suggs states that, for the Gospel of Matthew, "Jesus is Sophia incarnate".[170]

In the Pauline and Deutero-Pauline epistles there are many allusions to Wisdom motifs, but in Paul there is also a critical juxtaposition of God's Wisdom with the wisdom of the world (1 Cor. 1:18–31; cf. also Mt. 11:25 and parallel passages). In 1 Cor. 1:24 Paul refers to Christ as God's power and God's Wisdom (θεοῦ δύναμις καὶ θεοῦ σοφία). The verses that refer to Christ as sent by God (e.g., Gal. 4:4; Rom. 8:3) take up the motif of Wisdom's mission (Wis. 9:10); her preexistence and her mediation of creation are also attributed to Christ. The incorporation of traditional Wisdom material is most pronounced in the Epistle to the Colossians. According to Col. 2:3, "all the treasures of wisdom and knowledge" (πάντες οἱ θησαυροὶ τῆς σοφίας καὶ γνώσεως) are hidden in Christ. In Col. 1:15–20, by speaking of the 'image of God', a designation of divine Wisdom is applied to Christ, since Wis. 7:26 calls Wisdom the image of God's goodness (in chapter 3.2.7.1 I already pointed out the reference to this verse in Heb. 1:3). Jesus is thus characterized as the personification of the Wisdom of God.

In the Gospel of John, Wisdom is completely absorbed into, or replaced by, the Logos. Many exegetes assume that the pre-Johannine template of the prologue did not originally speak of the Logos, but of Wisdom, and that her characteristics—preexistence and mediation of creation—were then transferred to the Logos. The result is that one can speak of a 'Logification' of Wisdom Christology.[171] This was related to the general rolling back of apocalyptic motifs. Feminist theologians suspect the reason behind this was to serve the interests of masculinizing female Wisdom.[172] The weightier reason,

---

169 Translated from Vollenweider, *Christus als Weisheit*, 29–52. See also Ebert IV, *Wisdom Christology*, 37.
170 Suggs, *Wisdom, Christology*, 58.
171 On the relationship between the Johannine Christ and Wisdom, see Scott, *Sophia and the Johannine Jesus*.
172 E.g., in: Johnson, *Die Weisheit ward Fleisch*, 148.

however, may again lie in the absorption of Greek/Hellenistic Logos philosophy. There, too (e.g., in Philo), Wisdom was practically identified with the Logos (see above). It was not only this identification which led to the transcending of early Jewish Logos-Wisdom theology; rather it was the idea of an 'incarnation' in a human being.

The relationship between God and Wisdom corresponds to the relationship between God's divinity and the Word and the Spirit of God. In early Jewish Wisdom literature, Wisdom is regarded as an expression of God's essence, but one whose activity does not exhaust that essence. What has been said about the unity in difference between the eternal Word of God and the Word 'made flesh' in Jesus Christ is also true in regard to Wisdom. Yet however much the New Testament sees the Wisdom of God personified in Jesus Christ, it does not actually make an undifferentiated identification of the two. There always remains a relational difference: Jesus acts with the authority of divine Wisdom. The Wisdom-inflected template of the Johannine prologue states that he is the incarnate figure of eternal Wisdom. As "Wisdom incarnate"[173] he is completely one with her, without her being absorbed or exhausted in him. Here again, therefore, we can assert the dual difference between the *repraesentandum* (in this case, the Wisdom of God and thus also God) and the representative (Jesus Christ). God hypostasizes Godself in Wisdom and Wisdom is herself personified in Jesus Christ. She is present in his person in all her fullness, but exists prior to this representation, just as God is prior to Wisdom as his hypostasis.

In her account of this identity-in-difference, Elizabeth Johnson seeks to point back to the experience of the first Christians:

> then *her* (sc. Wisdom's) intimate relationship with God was also seen to be manifested in *him* (sc. Jesus), *her* activity in the world embodied in *his* work, *her* spirit poured out in *his*.[174]

It is for this reason that Paul could confess that Christ becomes Wisdom 'for us' (1 Cor. 1:30).

4.5.2 *The Ambiguity of God's Wisdom in the World, Represented by the Cross*

The dimension of "the Wisdom of God in its rich variety" (Eph. 3:10: ἡ πολυποίκιλος σοφία) has been and continues to be rediscovered in recent Christological debates. Jesus has been understood as a teacher or personification of God's

---

173   Dunn, *Let John be John*, 331.
174   Translated from Johnson, *Die Weisheit ward Fleisch*, 149 (emphasis in original).

Wisdom by scholars of feminist theology (e.g., Elisabeth Schüssler Fiorenza[175]) and by branches of Charismatic theology, as well as by prominent representatives of recent research on Jesus (e.g., James Robinson[176]) and Pauline exegesis (e.g., James D. G. Dunn[177]).

However, the connection of Wisdom with apocalyptic literature is mostly neglected. Wisdom appears as the creative and illuminating power of God that gives structure and orientation to the world, while Jesus is the one who teaches about Wisdom and puts her into practice. His action and his proclamation are at the center of interest—the 'prophetic office'. The moment of truth contained in the 'critical Wisdom', as it is articulated in Job and Ecclesiastes, recedes. It consists in the application of Wisdom to the world in a way that is not affirmative, but critical. For example, in the prophetic judgment sermon of the *Logia* source (Q), the world is not only a manifestation of God's Wisdom but is also filled with powers that oppose this Wisdom and bring injustice, suffering, and death in ruthless self-assertion of their own power interests. The passion narratives show where the 'wisdom of the world' can lead. Here the world's need for redemption is starkly revealed. A Wisdom Christology which downplays these dark themes deprives the Gospel of its liberating power and leaves it with only one remaining (albeit important) function, namely of directing human life.

We must keep both sides in view—that Wisdom confronts the malaise of the world, and that she gives voice to the world's true *nature* as a home (οἶκος) founded by, and in, God. Both sides are represented in Christ as the "Wisdom messiah".[178] Like Logos Christology and Spirit Christology, indeed perhaps more clearly than either of these, Wisdom Christology confesses that God weaves into the whole cosmos with his creative, ordering, enlightening power, and that this power is personified in Jesus Christ.

Thus, even quite mundane abilities and accomplishments, such as an artisan's creative work or a teacher's intelligence, are related to Christ (as with the Greek term σοφία in general as Plato had already used it). In the relationship between God, the world, and humanity, there is no salvific inner sphere over against the worldly outer sphere.

Paul brings the two together—the Wisdom of God *in* the world and her critical opposition *against* the world—by relating her to the cross and 'resurrection'. In these is revealed the Wisdom of God which opposes the wisdom of the world (1 Cor. 1:18–25). The new creation is not in tension with creation at large,

---

175 Schüssler Fiorenza, *Jesus*.
176 Robinson, *Jesus*.
177 Dunn, *Christology*, 163–212.
178 Moltmann, *The Way of Jesus Christ*, 309.

but in tension with its perversity. It does not question the order of the world based on God's Wisdom, but it does question human orders of knowledge and values which close themselves off from Wisdom. Christ is, so to speak, the crucified Wisdom. He not only represents the Wisdom of God, but also becomes the victim of the world's wisdom.

As regards *recognition* of the Wisdom of God, this means that Christ not only reveals Wisdom but also reveals her hiddenness in the world. This hiddenness is mentioned in Job 28:12–21. She cannot be unambiguously recognized in the concrete phenomena or structures of this world, nor in human abilities like rationality, ethical consciousness, or artistic creativity. Under 'worldly' conditions she only ever manifests herself in a fractured, fragmentary, at best allegorical way. A theology referring to the Wisdom of God in the world (and thus a 'natural' theology), which regards natural and historical phenomena as unmediated communications of God, will therefore always be doubtful and questionable. All worldly phenomena are ambiguous. The structures of reality are in principle 'wonderful' (Ps. 139:14) but they also harbour enormous destructive potential. Human rationality and creativity can be used for the good of human beings but also to develop weapons of mass destruction.

To summarize, Wisdom Christology presents Jesus Christ as the representative of God's Wisdom, who fills him completely and which he embodies in his whole person, without simply becoming identical with him. With his suffering and his brutal execution, however, he also represents—negatively, as it were—the consequences of a self-centered worldly wisdom: he reveals the tension between God's Wisdom and the world's wisdom and emphasizes the former's hiddenness in the world. It is 'under the cross'.

4.6 Word, Spirit, and Wisdom—an Interim Evaluation

In chapters 4.3, 4.4, and 4.5, I (a) answered the question of how we should regard the presence of God in Jesus (and thus his representation of God); and (b) defined the relationship between God as the one who is represented and Jesus as the representative.

(a) Regarding the first question, I have suggested that, rather than describing this presence of God using *one* model, multiple types of description should be applied instead. Of these, 'Word' ('Logos'), 'Spirit', and 'Wisdom' have the greatest prominence, due to their importance in the biblical tradition and in early Christianity. 'Word', 'Spirit', and 'Wisdom' designate aspects of God's *one* self-communication in the world; aspects anchored in God's being, which cannot be clearly distinguished either in content or in the historical tradition.

Rather, they overlap and interpenetrate. The concept of representation allows us to understand Jesus Christ as the realization of God's self-communication in the creative and directing Wisdom, in the redeeming and salvific Word, and in the strengthening and sanctifying Spirit.
- Referring to God, talking about the 'Word' emphasizes the specific *performance* of God's self-communication (the Word is a word of action or power); talking about the 'Wisdom' emphasizes God's *reason* expressed in her; and talking about the 'Spirit' emphasizes the *power* in and with which this self-communication happens, and which radiates from it.
- Referring to the world, the Word relates to *specific* demonstrations of God's power in nature, but especially in history and in addressing humans. Wisdom manifests herself more in the *general* structures of creation, as well as in enabling humans to understand God's will and to shape the world in its light. The Spirit is the enlivening and illuminating power of God, which comes into effect by bestowing vital energy and spiritual gifts, as well as in 'inspirations' that are possible everywhere and always arise anew. Framing things in terms of the 'Word', the 'Wisdom' and the 'Spirit' of God gives expression to God's universal grace and salvific commitment to the world.

In theology, the Word, the Spirit, and the Wisdom of God were and are often spoken of substantively and handled in an essentialist way. They appear as distinct entities, as hypostases with their own characteristics, each with their own modes of action and impact attributed to them. Within the doctrine of the immanent Trinity, the classical notion of the 'person' is used to describe *the* 'Word' and 'Spirit'. As theological terms, they are defined as clearly as possible and distinguished sharply from each other. In contrast, my understanding is that the Word, the Spirit, and the Wisdom of God are terms of reference rather than definitive concepts for comprehension. They are biblical modes of expression for the one creative and salvific self-communication of God (in the Word), self-manifestation (in the Spirit), and self-disclosure (in the Wisdom). They are not to be understood as entities, but as biblical perceptions and means of expression. They give voice to the fundamental experience and conviction that God does not (as with Aristotle) rest in Godself remote from the world, but rather 'goes out of Godself' to create a counterpart and to guide this creation towards the fulfilment of God's saving purposes. In this way, they variously express experienced, understood, and conceived forms of God's presence. These would be better described not substantively, but verbally or adjectivally (e.g., 'creative', 'salvific', 'inspiring').

The Christian faith sees in Jesus Christ the personification of the Word, Spirit, and Wisdom of God. These terms describe the presence of God in him and thus what makes him God's representative. Christologies based on incarnation, inspiration, and in-dwelling do not, therefore, represent mutually exclusive alternatives, but overlapping interpretations of the same fundamental proposition that God was and is in Jesus Christ. His Christhood existed and exists in this in-dwelling of God in him.

The question now arises whether the three ways of making God present *ad extra*—Word/Logos, Spirit, and Wisdom—could and should not be bound together in trinitarian terms, so that Christology would in itself have a trinitarian structure. This would not so much be a matter of embedding Christology in the doctrine of the Trinity as a framing theory, but rather of a Christology which is itself conceived along trinitarian lines. The Wisdom 'in-dwelling' in Christ in its role as mediator of creation can be connected with the work of the first trinitarian 'person'; the Word 'incarnate' in him is the self-communication of God in the Son or Logos, i.e., the second 'person'; and the Spirit 'inspiring' him is the Holy Spirit, i.e., the third 'person'.

I have reservations about such a systematization, however. It would reduce to a closed system the variety of forms in which the making present of God occurred and is occurring, the ways of thinking through which it has been and is being opened up, and the ways of speaking in which it has been and is being articulated. Other forms, analyses, and *modi loquendi* (such as reference to the 'Shechina' of God) would either need to be traced back to these three figures or eliminated. Moreover, the three would have to be defined against each other. It is important to me, on the other hand, to give space to diverse forms of thought, speech, and event, and not to clearly demarcate them from each other. Only in this way does the path remain open for the possibility that God's presence also occurs in ways that cannot be adequately represented in the expressions and language of biblical and Christian traditions—because these would restrict their otherness.

The three forms of expression—Word, Spirit, and Wisdom—are therefore not to be played off against each other but to be regarded as complementary. In the biblical and early Christian traditions, too, they do not stand side by side, as entirely distinct entities, but overlap, interpenetrate, comment on, and correct each other. Secondly, they are not intended to form a comprehensive trinitarian classification. Other, more pictorial forms of speech—e.g., about the 'Light' of God—can come alongside them or be used to illustrate particular interpretations. In this context, reference back to God's self-communication in the Torah must always be considered. A deliberate renunciation of sharp distinctions is theologically appropriate and should be taken into account more strongly in Christology than was and is often the case in dogmatic approaches.

(b) The relationship between God (from whom the Word, the Spirit, and the Wisdom originate) and Jesus (who is filled with this divine Word, divine

Spirit, and divine Wisdom) consists of two relationships and thus also of two distinctions. On the one hand there is the relationship/distinction between God (or the very being of God) and his utterance (or his self-communication; or his revelation in Word, Spirit, and Wisdom); on the other hand, there is the relationship/distinction between these expressions of God's being and their personification in Jesus, who thereby becomes the Christ.

The formal definition of each of these two relationships is analogous to the other: it can be described as unity in difference. For the first of the two relationships, this is expressed in both components of the word 'self-communication'. It is God*self* who communicates through Word, Spirit, and Wisdom (therein lies the emphasis on unity), but the *communication* consists in a kenosis in which the self 'gives itself away' (therein the element of difference). In the second relationship, the unity of difference consists in the presence of the Word, Spirit, and Wisdom in the person of Jesus. On the one hand he is filled so completely with this presence that one can say, 'God is in him' (emphasizing the *unity* of the person of Jesus with God's Word, Spirit, and Wisdom). On the other hand, the Word, Spirit, and Wisdom of God all extend beyond this representative—and therein lies the difference. This articulates the conviction, fundamental to the Christian faith, that God has communicated Godself in its creative saving presence, and in the power of the Spirit in the person and work of Jesus Christ. However, this still preserves God's transcendence and keeps open the possibility that this presence of God can also occur outside God's self-communication in Christ and its influence throughout history.

Such self-manifestations of God *extra Christum* do not have to be devalued *a priori* in relation to the representation of God in Christ, e.g., by downgrading them to a merely diffuse, general, indirect revelation in nature and history. One must assume the possibility that God, in making Godself present, also draws on the sources and streams of tradition of non-Christian religions, as well as on non-religious phenomena.

I am not yet concerned with whether this is in fact the case, but only with the question of which basic Christological decisions would support this line of thinking. The doctrinal formulation found at the Council of Chalcedon leaves less room for maneuver in this respect than approaches to Christology that are even more strongly connected to Jewish tradition and have a broader biblical foundation than Logos-Incarnation Christology (which referred primarily to John 1:14). This is truer still of that doctrine's post-Chalcedonian reception. In contrast, the concept of representation enables us to integrate ways of thinking about the identity of God's being, God's self-communication, and its historical manifestation, while yet allowing a double difference between these three dimensions. Under the aegis of this main concept it is then also possible to speak of a relationally defined consubstantiality between Jesus and God which, however, is not at the expense of the necessary distinctions.

4.7 The Revelation and Withdrawal of God

The term 'revelation' has the same configuration as that of representation. It summarizes two relationships in one act: the relationship between the revealer (God) and the historical medium of God's self-communication (Jesus Christ) as well as the relationship between this medium and the revelation's recipients. One also can distinguish between the source, the content, and the act of revelation. If revelation is understood as self-revelation, the source and the content coincide: in which case it is not some*thing* which is revealed, but the self of the revealer. The concepts of self-revelation and representation resemble each other in a further way: the self-revealing God not only shows but *gives* Godself. Revelation is not purely an epistemic but also a relational act—one which, by God making Godself known, constitutes a relation.

The same dialectic is thus at work in both the concepts of revelation and representation:

- 'Revelation' means the 'opening'[179] of God's hiddenness by Godself, and consequently the epistemic self-representation of God. But that does not mean that the fullness of God's being is now bared to the light. Revelation is rather a knowledge of God's *hidden* presence, unveiled in a creaturely medium. This revelation opens itself only to understanding based on faith. The reception of that unveiling does not lead to a rational knowledge but to a faithful certainty. This involves an awareness that God is not an 'object' of understanding.
- 'Representation' of God does not mean standing in for the absent God, but rather making God's presence experienceable. However, the experience of being present must not be equated with the availability of that presence. It remains a hidden presence (itself already widely attested in the Old Testament, e.g., Isa. 55:8f.).

Only if understood in this balanced way is it possible to speak of the presence and revelation of God. They are a presence and revelation within a permanent hiddenness, an immanence with permanent transcendence. This hiddenness holds true even when representation has taken effect. God dwells "in an

---

179 The German term "Offenbarung" has the connotation of "laying open".

unapproachable light" (1 Tim. 6:16). The light may be unapproachable, but it nonetheless shines and illuminates.

The concept of God's 'self-revelation'[180] (or 'self-communication'), which has been central to understanding revelation in Protestant theology since the nineteenth century,[181] is not one that we should understand as meaning that God reveals Godself *directly* as God. Rather, the revelation occurs in the *Word* of God, i.e., in an act of utterance in which the revealer, on the one hand, communicates themself in the revelation, but on the other hand also remains distinct from it.[182] The 'Word' of God, in turn, goes forth through the media of history. God thus 'speaks' as Godself through the 'other' of that self. In this process of becoming immanent, God remains transcendent. God becomes present in revelation but just as significantly remains *distinct from* this self-communication. Even there, where God makes Godself present, this presence is not simply evident; it must reveal itself as such. The concept of representation also expresses this dialectic of being present and withdrawing, of revelation and hiddenness.

This dialectic is summed up by the statement "Christ is the manifestation of God's hiddenness",[183] formulated by Norbert Bolz following Blaise Pascal. Revelation does not do away with hiddenness but makes manifest that which is hidden without it losing its hiddenness, such that it remains abidingly mysterious. God reveals Godself *as* hidden, withdrawn, unfathomable, immeasurable, inexhaustible. Even in God's revelations, God remains a mystery. Revelation and God's hiddenness are dialectically connected with each other. On the one hand, representational Christology expresses this dialectic and protects us from reifying how we speak of God. On the other hand, this representational Christology enables us to think of the historically mediated presence of God as an authentic experience of God's real presence.

Perceiving and understanding are key to the event of revelation. A revelation that is not perceived and understood as such is no revelation at all. 'Revelation' does not mean the transmission of supernatural information; rather, it is an event of opening up that takes place in one who understands.[184] In the same way, representation depends on being recognized and acknowledged for what it is.

---

180   See chapter 3.2.7.4.
181   See Bernhardt, *Offenbarung*.
182   Luther differentiated particularly clearly between God *Godself* (Deus ipse) and the Word of God, e.g. in WA 18, 685.
183   Translated from Bolz, *Interlinearversionen*, 33.
184   See also Bernhardt, "Da wurden ihre Augen geöffnet".

The revelation of God in Jesus Christ not only *proclaims* the overcoming of humanity's distance from God; it is the *realization* of this overcoming. In this, too, 'revelation' agrees with 'representation'. 'Revelation' denotes God's making Godself known in all aspects of the divine relationship with humanity. It is not, therefore, a distinct act of proclamation alongside other acts of God's self-communication; it is the epistemic side of that self-communication. It reveals itself in the 'eye' of the believing observer—in the spiritual contemplation of those who 'see' the world and life through the lens of God. Revelation leads to insights that are fundamentally hermeneutical. This understanding does not open itself up as knowledge (resulting from intellectual discoveries), but as certainty (becoming aware of the presence of God).

Knowledge derived from revelation is not in opposition to that which stems from reason. Rather, it employs reason in a broader sense that goes beyond the rational processing of empirical data. The use of reason appropriate to insights gained from revelation can be called "perceptive reason" ("vernehmende Vernunft").[185] This understanding of reason was advanced by Hamann, Herder, and Jacobi in particular in opposition to Kant's 'critique of reason'. They regarded reason ('Vernunft') as the organ of perception of the absolute. According to Herder, the very term 'Vernunft' ('reason') points to the act of 'Vernehmen' ('perceiving').[186] Belief in revelation therefore does not mean irrationally believing in supernatural truths, but rather perceiving the powerful self-communication of God.

Revelation does not entail disclosing a secret but allowing the recipients to participate in a mystery. Experiencing the presence of God includes the knowledge that God 'as such' cannot be experienced. Friedrich Naumann conveys this insight using the image of a 'seafarer' who sees the visible surface of the water, but to whom the depths of the sea remain hidden.[187] Another image for divine withdrawal is speaking about God as a 'person'. We ought not to understand this in the literal sense of God being a person, as human beings are persons. The designation of God as a person is not a factual statement about God's inner 'being' but a figure of speech for the 'face' of God that is turned toward the human and yet always remains hidden: God's revelation in permanent hiddenness. This is also true in relation to human beings: the dignifying title 'person' points to the unavailability of the human being, who is ultimately beyond the reach of all cognitive capabilities (as emphatically pointed out by the philosophical and theological Personalism of the twentieth century—and

---

185 See also Kamlah, *Der Mensch in der Profanität*.
186 Herder, *Ideen*, Vol. 1 (1784), Book 4, Ch. 4.
187 Naumann, *Briefe über Religion*, 34.

above all by Emmanuel Lévinas[188]). Here, too, the being of a person is not exhausted by everything that the person reveals about themself and that others recognize about them. Instead, as one's knowledge of the person deepens, they become more mysterious. There is a difference between the person and the various ways in which they express or reveal themselves.

We can therefore only talk of God's presence in a dialectic of transcendence and immanence, of withdrawal and self-communication, of irrevocable mystery and revelation in history. Because of this dialectic, all human speech about God occurs with an 'eschatological caveat'. No form of language can conceptualize the reality of God; nor can any other symbolization depict it. The ultimate reality—God as 'eschatos'—remains beyond all 'penultimate' representations, even if these refer to revelation, i.e. to God's self-representation. They are, and always remain, ideas and conceptions expressed through the media of human religion(s).

The emphasis on God's ontological and epistemological withdrawal, i.e., God's unknowability and ineffability, was and is the concern of 'negative' (that is to say, apophatic) theology. This involves pointing to the inadequacy of all attempts to describe God in positive terms; only negative statements are considered possible, i.e., statements about what and how God is *not*.[189] God is neither spatial, nor temporal, nor finite, nor limited, etc. This has consequences for Christology, too. For however much every Christological approach strives to produce intelligible and plausible lines of thinking about the person and significance of Jesus, they all inevitably feel the sting of negative theology. This sting says, in effect: "in Christology, God's inexpressibility becomes expressable, as inexpressibility".[190]

These limitations in talking about God counteract all absolutizations and sharpen our awareness that the 'object' to which we intend to point ultimately eludes all human speech. If we retract this symbolic difference, i.e., the difference between symbolized and symbol (or between represented and representing reality), theological absolutism rears its head, one which claims for itself exact knowledge of God and condemns all other ways of speaking about God.

Zen Buddhism warns against confusing the finger pointing at the moon with the reality of the moon to which it points. Aldous Huxley echoes this image:

---

188 Lévinas, *Die Spur des Anderen*, 209–235.
189 E.g., from Pseudo-Dionysius the Areopagite: "in relation to divine things, the negations are true, but the affirmations are inadequate [...]" (translated from: "De coelesti hierarchia" / "De ecclesiastica hierarchia" / "De mystica theologia", ch. II, 3 [12, 20–13, 1]). However, we must bear in mind that the negations were ultimately also aimed at positive statements. The naming of what God is *not* helped us to see more clearly what God *is*.
190 Hoff, *Wer ist Christus?*, 199. See also *id.*, *Aporetische Theologie*.

the atrocities of organized religion (and organized religion, let us never forget, has done about as much harm as it has done good) are all due, in the last analysis, to 'mistaking the pointing finger for the moon'—in other words to mistaking the verbalized notion for the given mystery to which it refers or, more often, only seems to refer.[191]

Whenever the (inevitable!) attempt to grasp the relation to the divine mystery in religious statements creates a situation in which these statements, confessions, and doctrines are no longer transparent to the mystery but rather elevate themselves to become the object of faith, the result is religious idolatry, i.e., turning religion itself into an idol. The divine mystery is absolute, but the symbol system that points to it is not; the latter must not be absolutized. This also applies to the symbol of Christ! Theology should raise a 'prophetic protest' against every objectification of God and so criticize religious idolatry on theological grounds. Paul Tillich, in particular, has repeatedly raised awareness of this:

> the protest against objectification is religion's heartbeat. Only where that pulse is absent is there nothing absolute left—religion has become wholly religion, wholly human.[192]

But if objectifying forms of representation, thought, and speech notoriously fails to capture both the essence of God and God's presence in Jesus, then speaking of God can only ever be stumbling, metaphorical, referential, and poetic, even when invoking revelation in Christ. This means there must be plurality to such discourse. The reality of God can only be spoken of through various forms of presentation, thought, and speech.

The plurality of ways of speaking about God, however, should be distinguished from the so-called pluralistic theology of religions. The representatives of the latter refer to negative theology and invoke the withdrawal of divine reality as an argument for their approach. They see the personal or nonpersonal conceptions of the divine in religions as expressions of the *one* divine reality that precedes them all. They propose that this one foundation of reality has made itself known through a variety of self-communications, which are in principle equally valid and which have become the sources of different religions' traditions.

---

191   Huxley, *Knowledge and Understanding*, Part I (1956).
192   Translated from Tillich, *Die Überwindung des Religionsbegriffs*, 383.

But this proposition is questionable, to say the very least. We cannot conclude, on the basis of God being ultimately withdrawn from all understanding, that these different religions are grounded in the same divine reality and that they have established equivalent relations with this reality. It is logically impossible to derive this pluralistic theology of religions from negative theology. Rather, pluralistic theology is superimposed on negative theology.

Negative theology is concerned with its *own* religion, in relation to which it insists that God is 'greater' than all religious testimony about God can possibly be. However, negative theology does not then proceed to the basic conviction of a pluralistic theology of religions, i.e., that this greater God has made Godself known in equally valid ways in the central revelations of all religions. This deduction *cannot* be made; it would not be conclusive.

Considering the divine reality in all its radical transcendence, mystery, withdrawal, and unavailability widens the horizon of expectation for manifestations of God's presence that go beyond the revelation of Christ. But this horizon must be kept open; we should not close it off with a theory of religious pluralism, as the pluralists do. One must not solidify *expectation* and *hope* into *actuality* without any reliable theological basis underpinning it. Vague inferences and quotations from selected biblical and theological traditions are not sufficient for this purpose. For good reason Catherine Cornille pleads for a "soteriological agnosticism".[193]

The 1989 World Mission Conference held in San Antonio expressed this openness:

> we cannot point to any other way of salvation than Jesus Christ; at the same time, we cannot set limits to the saving power of God. We appreciate this tension, and do not attempt to resolve it.[194]

Accordingly, it is necessary to respect the freedom with which God's self-communication takes place and to be sensitive to discovering traces of God's presence even where one does not expect them.

4.8 The Work of Jesus Christ and Its Effects

In this chapter Jesus' soteriological 'function' is at stake. How does the concept of representation spell out the 'salvific significance' or 'salvific mediation' of

---

193 Cornille, *Soteriological Agnosticism*, 201–215.
194 WCC, *The San Antonio Report*, 1990, 31–33.

Jesus Christ? The core statement of the concept of representation in relation to the *person* of Jesus is the confession 'God was in him'; the core statement in relation to the *work* of Jesus consists of the promise that this presence of God is not *a se*, but *pro me* or *pro nobis* (*for me / for us*). It can be formulated as follows: God's salvific commitment to humans appeared in Jesus Christ and radiated (and indeed still radiates) from him. Jesus represented (and continues to represent) this commitment.

A central biblical point of reference is Jn. 10:37ff., namely Jesus' comment that he was doing the 'works' of God. The earliest witnesses speak of Jesus as a man authenticated by God, through whom God worked powerfully (Acts 2:22). The effectiveness of salvation must not be reduced to Jesus' suffering and death alone; it should also include his words and actions. Because this work not only *corresponds* to God's will for salvation, but also *springs from it*, Jesus represents this will in his ministry. And because this saving will defines the *being* of God, this work also entails representation of this being, i.e., the 'Godness' of God.

With regard to Jesus' 'works' and their effects, too, the movement of representation takes place in both directions: firstly, as an active manifestation of God's salvific will and action toward human beings; and, secondly, as a representation toward God of humanity's despair, experience of suffering, fear of death, and need for salvation. Jesus Christ is both the real symbol of God's saving fellowship with humans and the real symbol of the profoundest human hardship which he brings before the face of God.

The concept of representation emphasizes that God's salvific presence is manifested in Jesus and affects those who are in relation with Jesus. It leads away from economic, legal, or cultic metaphors and expresses a personal presence. The efficacy of Jesus therefore does not consist in *acquiring* and *distributing* a 'benefit of salvation', nor in his *vicarious penal suffering* or the *provision of satisfaction*, nor in an *atoning sacrifice*, but in the *re-presentation* of God's eternal act of salvation in his person.

The radiance of God's salvific presence leads to a new (or renewed) relationship with God for those who allow themselves to be taken hold of by this representation. This can be understood as a pneumatological event. Through his personal presence (during his lifetime and then beyond his death as *Christus praesens*), Jesus draws human beings who open themselves to this spiritual radiance into its energy field; helps them orientate their existence toward God; establishes a community among those who gather in his name; and, with his own overcoming of death (symbolized as 'resurrection'), guarantees that this community with God and with one another will continue beyond death.

From the perspective of the Christian faith, God's salvific self-manifestation has occurred in Christ both normatively and sufficiently, i.e., it needs not be supplemented. However, this does not exclude the possibility that there may be other representations of God. Even if (viewed from the standpoint of Christian faith) they can only be identified as such through the knowledge of God that Christ brings, they nevertheless occur independently of that knowledge. Christ, therefore, should not be considered as the one and only constitutive ground for any salvific relationship with God, so that beyond him no such relationship would be possible. Rather, his relevance in that regard is an epistemic one: his way of representing God allows us to see "manifestations of grace"[195] also in non-Christian relationships with God.

Jesus Christ's salvific significance is therefore not causative but representative and functional. This means that he is not the *origin* of salvation—this origin lies in God's will for salvation and thus God's nature of love; rather, Jesus is the *enactor* of salvation. He reveals and mediates it for those who follow him. According to the Gospel of John, Christ performed a mediatorial service by conveying the Logos, or the self-communication, of God out into the world. The Logos is not a 'message' distinct from God, but God in the mode of self-communication. In its origin, this 'Word' is none other than the Word of creation.

4.8.1   *The Death of Jesus as a Saving Event or as Desolation?*

The following interpretation detaches both the cross and the 'resurrection' of Jesus Christ from economic, legal, and cultic frames of reference and replaces them with a relational, existential one. The terms characteristic of the former frames of reference, whether economic ('benefit' or 'ransom'), legal ('guilt', 'law', 'accusation', 'judgment', 'punishment', 'grace', 'justification') or cultic ('sin', 'sacrifice', 'lamb', 'blood', 'atonement', 'cleansing', 'forgiveness', 'reconciliation'), are transformed into terms that describe a relational event.

This transformation is founded on the hermeneutical assumption that these terms and 'language games' do not express an objectively given meaning of the Christ-event as such. As a metaphorical *modus loquendi*, they instead represent a specific reading of this event that is embedded in a contemporary context. If such a reading is no longer intuitive in today's experiential context without significant explanatory and interpretative effort, however, a *modus loquendi* with greater plausibility can and must take its place.

---

195   Translated from Tillich, *Protestantische Gestaltung*, 57–61.

4.8.1.1 New Testament Interpretations of the Death of Jesus

In its interpretations of the death of Jesus, the New Testament incorporates different lines of tradition and draws on real-life experiences:

– the *salvation history* interpretation, which saw in Jesus' death an eschatological event predetermined in God's plan of salvation, one which had to take place 'according to the Scriptures'. Jesus' death as such has no intrinsic significance for salvation; rather, it is a passageway to glory (especially in John[196]). Jesus is a 'forerunner' of those who follow him (Heb. 6:20) and prepares the way to God for them (Heb. 10:20).

– the *martyrological* interpretation, which understands Jesus' death as analogous to the persecution and murder of the prophets sent by God. It was not God but human beings who were responsible for his death. This interpretation can be found in the vineyard parable (Mt. 21:33–41 and parallels), in the contrast scheme (see below), but also in the Philippians hymn (Phil. 2:5–11), which speaks of the self-abasement of Jesus Christ and his exaltation by God, as well as elsewhere in Paul's writings (1 Thess. 2:15f.).

– the interpretation of *'passio iusti'*, following the songs of the servant of God in Deutero-Isaiah. Jesus died the death of the suffering righteous. Here, too, the death of Jesus has no salvific significance in its own right. It *becomes* an event of salvation in that God allows the unjust death of the righteous to benefit the unrighteous. By turning it *post factum* into an act of substitution, it has the effect of justifying sinners. In this way, it becomes a death *for* us.

– the *soteriological* interpretations (above all those pertaining to atonement theology), which see Jesus' death as a self-sacrifice he performs in conscious and voluntary obedience 'for our sins'. He 'died for us' in order to avert God's judgment of destruction imposed on sinful humanity and to reconcile us with God (interpreting his death as atonement, Rom. 3:25), to redeem us from the power of sin (interpreting it as ransom, Mk. 10:45), and/or to swallow up death (interpreting it as struggle and victory, 1 Cor. 15:54f.).

The interpretation I propose in this chapter draws on the resources of past interpretations, but also transforms them into a relational and existential theological perspective on Jesus' death in the overall context of his life's work and the eschatological action of God laid on him (symbolized by the term 'resurrection'). It thus ties in with Luther's tropological interpretation of Scripture,

---

196 The interpretation of Jesus' death as a sacrifice or atonement is not found in the Gospel of John. John 3:16 does not say that God "gave away" (παραδίδωμι) his Son, but that he "gave him" (δίδωμι). The "lamb" is not a sacrificial lamb but refers to the liberation experience of the Exodus.

in which he relates the biblical traditions to the existence of the individual, but also keeps in view their cosmic dimensions (i.e., those relating to the 'world').

While medieval and Reformation theologies of the cross generally follow soteriological patterns of interpretation, my proposed approach takes its starting point from non-soteriological viewpoints. The thesis is that Jesus' death in itself has no significance for salvation. It is not a saving event but rather a tragedy, caused by human sinfulness: "the death of Jesus was a sin and therefore against the will of God".[197] Soteriology should therefore take its starting point less from the cross and more from the 'resurrection'—as both confirming and anticipating communion with God, communion which is protologically founded and will be eschatologically fulfilled.

Therein lies this approach's decisive difference from the 'constitutional Christologies' (strictly speaking: 'constitutional *soteriologies*'), which ascribe a soteriological quality to Jesus' death—in the sense of a causality that brings about salvation.

4.8.1.2   The Death of Jesus Christ as a Saving Event: Constitutive Soteriology

By 'constitutive soteriology' I mean approaches that consider the death of Jesus to be the decisive event in salvation history. According to such approach, this death is constitutive, or causal, for the salvation of humanity. We can identify two basic types of constitutive soteriology; in Protestant theology, one is more predominant in so-called 'Old Protestantism' before Schleiermacher and the other in 'New Protestantism' from the nineteenth century onward.

(a) The first type assumes that God's saving will had to be restored before reconciliation between God and human beings could take place, and that this restoration took place through the death of Jesus. He therefore brought about a transformation in God which resulted in the salvific transformation of God's relationship with human beings. This 'transformation in God' consists of the appeasement of God's wrath, making it possible for humans to be saved from the judgment to come (Rom. 5:9). Jesus death on the cross was necessary to make God's love manifest once again.

This view is widespread in sixteenth-century Reformation theology and beyond. It states that, due to humanity's original sin, God's will for salvation was obscured by God's wrath and had to be uncovered or reinstated through Jesus' sacrificial death. This restitution is itself rooted in God's original will for salvation; God has chosen this way of reinstating that will.

---

197   Translated from: Johnson, *Die Weisheit ward Fleisch*, 150.

In his 1521 work 'The Misuse of the Mass', Luther wrote about the Lord's Supper: "the body of Christ is given and his blood poured out, and thereby God is reconciled [...] so that he may avert from us the wrath of God which we by our sins have deserved".[198] The salvific event consists of Jesus taking upon himself what is due to the sinner—the death penalty—and suffering it vicariously. Because the debt is settled, God can be reconciled with the world, and sinners are freed from the consequences of sin. On the other hand,

> all outside of Christianity, whether heathen, Turks, Jews, or false Christians and hypocrites [...], abide in eternal wrath and damnation. For they have not the Lord Christ, and, besides, are not illumined and favored by any gifts of the Holy Ghost.[199]

Luther describes this salvific event through the twin lenses of (i) the reconciling work of God and (ii) redemption from the powers of corruption (as Paul describes them e.g. in Rom. 7:7–25):

> Saint Paul [...] relates three things which Christ has overcome and from which He has released us, as death/sin/law. [...] God's people can have no other peace or joy without these three, death, sin, and the law being overcome.[200]

Reconciliation overcomes separation from God, while redemption frees humanity from the powers of corruption that hold it captive. In this way, Luther builds on the redemption soteriologies of the Early Church (e.g., Athanasius) and the reconciliation soteriologies of the Middle Ages (e.g., Anselm).

Calvin puts it very similarly in his description of the priestly ministry of Jesus Christ:

> But God's righteous curse bars our access to him, and God in his capacity as judge is angry toward us. Hence, an expiation must intervene in order that Christ as priest may obtain God's favour for us and appease his wrath. Thus Christ to perform this office had to come forward with a sacrifice. [...] [believers/human beings] could not propitiate God unless their sins were expiated.[201]

---

198   WA 8, 519. LW 36: Word and Sacrament II, 177.
199   Luther, *The Large Catechism*, 2nd part, 3rd article.
200   Luther, *Christmas Sermon on Isaiah 9*, 71ff.
201   Calvin, *Institutes* II, 15,6.

Confessio Augustana 3 explains that Christ "was a sacrifice not only for original sin, but also for all other sins, and to conciliate God's wrath".[202] Here, too, it becomes clear that this understanding of soteriology is linked to the doctrine of original sin: the idea that human nature is so corrupted by this turning away from God that human beings cannot on their own overcome the abyss that separates them from God and are also unable to act in a good and God-pleasing way. Constitutive Christologies see Jesus' death on the cross as the overcoming of human sinfulness and 'fallenness'.

In response to the first question of the Heidelberg Catechism ("What is your only consolation in life and in death?"), the answer is given:

> That I [...] belong to my faithful Savior Jesus Christ. He has fully paid for all my sins with his precious blood and redeemed me from all the power of the devil.[203]

It describes the salvific significance of Jesus' death using the 'ransom' motif.

All these soteriological perspectives agree that the death of Jesus constitutes the reconciliation of God, which in turn constitutes God's reconciliation with human beings. Both sides of the reconciliation are founded in the sacrificial death of Jesus.

(b) The second line of argument largely removes from soteriology the motif of appeasing God's wrath. *God's* reconciliation is therefore no longer necessary; God's salvific will does not need to be restored. The constitutive function of the death on the cross is now seen as enabling God's reconciliation with human beings, as the way in which God's salvific will is accomplished. Without this fulfillment, there would be no salvation. This sacrifice was not made *for* God, but *through* God. God's will to save is the reason for the Christ-event, including the death on the cross, not the other way around. Jesus' death on the cross must not be understood as the *cause*, but as the *consequence* of God's will to save. Christ is not the cause, but the mediator of salvation.

This version of constitutional Christology is found above all in (and since) Schleiermacher; in his wake, Albrecht Ritschl notably described it. Ritschl rejects a constitution of the divine will for reconciliation through Jesus' death on the cross, but nevertheless teaches that reconciliation of humanity with God is constituted in Christ. According to him, the divinity of Jesus is proven in the content of his proclamation, which he authenticated through his life and death. This is also the position of most recent soteriological approaches.

---

202 Cited from Wengert, *The Augsburg Confession*, 42, 45.
203 Heidelberg Catechism, § 1.

The idea of atonement continues to play an important role in many approaches that argue along these lines. They interpret the death of Jesus as a salvific event that was necessary for the forgiveness of sins. The *objective* possibility of salvation for humans is constituted in him.

This type of constitutional soteriology is also widespread among Catholic theologians, e.g., Karl Rahner. He, too, understands Jesus' death on the cross not as the cause but as the consequence of God's will to save; as such, Jesus' death represents the constitutive basis of human salvation. As Rahner puts it:

> [because] there is a salvific will of God, there is the cross and resurrection of Jesus; but not: because there is the cross, there is God's salvific will toward us. God is not changed by the cross from wrathful justice to forgiving love; rather that God, who forgives a priori and without reason, who communicates Godself to and overcomes the world despite its guilt, brings about the Christ-event.[204]

Accordingly, there is no change in God's nature from wrath to love. The salvific event does not consist only of the death on the cross; according to Rahner, the entire Christ-event is the universal and primordial sacrament of salvation.

Otto Hermann Pesch interprets Thomas Aquinas' position in this sense:

> the satisfaction of Christ does not *bring about* the love of God (for example by 'reconciling' a God who is offended and angry) but is *brought about by it*, namely as the path by which the love of God, which had never ceased, reaches humanity again.[205]

Bernd Janowski explains it in a very similar vein:

> by dying 'for us', [Jesus] 'took our place', i.e., the place of hopeless remoteness from God and the fallenness of death. The fact that he came to this place is a *consequence*—and not the intended aim!—of his life, and thus the extreme form of his 'devotion'.[206]

In emphasizing that it was not *God* who had to be reconciled, but God who reconciled *humans* with Godself, this type of constitutional soteriology offers

---

204 Translated from Rahner, "Der eine Jesus Christus und die Universalität des Heils" in *Sämtliche Werke* 22/1b, 892.
205 Translated from Pesch, *Thomas von Aquin*, 325.
206 Translated from Janowski, *"Hingabe" oder "Opfer"?*, 109.

a significant correction of the medieval and Reformation soteriologies influenced by Anselm's doctrine of satisfaction. It remains the case, however, that the efficacy of God's saving work was only made possible and realized through the death of Jesus Christ on the cross. God's salvation comes into the world and to humanity solely (at least in its fullness and entirety) through the Christ-event, especially through the death of Jesus Christ on the cross. Jesus' death is an act of atonement, without which salvation for humanity would not be possible.

This interpretation aligns with representational Christology firstly in attributing a soteriological effect to Jesus' death only in relation to *humanity* (and not in relation to *God*). God is not the object but the subject of reconciliation. The second point in common is the emphasis on the antecedent reality of God's salvific will—it comes before Jesus' passion, not after it.

These approaches, however, differ from representational Christology's understanding of soteriology in ascribing to Jesus' death a salvific significance in itself, in the sense of an act of atonement or satisfaction performed by Jesus. For representational Christology, on the other hand, this salvific significance lies not in the event itself but in its reception. Retrospectively it was *turned into* a salvific event. In itself, it is a traumatic event.

We can dispense with the idea that God's will to save was suspended by humanity's original sin and had to be reactivated. Jesus' suffering and death neither constituted nor restored God's will to save. Rather, it was this eternally existing will which turned this path of desolation to a salvific end—on the one hand by proving that God was also present in Jesus' suffering, and on the other by continuing and consummating God's salvific fellowship with the one who felt abandoned by God, beyond his death. In this sense, one can even speak of a 'reconciliation' of Jesus with God, the 'Son' with the 'Father'. 'Reconciliation' should not be understood as overcoming guilt, but as healing a wound of separation.

4.8.1.3   The Death of Jesus as a Catastrophe

Both lines of argument presented in the previous chapter focus on the message of salvation in contrast to its opposite: the miserable, fallen human condition.' The representational Christology presented here differs from these constitutive soteriological approaches in emphasizing that God's salvific action does not primarily consist in overcoming a metaphysical guilt and its consequences. There is no need to deal with an original sin of superhuman proportions; there is no need to pay a penalty; there is no need to appease God's wrath; there is no need to 'change God's mind' through a sacrificial death; there is no need to restore corrupted human nature and regain the lost image of God; there is no need to overcome a primordial sinful breach of relationship between God and humans. Therefore, there is also no need for a once-and-for-all act of satisfaction and reparation. An atoning sacrifice does not have to be offered to bring about reconciliation with God. All these ideas interpret the Gospel personified in Jesus Christ in the paradigm of (original) sin and its overcoming (atonement through sacrifice), i.e., as 'repairing' a fundamental damage. But was this the central message of Jesus, for which he lived and died?

In my representational Christology I do not attribute any salvific effect to Jesus' death as such, let alone any soteric effect *pertaining to God*. The salvific will of God does not need to be restored, reconstituted, brought forth, or re-enacted by the Christ-event—because it is already intrinsic to God. It has its foundation in the divinity of God and has existed unbroken from eternity.[207] It seeks the completion of the work of creation in an all-encompassing *shalom* as well as perfect communion with and between creatures. This also requires liberation from everything that stands in the way of this aspiration. But this liberation *from* the 'powers and authorities' (Eph. 6:12; Col. 1:16; 2:10; 2:15; 1 Pet. 3:22) is geared to a liberation *toward* the envisaged state of salvation. The act of salvation itself acts with resistance against the resistance that created beings mount against the realization of salvific intent. However, soteriology must not limit itself to this aspect. Soteriology is about becoming and being saved in a comprehensive sense: not only overcoming the negative, but above all about embracing the intended positive.

Overcoming these 'powers and authorities' is not a one-off event but must happen again and again. For as long as the world exists, these powers will also continue to exist. They are not supernatural entities, but powerful dispositions in human beings, above all their individual and collective self-centeredness, misanthropic ideologies, social and mental structures of coercion, addictions, desires, obsessions with power, etc. These 'powers' can seize a person's center of personality and keep possession of it. They can disrupt and damage the basic relationships in which human beings live, including first and foremost the relationship with God as the basis of both one's own existence and all else that exists. Wherever such disruptions occur, as they do constantly, God's will for salvation aims to remedy them, above all to create a community of God that is 'free of all barriers'.

In the sense of a *subjective* participation in the salvific event represented in Christ, representational Christology can also speak of a 'constitution' of

---

207 Through this concept, representational Christology agrees with Abelard's Christology and soteriology.

salvation in Christ. In his relationship *with humanity*, Jesus Christ is therefore not merely the *causa exemplaris* (an example) of salvation (from which a 'model Christology' would arise), but the mediator of God's salvific presence. However, this 'salvific effectiveness' must not be transferred to Jesus Christ's relationship *with God*, such that, for example, the death on the cross gains the significance of having brought about a transformation in God—from a will to do harm to a will to save (as the doctrine of satisfaction would suggest).

4.8.1.4   The Death of Jesus as the Consequence of His Mission

To understand Jesus' death, one must start with his mission and view it in its historical context (as far as the New Testament sources allow). Jesus represented God's eternally existing and constantly renewed relational will towards human beings, as paradigmatically depicted in Luke's parables of the lost sheep (Lk. 15:1–7), the lost coin (Lk. 15:8–10), and the prodigal son (Lk. 15:11–32). This representation of God's unconditional and universal will to save took place not only in his preaching, but also in his practice, especially in the forgiveness of sins that he granted in God's name. In his healings, raising the dead, and casting out demons, Jesus acted with the authority of God. This symbolic act of salvation was not dependent on the 'religion' of those he healed or whether they were members of the people of Israel. With sovereign power, Jesus transcended social, ethnic, and religious boundaries. He cultivated communion with sinners and promised them participation in the reign of God. His proclamation and practice of unconditional love towards neighbour, stranger, and enemy alike proved him to be a representative of God, a real symbol of the divine will for salvation. According to Thomas Pröpper, "Jesus' love 'did not require the death of the cross in order to be itself'".[208]

In his charismatic manner and in his speaking and acting with the authority of God, Jesus collided head-on with the official authority of the priests and scribes who invoked the Mosaic Torah. The Romans saw him as a political insurgent who threatened their rule. This provoked resistance from those in power, which in turn led to his execution on the cross. He fell victim to the sin of those who allowed themselves to be guided by the interests of power politics and who saw the presence of God in him as sinful hubris and as a political danger.

My thesis is that there is no divine necessity in Jesus' death; it was not ordained, willed, or even wrought by God for the sake of reconciliation with human beings. Rather, it is the epitome of senseless violence, to which God

---

208   Translated from Pröpper, *Erlösungsglaube und Freiheitsgeschichte*, 97.

does not react with destructive counter-violence, but with an offer of relationship ('resurrection') that overcomes the violence. Jesus did not 'obtain' or 'acquire' salvation for human beings; he made present, even in his death, the salvific presence of God.

In the act of *overcoming* this death, an act which does not take place *in* the death or *through* it, but *against* it, God's eternal, universal, and unconditional will for salvation is applied and thus revealed. This revelation enacts that which it also reveals: community between humanity and God, even beyond the boundary of death. This community is not brought about by the death of Jesus but is demonstrated in it—through a reversal of meaning.

4.8.2   'Resurrection' as a Reversal of Meaning

There is no salvation for humanity in the historical event of the crucifixion. It is the real symbol of the sheer evil that human beings can do to other human beings. Such actions reveal ignorance of, and hostility toward, God. For the victim, it means the eclipse of God. Hans Iwand rightly described the cross as the "night of separation from God: real, ultimate separation of which no sense can be made".[209] Just as 'Incarnation' stands for the greatest closeness to God, the cross stands for the deepest separation from God: "A theology of the cross without the resurrection is hell itself".[210]

Only in the light of God's creative act, symbolized as 'resurrection', does it become clear *retrospectively* that God was also present in Jesus' utmost remoteness and separation. The fact that God was 'in' Jesus applies not only to his life, to his words and actions, but also to his suffering and death. It is only from the 'resurrection' onward that a salvific significance is linked to the horror of the cross. This message asserts that God is also present where all human possibilities of being and acting end, where humans are dehumanized, and where, like Jesus on the cross, they experience only the eclipse of God. Moreover, the radical nature of God's will for salvation is seen specifically in the senseless, disastrous event of Jesus' death by torture. God embraces this meaningless event and *gives* it a salvific meaning.

Everything that separates us from God—the guilt of those who put Jesus on the cross, as well as the guilt of all those who impose crosses on other human beings; Jesus' despair, fear of death, and feeling of being abandoned by God, like all people's suffering on their respective crosses; the power of death as the 'last enemy' of God (1 Cor. 15:26) with the fear it spreads—none of this can ultimately separate us from God (Rom. 8:38). The message of salvation is that God

---

209   Translated from his Christology lecture printed in Klappert, ed., *Diskussion*, 288.
210   Moltmann, *The Trinity and the Kingdom*, 41.

is close even in the experience of deepest separation from God, abandonment by God, and eclipse of God. But if God is also present even there, then it follows that "from then on, nothing human, even at the lowest and most miserable level, can be alien to God".[211]

Thus, even in the greatest possible alienation from God, in which God is experienced as unrevealed because absent, God is revealed as being nevertheless present. There can then be no ultimate abandonment of human beings by God, not even of those who have brought guilt upon themselves. This does not mean that a cheap promise of forgiveness has been given and that guilt has been wiped away. Even though Mt. 5:45 states that God "causes his sun to rise on the evil and the good and sends rain on the righteous and the unrighteous", this does not mean zero difference between evil and good, between righteous and unrighteous. Whatever does not stand up to God's scrutiny will 'burn up'. The deeds of those who are unrighteous will burn up and they will "suffer loss ... [they] will be saved, but only as through fire" (1 Cor. 3:15).

The fact that God is not absent even in the deepest eclipse of God, but is in fact present to bring salvation, is not revealed on the cross itself, but only in the light of Easter—not on Good Friday, only at Easter Sunday. Only the light of this reversal of meaning opens our eyes to the fact that the eschatological promise of salvation does not come to an end with the crosses that we impose on others and on ourselves. Equally, and in positive terms, the light of this reversal opens our eyes to the fact that this promise will only be fulfilled when the world and all the crosses in it have come to an end. Rather, it is fulfilled in a fragmentary and anticipatory way, in the certainty of faith that God is also present in these sufferings. In the light of the 'resurrection' experience, it becomes clear that God's will to save means that desolation does not have the final word.

The 'resurrection' of Jesus means that relationship with God continues beyond the threshold of death and so completes it. Out of the total eclipse of God (Mk. 15:34), the one who has died passes into God's light, i.e., into the eternal communion with God of the living and the dead. This proves that the final boundary of human existence is no boundary for God. God remains God even beyond death, i.e., beyond everything that destroys life. This guarantees the hope of the ultimate eschatological overcoming of all desolation. As the "firstborn from the dead" (Col. 1:18), Jesus represents the basis of this hope.

In a sense, there is an 'application' of God's eternal will for salvation to the event of Jesus' death, which is turned to a particular purpose. God demonstrates, carries out, and thus confirms his will for salvation in overcoming this

---

211 Translated from Deuser, *Kleine Einführung*, 103–4.

death. This happens in the belief that God grants it a meaning it did not (originally) have. This reversal of meaning turns an event of desolation into an event of salvation. Jesus' death is therefore not *necessary* for salvation, but it does have a *post factum* salvific *significance*. The *necessity* of salvation would underlie and precede the event, whereas the *significance* of salvation can be attributed to it afterwards. We can therefore apply to the death of Jesus Bonhoeffer's words: "I believe that God can and will let good come out of everything, even the greatest evil".[212]

This does not mean that evil is declared good or that desolation is declared salvation. Desolation remains desolation, but the consequences of desolation can be healed. In this way, salvation can *arise* from desolation. The senseless can be *given* meaning. The experience of suffering can *benefit* others.

According to this understanding, the salvific significance of Jesus' death on the cross therefore does not arise from a Christocentric view of this event, one which sees it as Jesus' achievement of salvation, but rather from a theocentric one. Not theocentric in the sense that this death should be interpreted as the fulfillment of a divinely imposed necessity in the history of salvation, but in such a way that God proves himself in his healing[213] action.

Exegetically, this interpretation can be based, among other things, on what New Testament scholars call the 'contrast-scheme'. This appears mainly in Peter's sermons in the Acts of the Apostles. There, the actions of the Jews who crucified Jesus are contrasted with the actions of God who "raised [him] from the dead" (Acts 4:10; 2:23f.; 3:13ff.; 5:30f.; 10:39f.). These statements are to be understood against the background of the Jewish Christian community's disputes with the authorities of the synagogues. The former counter the latter's criticism of Jesus' Messiahship with the accusation that they are to blame for Jesus' death. (The guilt of the Romans goes unmentioned.) However, God's action in the form of Jesus' 'resurrection' had put them in the wrong and thus also shaken the authority of the law to which they had referred in their own actions. The human act of evil that led to Jesus' death on the cross is thus contrasted with the divine act of salvation that brought Jesus through this death into eternal communion of God. Believing participation in this event,

---

212 Bonhoeffer, "After Ten Years. An Account at the Turn of the Year 1942–1943", DBWE 8, 46. Compare Gen. 50:20a and the response to question 26 in the *Heidelberg Catechism*. It expresses the trust that God "will turn all evil [...] to my good".

213 In the context of his doctrine of providence, Karl Barth distinguished between God's preceding, accompanying, and following activity (praecurrere, concurrere, and succurrere) (Barth, CD III/3, 119ff., 131ff., 151ff.). I take up the idea of God's following, post-curative, uplifting action and apply it to Jesus' death on the cross.

participation which God makes possible, also grants believers a share in this communion with God.

4.8.3 *A Paradigm Shift: Focusing on Suffering Instead of Sin*

Emphasizing that a salvific relationship with God is constituted by God's eternal grace does not mean, however, downplaying the concrete experiences of desolation, of suffering and death. My line of thinking does not lead to a *theologia gloriae* that the promised overcoming of all that is negative has already happened. The promise of salvation remains related to existence 'under the cross'. In fact, it only really comes into play when Christ's death on the cross is understood as the epitome of the human experience of desolation, rather than as the climax of a drama of salvation staged by God and made necessary by human sinfulness.

To this end, Jesus' death on the cross must first be interpreted in the paradigm of suffering and God's presence within suffering, rather than in the paradigm of guilt, atonement, forgiveness, and reconciliation. An interpretation of the salvific significance of Jesus' death based on the theology of *sin*, which understands this death as atonement, vicarious punishment, or victory over the power of sin, takes a back seat for the moment to an interpretation grounded in the theology of *suffering*. However, the former immediately comes back into play in a re-reading based on existential theology.

The *theology-of-suffering interpretation* sees the death on the cross as the deepest reaches of God's *kenosis*. In Jesus' surrender of himself, God's surrendering "is taken up in exemplary fashion and in reality".[214] Through the power of the Spirit, God participates in Jesus' path of life and suffering. Using anthropomorphic metaphors, we can say that God made human experiences in Jesus, even to the point of suffering and dying. This changed God, not in such a way that an angry God became a loving God, but rather a God who is no stranger to the abysses of human existence and whose salvific work begins at the deepest depths of this abyss. Albert Camus writes:

> The night of Golgotha is so important in the history of man only because, in its shadow the divinity abandoned its traditional privileges, and drank to the last drop, despair included, the agony of death.[215]

---

[214] International Theological Commission, Selected Questions on Christology, § 3.5.
[215] Camus, *The Rebel*, 32. The quotation continues: "This is the explanation of the *Lama sabactani* and the heartrending doubt of Christ in agony. The agony would have been mild if it had been alleviated by hopes of eternity. For God to be a man, he must despair" (ibid.).

In the Christian understanding, God's salvific action is thus linked to Jesus' concrete experience of desolation. Yet this does not mean that this action is brought about, constituted, or restored by this experience. God's will to save exists since all eternity. But it gains its 'Christian' manifestation in and through a specific situation in history. This, in turn, shapes the Christian understanding of God—as one proven to be both compassionate and close by, whose reign takes place in the deepest *kenosis*, right down to the remotest corner of human suffering. God's self-revelation in Christ consists in this devotion.

The salvific will of God in itself is unconditional: it is not conditioned by a particular historical situation. Its starting point and its end goal both exist within God's nature. In the Christian understanding, however, this salvific will occurs normatively in the Christ-event, namely, Jesus Christ's life, work, suffering, death, and 'resurrection'. From there it reveals itself in its cosmic universality and unconditionality.

Yet this event is not accompanied by a triumphant overcoming of evil. It takes place proleptically under the miserable conditions of existence, above all in the face of suffering and death. From a 'pre-Easter' perspective, the powers of corruption that Jesus confronted with his words and deeds triumphed over him. Not only did he represent to humanity God's will for salvation, but also, to God, the calamity that threatens human existence. He bore this calamity before God and (through his intimate relationship with God) also in God, so that one can say that the other side of the event of salvation in Jesus is the presence of misery in God. Formulated in anthropomorphic metaphors once again we can say that God came to know 'in God's own body' what desolation is and what human beings are capable of doing to other human beings. God 'felt', in all its terrible consequences, that opposition to God which we refer as 'sin'. God allowed Godself to be 'affected', whereby the work of salvation became historically concrete and close to the human experience of life. This insight should not be withheld from interlocutors from other religions.

The *theology-of-suffering* interpretation of Jesus' death on the cross expresses the Gospel of God's saving presence in the furthest, most traumatic abysses of human existence. The *theology-of-sin* interpretation complements this. It expresses the Gospel that all disruptions of basic human relationships ultimately have no validity in the face of God's healing action.

According to Paul, human existence means exposure to the corrupting powers of sin, law, and death. If the content of these terms is translated into an existential theological frame of reference, they are very well suited to expressing the depths of the human experience of desolation.

- 'Sin' is therefore to be understood as the individual and collective self-centeredness of human beings, which on the one hand leads to self-exaltation and even self-deification, and on the other hand to self-devaluation and even self-contempt.
- 'Law' stands for all forms of internal and external constraints and coercive structures that subjugate human beings and prevent the free development of life.
- 'Death' can refer to the destruction of life (biological death), living spaces (ecological death), and relationships (social death).

The interpretation from the theology-of-suffering perspective emphasizes the omnipresence of God, even and especially where this presence is not experienced. The theology-of-sin interpretation refers to how Almighty God has overcome everything in the human situation that stands in the way of God's reign (that is, the implementation of God's unconditional and universal will for the well-being and salvation of humankind).

In the crime committed against Jesus there was manifested an orientation of existence that was aligned with religious and political power interests instead of with God's will for salvation. Sin likewise manifested itself as that which separates from God; and Jesus became a victim of this sin. His opponents declared him to be a sinner and, as Paul says in one of his boldest assertions, even God made him to be sin (2 Cor. 5:21). The sinless person represents sin and suffers the separation from God that is the essence of sin. God's salvific presence strives to overcome this separation, whether it be the separation from God that human beings *suffer* (like Jesus), or the *self-inflicted* separation from God (sin). In the faithful participating in this event, Christians live in the certainty that, faced with this human existential orientation that repeatedly turns away from God, God in turn repeatedly meets it with a lasting offer of relationship. That which separates from God is that which can be overcome by God, again and again.

The theology-of-sin interpretation recognizes Jesus in his relationship with God as the representative of injustice suffered, as the victim of cruelty, and as humankind dehumanized. This interpretation also lays bare the self-inflicted separation from God in those who put him on the cross. In relation to humanity, Jesus Christ's 'resurrection' represents the hope that injustice, cruelty, and dehumanization cannot ultimately separate us from God, and that God's unconditional and universal will for salvation has the last word.

In the framework of the theology of sin, Jesus represents the overcoming of everything that separates us from God. In the framework of the theology of suffering, he seals the promise that "[God] will wipe every tear from [our] eyes" (Rev. 21:4), suffering and its causes will be abolished, and creation will be consummated.

We can relate the interpretation of the ministry and impact of Jesus Christ presented so far to the classical doctrine of his three 'offices'. In the history of Protestant theology, at least until the Enlightenment (but also beyond), the priestly office of Jesus Christ was very much in the foreground, while Enlightenment theology placed a strong emphasis on the prophetic teaching office. In contrast, the representational Christology presented here attempts to maintain a balance between the concerns that are associated with the three offices. The *single* act of the representation of God to humanity and of humanity to God takes place, in terms of Jesus' ministry and its impact, in three modes:
– through his speech and actions, in which he proclaims and practices the unconditional and universal salvific will of God in the face of human evil (prophetic office);
– through his suffering the experience of the total eclipse of God and abandonment by God as the lowest point of human suffering (priestly office, as the theology of suffering understands it), which is the result of sinful transgressions by perpetrators and passive onlookers; and by God overriding this transgression and demonstrating the salvific will directly through it (priestly office, as the theology of sin understands it);
– through his exercising the ruling, liberating, and redeeming power of God as the one exalted at God's right hand, in the face of human interests which are contrary to God and their resulting actions and structures (kingly office).

4.9 Christ-Event and Christ-Content

This chapter addresses the relationship between the Christ-event (i.e., the overall context of Jesus' life, work, suffering, death, and 'resurrection') and the content within this event. It is therefore about the relationship between manifestation ('Gestalt') and content ('Gehalt'). 'Manifestation' here covers not only the historical person of Jesus, but also the historical formations of the *Christus praesens* grasped in faith. The term 'Christ-*event*' refers to the actuality of the Christ figure, and the effects emanating from him. The term 'Christ-*content*' refers to what is represented in this overall context.

The question now is this: Is the content ontologically and epistemologically identical with the 'Christ-event', or can it be distinguished from it? In the *identificatory and constitutive* model, the content consists *in* this event and vice versa. The two are coterminous. This content—God's will for salvation—exists only as this event. The Christ-event is the one and only realization of God's universal salvific will. In the *representative* model, however, event and content are not coterminous. The content takes place here in all its authenticity, but it also exists before this event and goes beyond it. The event represents the content, in the mode of making it present.

Here the polarity of particularity and universality which was developed in terms of the theology of religions in chapter 2.4 reoccurs in a Christological application. If we one-sidedly emphasize the realization of God's will for salvation at a specific place and time in history, namely the Christ-event, and if we declare believing participation in this event to be the only medium through which God's salvation occurs, then the universal content of Christ is restricted to a historically particular form of event. If we apply this one-sidedness in the other direction and detach the universality of the divine will for salvation from its specific representation in Jesus Christ (e.g., through spiritualizing the Christ-content so that it is not tied to a historical medium), then Jesus Christ becomes a mere example of this immediacy in the relation to God.

Christology has always struggled with the question of whether and how the singular historical event of Christ can have a validity that transcends history. The concept of revelation and the key soteriological terms ('salvation', 'reconciliation', 'redemption', etc.) were and are generally used in answering this question. These terms indicate an identity of (historical) realization and (transtemporal) significance.

We can distinguish between two basic models of classification of Christ-event and Christ-content:

(a) Christological approaches which see the Christ-content in the Christ-event itself (i.e., identifying the two with each other) start by treating God's self-communication in Jesus Christ as an historically unique event that cannot be derived from any 'higher' principle. The question then arises as to whether the revelatory significance of the unique (non-analogous) event can be recognized by means of rationality working through historical research (as Pannenberg argues)[216] or whether it must be revealed by God, through the Spirit, in the "subjective reality of revelation" (as Barth argues).[217]

Pannenberg accused theology of the Word of God of a subjectivist *Dezisionismus* or fideism, i.e., the justification of the validity of faith from within faith itself, ultimately consisting of a mere assertion without proof.[218] However, the objection to Pannenberg's approach must also be raised, namely, that

---

216   Pannenberg, *Systematic Theology*, Vol. 1, 230–57.
217   Barth, CD I/2, 203–79.
218   Pannenberg, *Problemgeschichte*, 197–204.

we cannot simply read the attribution of revelatory meaning and soteriological relevance from the Christ-event. It is a postulate of faith that the divinely ordained destiny of history takes place in advance in Jesus Christ. This assumption requires still greater justification when it is called into question, e.g., by a positivist interpretation of history that is critical of religion, or by competing religious views that attribute revelatory character to other historical events (such as the descent of the Qur'an). Pannenberg recognizes this necessity but underestimates faith's constructive contribution to an interpretive understanding of the Christ-event *as* an event of revelation. Faith 'sees' this added value of meaning—in the sense of 'seeing as'.

(b) Christological approaches that distinguish the Christ-content from the Christ-event, on the other hand, take as their starting point what they understand as the general content across time. They view the Christ-event as a manifestation of this content or principle (e.g. the principle of mediation between God and human beings). This content can be attributed a general validity that transcends space and time. This 'idealistic' view seems to lead to the danger of Docetism, which devalues the life, work, death, and 'resurrection' of Jesus by presenting it as the historical 'appearance' of the divine principle. However, this is by no means necessarily the case—for without this event, the content of Christ would remain abstract and without historical reality.

The distinction between the event of Christ and the content of Christ does not devalue the event, but points to its historical contextuality (as the term 'incarnation' in a broader sense indicates). Even if the Christ-event has a meaning that extends far beyond the historical person of Jesus, it always remains bound to the that person and its context. By maintaining such a historical grounding, we can also counter the danger of elevating the Christ-content into philosophical speculation. This danger arises when attempts are made to define the Christ-content independently from the Christ-event.

Theologians who oriented themselves towards the philosophy of German Idealism, such as Alois Emanuel Biedermann, tended to see Jesus Christ as manifesting a principle of mediation between God and humanity. In the last third of the nineteenth century, philosophy (e.g., Kierkegaard) and theology (especially Albrecht Ritschl) sharply distanced themselves from such idealistic approaches. The starting point of Christological doctrine was now the historical: the concrete self-communication of God in Jesus Christ. Accordingly, there is no Christ-content that can be distinguished from this event.

In twentieth-century theology, the two methods of relating content and event were expressed, by Karl Barth and Dietrich Bonhoeffer on the one hand and by Paul Tillich on the other.

(a) For *Karl Barth*, who follows Ritschl on this point, it is clear that the revelation attested in the biblical tradition has the character of an event. According to him, "there is no second question as to what its content might be. Nor could its content be equally well manifested in another event than this",[219] and *"the content of the New Testament is solely the name of Jesus Christ [...]".*[220] All Christological definitions are secondary to the fact of this name. Dietrich Korsch writes that Barth develops a "theory of the principal (singular) fact" of God's incarnation in Jesus Christ in *Church Dogmatics*.[221] As Barth sees it, the identity of God is to be understood from this 'fact'. In §33 of the *CD* he writes, "There is no such thing as Godhead in itself".[222] The content of God's nature must not be subordinated to God's selfhood. It constitutes this selfhood— which is only revealed by Christ.

Similarly, *Dietrich Bonhoeffer* banished the idealistic approach from Christology: "God did not become an idea, a principle, a program, a universally valid belief, or a law; God became human."[223] What is decisive is not the supra-historical general but the historically singular; not an ideal content, but a concrete person; not a being, but an act. It is not a question of the 'what', but of the 'who'. The 'what' *is* the self-communication of God in the person of Jesus Christ.

(b) *Paul Tillich*, on the other hand, who was influenced by Schelling's late philosophy, understands the Christ-event as the historical manifestation of the 'new being'—by no means without history, but also not exclusively bound to a particular event. Rather, it is simultaneous to all historical events. Jesus as the Christ functions as the *bearer* and *mediator* of the essential unity between God and humanity, and as such as redeemer. Tillich speaks explicitly of representation in this context:

> he represents God to man [...] He represents the original image of God, embodied in man, but he does so under the conditions of estrangement between God and man.[224]

As Tillich sees it, when we talk about the 'Incarnation' we are talking about the "assertion that God is manifest in a personal life-process as a saving participant

---

219   Barth, *CD* I/1, 309.
220   Barth, *CD* I/2, 17.
221   Translated from Korsch, *Dialektische Theologie*, 170.
222   Barth, *CD* II/2, 116.
223   Bonhoeffer, *Ethics* (DBWE 6) 99.
224   Tillich, *Systematic Theology*, Vol. 2, 93–4.

in the human predicament".[225] Jesus acts as the Christ in the power of that which manifests itself in him but is distinct from him: the eternal relationship of God to humanity. Event and content are not identical, but neither can they be separated. The content must occur in the form of an event in order to become effective:

> Only if existence is conquered concretely and in its manifold aspects, is it actually conquered. The power which has created and preserved the community of the New Being is not an abstract statement about its appearance; it is the picture of him in whom it has appeared.[226]

The reflections that Tillich offers in his essay 'A Reinterpretation of the Doctrine of the Incarnation' are also significant in this context.[227] To summarize his central thesis: He does not want incarnation to be understood *mythologically*, i.e., as a proposition that God became human. "The proposition that God became man, or 'became flesh', is definitely not biblical".[228] The *metaphysical* understanding of Incarnation as a mediation of the finite with the infinite is also misguided. The meaning is instead a *soteriological* one, concerning the tension between essence and existence: "The Incarnation is the manifestation of original and essential Godmanhood within and under the conditions of existence."[229] The New Being is represented in Jesus as the Christ.

In contrast to representational Christology as I present it in this book, Tillich assumes that Jesus Christ represents God to human beings, but not human beings to God.[230] In Jesus, the essence of humanity is revealed, but not the depths of its fallenness. This removes from the representation his experience of suffering, and within that suffering his encounter with human desolation. Representational Christology goes beyond that approach.

My model of representational Christology defines the relationship between the event of Christ and the content of Christ in terms of a difference with close interconnection. The content is realized in the event; it does not merge into it but exists before it and extends beyond it. The event is the symbolic realization of the content that transcends that very event. The Christ-event is the representation of the fellowship with humanity opened up by God, the representation

---

225   Tillich, *Systematic Theology*, Vol. 2, 95.
226   Tillich, *Systematic Theology*, Vol. 2, 114.
227   Paul Tillich, *A Reinterpretation*, reprinted in *Paul Tillich Main Works*, 305–318.
228   Paul Tillich, *A Reinterpretation*, reprinted in *Paul Tillich Main Works*, 310.
229   Paul Tillich, *A Reinterpretation*, reprinted in *Paul Tillich Main Works*, 310.
230   Tillich, *Systematic Theology*, Vol. 2, 93.

of God's will for salvation and covenant that undergird this fellowship, and the representation of God's nature, characterized by love and justice, which constitutes this fellowship. This nature, this will, and the relationship between God and humanity that emerges from them both are realized in Jesus Christ but are not exhausted in this realization. By their nature they are universal. Therefore, they cannot be connected to or originally constituted by a historical event such that they consist entirely in it, or such that their entire reality is revealed here and only here. God's saving purposes are not seen merely partially, but entirely, in the person of Jesus and his ministry and impact. However, these same saving purposes of God are neither founded on nor limited by the person, ministry, and impact of Jesus.

CHAPTER 5

Selected Approaches to a Representational Christology

In this part of the study, I discuss two approaches from recent North American theological history. They take a similar direction to the representational Christology presented in this volume, which can thus be refined through entering into conversation with them. The first is the approach of the Protestant theologian Schubert M. Ogden (5.1), who was influenced by Rudolf Bultmann and process theology. The second is that of the Jesuit Roger Haight (5.2), whose book *Jesus Symbol of God*, published in 1999 and awarded a prize by the Catholic Press Association, prompted the Vatican Congregation for the Doctrine of the Faith to ban him from teaching.

5.1 Schubert M. Ogden's Concept of Representation

As part of his examination of Bultmann's program of demythologization, Schubert M. Ogden introduced into the discussion the distinction between the *constitution* of salvation and the *representation* of salvation. The substance of this idea, if not the exact terminology, can already be found in Paul Tillich,[1] Donald MacKinnon,[2] John Macquarrie,[3] and Maurice Wiles.[4] This distinction is entirely based on soteriology, i.e., the significance of Jesus Christ to God's saving action. The basic question is this: Do Jesus' actions (especially his death on the cross) *constitute* the justification of human beings by God and thus their salvation, or does Jesus (especially in his preaching and practice) *represent* God's eternal salvific will? Ogden's thesis is that the salvation of humanity is founded on the eternal salvific will of God and represented by Jesus.

---

1 See especially Tillich, *Systematic Theology*, Vol. 2, 165–80.
2 MacKinnon, *The Relation*, 145–67. See also Sherry, *Modes*, 34–48.
3 Macquarrie, *Principles*, 269.
4 Wiles, *Remaking*, 79–82.

5.1.1 Jesus-Kerygma and Christ-Kerygma

As Willi Marxsen does,[5] so too Ogden distinguishes between the Jesus-kerygma of the contemporary followers of Jesus, revealed above all in the synoptic Gospels, and the Christ-kerygma related to Good Friday and Easter. The Jesus-kerygma consists of the message that:

> Through Jesus himself [...] God's own love continues to be decisively re-present as the gift and demand that authorizes us to exist in obedient faith in God and in love both for God and for all whom God loves.[6]

Jesus is thus "the decisive re-presentation of the meaning of God for us".[7] According to Ogden, the meaning this had for believers lay in the message of God's saving presence and in the symbolic actions through which Jesus put this message into practice. The believers proclaimed this meaning in their own preaching. The Jesus-kerygma was therefore entirely oriented toward the proclamation and practice of Jesus.

The Christ-kerygma, on the other hand, is focused on soteriological interpretations of the death and 'resurrection' of Jesus. Ogden sees this kerygma as the result of a post-Easter contemplation which hones the implicit Christology of the Jesus-kerygma into explicit Christologies—ones which see the crucifixion and 'resurrection' as "god's liberating judgment of the world, through which all who are willing to die with Christ are given to rise with him to newness of life".[8]

Ogden draws on the history of theological tradition to show that these explicit Christologies—which see Jesus' death as constituting three elements of reconciliation with God, redemption from the corrupting power of sin, and salvation for humanity—are not yet present in the earliest books of the New Testament. The implicit Christology found there relates instead to the effect of the person of Jesus on his community of followers. However, the focus on the salvific significance of the cross and 'resurrection' can already be seen in pre-Pauline sources and Paul then expands upon them in his letters.

Ogden writes that there are only two instances of Jesus referring to the salvific significance of his death in his own words: in Mk. 10:45 (Mt. 20:28), where he refers to his death as a 'ransom', and in the words of the Lord's Supper (Mk. 14:22–24 and parallels; 1 Cor. 11:23–26). However, these words did not

---

5 Marxsen, *Die Sache Jesu geht weiter*, 39ff.
6 Ogden, *The Understanding*, 74.
7 Ogden, *The Understanding*, 74.
8 Ogden, *The Understanding*, 75.

originate from the early Palestinian Christian community, but from Christians shaped by Hellenistic influence. In contrast, there is no soteriological interpretation of the death and 'resurrection' of Jesus in the Q source,[9] not even an explicit proclamation of the 'resurrection'. According to Ogden, the later Christologies were based on the original Jesus-kerygma. This was the *'christologia normans'*.[10]

I will set to one side the exegetical difficulties arising from such a distinction between the Jesus-kerygma and the Christ-kerygma. By referring to both views of Jesus' salvific significance as 'kerygma', Ogden makes it clear that he does not want to contrast the (pre-Easter) authentic self-understanding of the historical Jesus with the (post-Easter) formulation of the confession of Christ. Both are post-Easter perspectives that differ above all in their understanding of the cross and 'resurrection'. The Jesus-kerygma is also formed in the light of the 'resurrection'; only from that point on the certainty for the followers of Jesus is confirmed that in encountering him they have encountered the saving presence of God.

However, both versions of the kerygma agree that God's salvific initiative is not founded on the Christ-event.[11] No event localized in space and time (even if it gains its significance through faith) can constitute God's will to save and thus the possibility of salvation for humanity. This will and this possibility are constituted by "the primordial and everlasting love of God, which is the sole primal source and the sole final end of anything that is so much as possible."[12] Otherwise, the offer of salvation would be limited to those humans who lived temporally *after* this event and spatially within its sphere of influence.

This means that soteriology is ultimately anchored in the first, not the second, article of the creed: the *source* of salvation lies in the eternal will of God. The *realization* of salvation, i.e., its being dedicated *pro me* and *pro nobis*, remains in the Christological realm. In Christ, God does not *bring about* salvation, but *reveals* and *bestows* it. Christ is the *mediator* of salvation. It is not what he is, does, and suffers *in itself* that is relevant to salvation, but what is made present in it.

Ogden rejects a constitutive function of Jesus Christ in relation not only to God but also to human existence. The revelation of Christ cannot be necessary for the *grounding* of human existence (in its relation to God) in its authenticity

---

9 Ogden, *The Understanding*, 75.
10 Ogden, *The Understanding*, 76.
11 Ogden, *Is There Only One True Religion*, 79–104. See also *id.*, *Christ without Myth*, 156–61; *id.*, *The Reality of God*, 164ff; *id.*, *Problems*, 493–507.
12 Ogden, *Is There Only One True Religion*, 92.

('Eigentlichkeit'), but only for the reflective *grasping* of this authenticity.[13] A few lines later, Ogden contrasts 'constitution' with 'explication': "Christian revelation is necessary to human existence [...] in the first instance not to the *constitution* of our possibility, but to its full and adequate *explication*".[14]

In relation to this argument, Ogden mentions John Wesley, probably reflecting his background of teaching at Southern Methodist University in Dallas from 1956 to 1969 and from 1972 to 1993. However, the argument is primarily to be understood against the background of Bultmann's understanding of revelation, to whose existential theology Ogden was committed.

5.1.2 *Connections and Demarcations*

Bultmann had rejected the view—held by Luther, among others—that the Christ-event expanded the content of the general revelation through creation (which reveals the pure *existence of God* as creator) by a special revelation in Christ which makes known the *grace of God*. The general revelation is under the 'law', while the special revelation shines forth from the Gospel. In contrast, Bultmann insisted that special revelation was in no way qualitatively different from general revelation. Rather, its uniqueness consisted in this truth of God being made present in the here and now of human existence—in a manner that was decisive but also demanded decisions from those who encountered it.[15]

Ogden agreed with this existential theological understanding of revelation: "the point of Christology is a strictly *existential* point".[16] The central Christological statement "Jesus is the Christ" says of Jesus "that what is re-presented to us in him is the answer to our question about God as the question of our own existence."[17]

> [I]t re-presents the word that is addressed to us and to all men in Jesus as the decisive word about our own human existence, as the Word that answers all our deepest questions about God because it tells us explicitly and finally who we ourselves are given and demanded to be.[18]

---

13 "[I]t can very well be necessary of the *objectification* of existence, in the sense of its full and adequate understanding at the level of explicit thought and speech" (Ogden, *On Theology*, 41).
14 Ogden, *On Theology*, 41 (emphasis mine).
15 Bultmann, "Offenbarung, IV. Im NT"; *id., Glaube und Verstehen*, Vol. 2, 252ff.
16 Ogden, *The Point of Christology*, 375 (emphasis in original).
17 Ogden, *The Point of Christology*, 378.
18 Ogden, *The Point of Christology*, 379.

This Word is present as an inner word in the depths of human existence and is therefore accessible to every human being. The external Word, which is embodied in Christ and in the historical Christ-event, is its representation.[19]

However, Ogden distances himself from a dissolution of the 'real' reference to God into a "pseudo-existentialist subjectivism, which collapses the important logical distinction between truth and belief",[20] thereby also distancing himself from Bultmann to some extent. The divinity of Jesus is the precondition for the salvation which he brings about *pro me*. Jesus is not the Son of God because he helps me;[21] rather, he can only help me because he is the Son of God. Ogden thus shifts the soteriological emphasis away from theology of the cross and toward the motif of the incarnation, understood as a representation of God's saving presence.

For Ogden, the foundational event *constituting* salvation consists in the self-identification of God, i.e., in his saving purposes, and the Christ-event *representing* salvation consists in the re-presentation, i.e., in the manifestation of God's salvific presence. This presence has its constitutional basis in God's nature rather than in a spatiotemporal event such as Jesus' suffering on the cross; but it can only be represented *in* space and time. That which is being represented is supra-historical and timeless, whereas the representation must be historical to achieve its goal, namely, the healing of human existence and of the whole of creation. Re-presentation therefore means 'making present again' God's creative and healing love that has gone forth with creation and is always going forth anew. By *revealing* the authenticity of existence in Christ, that which is inherent in human existence as an inner 'word' is made real.[22] In other words, the authenticity of existence is not first and foremost laid down as a foundation, nor is it merely indicated: it is made present.

Behind this approach lies not only the critical reception of Bultmann, but also the distinctive understanding of incarnation promoted by process theology: God unfolds Godself by stimulating the cosmic process to develop ever greater complexity, harmony, and beauty. The continuous incarnation of God and the humanization of humanity toward its true self both reach their full realization in Jesus. In him, therefore, there is no supernatural disruption of the nexus of historical events, but rather the realization of humanity's purpose. This interpretation allows the claim to universal significance, uniqueness, and

---

19 Ogden, *On Theology*, 41.
20 Ogden, *The Point of Christology*, 389.
21 As Bultmann frames it in *Glaube und Verstehen*, Vol. 2, 252.
22 In "Christ Without Myth", Ogden spoke of an "original possibility of existence *coram Deo*", which is inherent to humans as such (156–7; 160–1).

normativity of the Christ-event to be upheld—without declaring Jesus Christ to be the constitutional basis of the divine will of salvation or the exclusive mediator of salvation. Divine action is not aimed at *him*, but at humanity; the content of revelation is not *him*, but God's will to save, which is demonstrated in him. We can no longer speak of his uniqueness in relation to the mediation of salvation, but of his relevance to the history of salvation, his universal significance, his 'centrality'.[23]

Like Bultmann, Ogden also distinguishes this conception of Christ from that of liberal theology, as found (for example) in Alois Emanuel Biedermann. Unlike Biedermann, Ogden assumes that Jesus is not the realization of a universal principle of mediation between God and human beings. The frame of reference for his thinking is not idealistic philosophy, but existential theology. At its center is the concept of 'faith', understood as an existential attitude. Ogden emphasizes that Jesus does not constitute the possibility of faith but represents it.[24] What is decisive for Ogden is not Jesus' *own* faith and Jesus' *own* love, so much as the love of *God* that shines through Jesus and reaches out to all human beings. Ogden is concerned with the possibility and reality of salvation, constituted solely by God, which is re-presented in a unique way by Christ and in him definitively made present. Jesus is not only the paradigm of the human being who is seized by God's creative and salvific power. Rather, this power *takes place* in him as the representative of God. Christ is not merely *exemplum*, but *sacramentum* of salvation.

In making this distinction against liberal Christology's idea of a perfect realization of the highest potential of humanity, Ogden essentially agrees with Bultmann. He rejects any constricted perspective on Jesus ('Jesuology'). The humanity and 'works' of the 'historical' Jesus are significant as *carriers* of the kerygma. Like Bultmann, Ogden shows no interest in the 'historical' Jesus and instead emphasizes the role of *God* as the subject of salvation.

At a point that is significant for our discussion, however, Ogden deviates from his spiritual father and pursues his own path. Bultmann had always emphasized that the revelation of Christ was the absolute (i.e., the eschatological, ultimate, and therefore unsurpassable) Word of God to all humanity; the continuing presence of this Word transcends all times and thus also

---

23 It is in this sense that Ogden writes: "the re-presentation of God [...] has taken place and continues to take place through the particular strand of human history of which Jesus is the center" (Ogden, *On Theology*, 29).

24 "Jesus is the Christ not because he *actualized* the possibility of faith and, unlike us, actualized it perfectly, but because he *re-presents* the possibility of faith and, for us, re-presents it decisively" (Ogden, *The Point of Christology*, 391 [emphasis mine]). See also Ogden's published notes in *The Notebooks*: Section 15: Christology: Miscellaneous, 555–76.

determines the future. Ogden rejects the claim to exclusivity implied therein, in order to cautiously open himself up to a pluralistic soteriology.[25] Although Christ is the only definitive representation of divine love *for Christians*, the possibility that there might be other equally definitive representations for followers of other religious traditions cannot be ruled out.

In allowing for this possibility, but not asserting it as fact, Ogden offers a critique of the representatives of a pluralistic theology of religions who also recognize other religions as fully-fledged paths to salvation. Like them, Ogden also states that their references to the divine reality are rooted in their being initially founded in God's universal and omnipresent commitment to humanity. But he does not want to generalize all these religions as paths to salvation (in full knowledge of the problematic manifestations in all religious practices). They *could* become such for their followers *if* they correspond to God's universal love. For Ogden, therefore, there *can* be several true religions. In the Christian understanding, the universal love of God is most authentically represented in Christ. Christ is not the ground for the existence of this love, but the ground for recognizing it. Paul F. Knitter has described this position as "cautious pluralism".[26]

Nevertheless, the question must here be posed in response to Ogden: Does the representative of God's commitment to humanity not also become the mediator and, in this sense, the constitutional basis of the *reception* of that commitment? In this respect, shouldn't a stronger distinction be made between Jesus Christ's relationship *with God* and his relationship *with humanity*? To criticize the idea that Jesus Christ constitutes salvation is to engage directly with his relationship with God. Its intent is to reject the idea that Jesus acquired salvation from God through his death on the cross. However, for those who believe and participate in the realization of this salvation in Christ (i.e., Christians), the Christ-event is the constitutional basis of their new condition of existence. One can speak of an *intermediate* constitution, i.e., one that in turn refers to an underlying ground. This is the view of the representational Christology advocated in this volume. It thus takes up one of the key concerns of constitutional Christology.

5.1.3 *Consequences for the Theology of Religions*

Two interests overlap in Ogden's approach. On the one hand, he seeks to retain the uniqueness of Christ (along with Bultmann and process theology). On the other, he seeks to fend off claims to exclusivity based on Christology and to

---

25 Ogden, *Christ without Myth*, 111ff.
26 Knitter, *One Earth, Many Religions*, 184, footnote 11.

avoid denying from the outset the truth claims of non-Christian testimonies to revelation. In contrast to a Christian claim to sole legitimacy, he emphasizes the universality of God's love, the effectiveness of which in other religions can never be fundamentally excluded. In contrast to a relativism concerning the ways of salvation, which wants to recognize other 'Christs' on an equal footing with Jesus Christ, Ogden is emphatic that the Christ-event is not *one* among many representations of God's love, but *the decisive representation*. It is not merely *a* sacrament of salvation, but (with clear echoes of Rahner) a unique primordial sacrament,[27] which makes the possibility of salvation—which is always already implicitly present for every human being—present again and explicit.[28] Ogden states that he finds Rahner's position "by far the most ingenious defense of the constitutive type of christology underlying inclusivism of which I have any knowledge".[29] Rahner's doctrine of God's universal will for salvation and the implicit faith of the 'anonymous Christian' is echoed in Ogden's 'implicit/explicit' pair of terms. Moreover, there are parallels to Rahner's existential theology in what Ogden says about the general revelation of God bringing about a quasi-transcendental orientation of the human constitution. He thus sees the task of Christology today as showing that Jesus brings to light the true condition of human existence.[30]

There is no tension between (a) emphasising the universal significance of the revelation of Christ *for every human being*;[31] and (b) the statement that Christ is the only definitive representation of divine love *for Christians*. The significance of the revelation of Christ as a representation of divine love is universal, but only for Christians is it the *decisive* representation. Beyond one's own religious tradition, the possibility of other *decisive representations* must be conceded. However, Ogden leaves open the question of how the *decisive* representation of God for Christians relates to the representations on which other religious traditions are based. The question must remain open because answering it would require a metaphysical point of view, which an existential, hermeneutical theology cannot admit.

Ogden differs in another way from Christological approaches which see in Jesus Christ (especially his death and 'resurrection') the culmination and turning point of salvation history. Unlike these, his representational Christology does not have to come to grips with the question of how God's salvific purposes

---

27   Ogden, *Is There Only One True Religion*, 97–8.
28   Ogden, *Is There Only One True Religion*, 100.
29   Ogden, *Is There Only One True Religion*, 94.
30   Ogden, *The Point of Christology*, 392.
31   On Christ's universal significance, see also Ogden, *On Theology*, 41; id., *The Point of Christology*, 379.

could reach people who lived *before* this culmination point and people who lived *afterwards* but remained unaffected by it. It can dispense with an inclusivist theology of religions that aims to bring non-Christians into relationship with God through the Christ-event. On the other hand, it can avoid falling into a pluralist theology of religions that declares non-Christian religions also to be divine paths to salvation.

According to Ogden, God's saving presence is universal, and it is in this universality that it is represented by Christ in history. Christ does not have to add anything to it because it already exists in all its fullness. He only needs to reveal and make present its essential universality. The fact that this process has taken place in him in a *decisive* way is of *existential* importance: a new orientation of existence towards God opens up, one which applies to all humans.

However, as a hermeneutical event, this opening up of God's gift of salvation represented in Christ is bound to the perspective of Christian faith. In addition, there can also be other disclosures which can be illuminating for Christians, even if not decisive. In this way, Ogden's Christological approach enables a theological appreciation of the sources and traditions of other religions. Appreciation does not mean blanket and *a priori* recognition, and it is certainly not to be conflated with a declaration of soteriological equivalence. How are we to determine the value of revelations, mediators of revelation, doctrines of salvation, etc., which different religious traditions regard as fundamental? There is no plausible method of determining value which will gain universal agreement. However, representational Christology cherishes the expectation of discovering in other religions the manifestation of God's presence, which, according to Christian belief, established itself decisively in Christ. This approach generates a *theological* motivation for dialog with non-Christian religions without having to make irresponsibly far-reaching pre-dialogical declarations about the validity of their claims to truth and salvation.

5.2   Roger Haight: Jesus as Symbol of God

On December 13, 2004, the Vatican Congregation for the Doctrine of the Faith declared that the book *Jesus, Symbol of God* by Father Roger Haight, SJ[32] contained

---

32 Haight, *Jesus*. See also Haight, *The Future of Christology*.

serious doctrinal errors contrary to the divine and Catholic faith of the Church. As a consequence, until such time as his positions are corrected to be in complete conformity with the doctrine of the Church, the Author must not teach Catholic theology.[33]

This notification was signed by the then Prefect of the Vatican Congregation for the Doctrine of the Faith, Cardinal Joseph Ratzinger.

Through such acts of censorship, the Vatican shows that it is only prepared to respect the freedom of theological scholarship so long as such freedom operates within Vatican-approved boundaries.

Roger Haight is one of the most renowned Catholic theologians in North America and was also president of the American Catholic Theological Society for several years. He had already outlined his theological approach and aims in *Dynamics of Theology*:[34] there, he sought to interpret the traditional doctrines of faith in a creative way that makes them fruitful for contemporary life and thought. The starting point of his reflections is not these doctrines of faith, but the situation of believers today. It is therefore not a doctrinal theology, but a contextual and 'apologetic' theology in the sense of Tillich, to whom Haight repeatedly refers: a theology that responds to the challenges of the world today. Theology must start 'from below', with the existential questions and experiences of humans, and bring the message of the Christian faith to the fore as an answer to these, in a language that is understandable to all.[35] Theology is the doctrine of faith, not in the sense of an ecclesiastical instruction of believers but as an explanation of the contents of faith that is plausible for the present-day existence of believers.

The approach 'from below' also means a Christology that must take the story of Jesus as its starting point. According to Haight, this has in fact always been the case throughout theological history: Christologies were and are based on an "ascending logic".[36] They start from the impression that Jesus made then as well as now, and from there they move on to asking about his divinity. Even

---

33 Congregation for the Doctrine of the Faith, Notification. Haight then moved from the Weston Jesuit School of Theology in Cambridge, MA to the non-denominational Union Theological Seminary in New York. In January 2009, a general ban on teaching and publishing was imposed on him, which also applies to non-Catholic institutions like Union.
34 Haight, *Dynamics of Theology*.
35 With regard to Barth and Moltmann, Haight laments "a hybrid language of history, doctrine and myth that robs the confession that Jesus is the Savior of credibility for a historically sensitive audience" (Haight, *Dynamics of Theology*, 339).
36 Haight, *Jesus*, 209. See also xii–xiii.

if they then take the opposite route in their presentation (from 'above' to 'below'), the interest which leads to this exploration and presentation is based on the "concrete imaginative memory of him".[37]

5.2.1 The Term 'Symbol'

As early as Part 4 of *Dynamics of Theology*, inspired by Eliade, Tillich, Rahner, and Ricœur, Haight took up the concept of the religious symbol. His initial, general understanding of 'symbol' was "that through which something other than itself is made present and known".[38] In *Jesus, Symbol of God*, his definition reads: "a symbol may be understood as something that mediates something other than itself. A symbol makes present something else".[39] For him, the term 'symbol' stands for a theology 'from below' that starts with humans, while 'sacrament' indicates a theology "from above".[40]

Haight distinguishes between religious symbols that are conceptual (in the sense of mental, verbal, pictorial) and those which are physical.[41] Conceptual symbols[42] are religious ideas, words, metaphors, parables, poems, stories, etc. They are localized in the consciousness and are articulated linguistically or figuratively. In contrast, *real* symbols referring to God (which Haight calls "concrete symbols") are part of material reality: objects, places, events, and people. At the center of the Christian faith is the person of Jesus as a symbol of God: "in the case of the concrete symbol Jesus, we are speaking of the real presence of God to him, and through him to the world, that is mediated by him".[43]

Like Tillich, Haight insists that an authentic symbol is not merely a designation or a sign; rather, it mediates and visualizes that which it symbolizes. However, the symbolic difference between the symbol and the symbolized (Jesus and God, in this case) always remains. The reality of that which is symbolized extends beyond the symbol. The symbol is what it symbolizes, and

---

37 Haight, *Jesus*, 209. "Imagination" here does not mean "fantasy", but an understanding or cognition that is always influenced by the cognitive subject's power of imagination. See Haight, *Jesus*, 37ff.
38 Haight, *Dynamics*, 130. This recurs almost word-for-word in Haight, *Jesus*, 8.
39 Haight, *Dynamics*, 197.
40 He thus understands the title of *Jesus, Symbol of God* as a counterpart to Edward Schillebeeckx's neo-Thomist classic *Christ the Sacrament of the Encounter with God* (New York: Sheed and Ward 1963) (Haight, *Jesus*, xiii, note 6).
41 Haight, *Dynamics*, 129–45; Haight, *Jesus*, 13, 197–99.
42 In *Dynamics of Theology* (140–45) he describes them as "conscious symbols", and in *Jesus, Symbol of God* (196–202) as "conceptual symbols".
43 Haight, *Jesus*, 189; "Jesus is the historical mediation of God to the Christian imagination" (Haight, *Jesus*, 112); "Jesus as symbol participates in God as Spirit, mediates God and makes God present" (Haight, *Jesus*, 458). See also Haight, *Jesus*, 14 and *passim*.

at the same time it is not; this dialectic is fundamental to the understanding of symbols. Haight describes his methodological approach as "symbolic realism".[44] The symbol refers to a reality, but only expresses it by way of reference. However, this is perfectly appropriate to the reality that religious language describes.

Symbols signify things and make them understandable; they do not interpret themselves. Rather, they need to be understood, and this in turn takes place from a certain perspective. Only in the perspective of Christian faith does Jesus appear as the symbol of God. Symbols are always multivalent and open to interpretation; they do not have single, simple meanings.

As Haight sees it, religious discourse is always symbolic communication because its 'objects' (God, the divinity of God's mediator, the salvific transformation of human existence, etc.) are transempirical realities. They can only be articulated in the symbolic language of faith, i.e., in a referential language, rather than in one which is conceptually descriptive and concerned with definition. The symbol is the transparent foil of these meanings and as such a carrier of meaning.

These carriers of meaning are only recognized as symbols of transempirical reality when, on the one hand, the cognitive subject participates in their meaning, and on the other, in the context ('Lebenswelt') from which the symbols originate. Tillich emphasized the former type: participation in the symbolized divine reality. Haight moreover emphasizes the second (which again indicates the historical reference of his theology): participation in the culture to which the symbol carriers belong. This shows the importance he attaches to the inculturation of the Gospel.[45] Where symbols no longer have a place in a culture and a religion, it makes no sense to use them in religious communication. Haight's aim is to present a plausible view of the person of Jesus and his meaning in the context of contemporary postmodern, pluralist culture.

In this intention, in his methodology, and in the development of its content, Haight's approach is close to the representational Christology I am developing here, even if 'representation' seems to me to be more suitable as a guiding concept of Christology than 'symbol' (for the reasons mentioned in chapter 3.2.7.3).[46] Both terms allow us simultaneously to express the presence

---

44   Haight, *Jesus*, 472 and *passim*.
45   See the contextualization in the introduction to *Jesus, Symbol of God* (Haight, Jesus, xi–xii).
46   However, Haight defines the concept of symbol more broadly than Tillich. Above all Tillich referred to what Haight calls "concrete symbols", while Haight includes everything that indicates a meaning: the whole area of analogical, metaphorical, poetic speech, pictorial representations, symbolic actions, etc. This includes the whole of theology: "because

and the transcendence of that which is symbolized, the recognizability alongside the hiddenness. Jesus represents God, i.e., he reveals the presence of God without this revelation abolishing the mystery of what is revealed. Haight also uses the concept of representation in various ways and makes use of other semantic equivalents, such as speaking of Jesus as a 'parable' of God.[47]

5.2.2   Elaboration of Haight's Approach

Haight develops his view of Jesus as a symbol of God via four lines of questioning. Firstly, in terms of the redemption of humanity, he asks about the 'objective' ground for redemption in Jesus' relationship with God and then about the 'subjective' events of redemption in the human world. In doing so, he particularly emphasizes the socio-political dimensions of redemption, i.e., as liberation from conditions which are dehumanizing and detrimental to life. Secondly, he asks about the person and significance of Jesus in view of religious pluralism; thirdly, about what constitutes Jesus' divinity; and, fourthly, about the relationship of Christology to the Trinitarian understanding of God. The second and third points are of particular interest to us; I will discuss the other two only relatively briefly.

5.2.2.1   Redemption

Haight writes that it was and is the *experience* of God's redeeming power radiating out from Jesus that underlies all Christology, Christian beliefs, and the Christian religion.[48] Jesus being a symbol of God is not the result of a revelation 'from above', but of an experience of encounter 'from below'. A transformative power radiated outwards from the encounter with him then and continues to do so throughout all time. It brings about 'healing' in the sense of making whole that which is broken and damaged. This concerns not only human spirituality or humanity's relationship with God, but also their entire physical and spiritual state of existence, which is characterized by ignorance, sin, guilt, suffering, and death.[49] Redemption also refers to the social, political, and economic living conditions dominated by injustice, discord, and oppression. This is where Haight brings the concerns of liberation theology into play. Redemption also includes nature in the face of ecological upheaval. Creation and redemption are closely related. Haight's holistic understanding of redemption is based on

---

theology deals with a transcendent reality, and the data of faith is received through revelation, theology is a symbolic discipline" (Haight, *Jesus*, 9).
47   Haight, *Jesus*, 112ff., and *passim*.
48   Haight, *Jesus*, 335.
49   Haight, *Jesus*, 354.

an anthropology that always sees humans as social beings that belong to the wider created order.

As opposed to an understanding of redemption as a supernatural 'mythical' event, as far as possible Haight wants it to be understood as something concrete, relevant to the present day, and true-to-life within our postmodern context. For him, it is not enough to hold out hope for redemption as the promise of a better future, nor even to relate it to an afterlife. Redemption must be discussed as a possible experience in the here and now—and not merely as an experience to be received passively, but as an impulse toward actively using one's freedom. Redemption (like revelation) is realized through historical media, in this case through the liberating actions of human beings.[50] The transformative power radiating from God motivates and enables those people affected by it to take action against conditions that are hostile to life and thus contrary to God. This 'worldly' understanding of redemption is diametrically opposed to all contempt for the world and flight from the world. It is not about redemption *from* the world, but redemption *in* and *with* the world.

Jesus is the *mediator* of redemption, the foundation and origin of which is Godself. Jesus mediates redemption by revealing God as the Redeemer, thereby placing the addressee of the revelation in relation to God, and himself appearing as the prototype of a human entirely related to God: "Jesus is salvation by being a revealer of God, a symbol for an encounter with God, and an exemplar of human existence".[51] If Jesus himself were the foundation and origin of redemption, it could not be conceived as universal and applying to all humans throughout all time. This universality does not end at the boundary of faith in Christ and the Christian religion. In thinking about soteriology, we must keep in mind from the outset how the transformative power radiating from God also reaches the followers of non-Christian religions and makes use of these religions' media. In Haight's understanding, there are also impulses toward holistic redemption in other religious traditions.

5.2.2.2   Religions

Haight observes that the attitude that non-Christian religions have "a validity rooted in God's providence"[52] is becoming more widespread among Christians.

---

50   "Jesus reveals a potential salvation that is dependent upon its being taken up in action by the follower. The possible meaning of history consists precisely in assuming in one's own life the value of the kingdom of God and acting them out in one's own history" (Haight, *Jesus*, 388).

51   Haight, *Jesus*, 357–8.

52   Haight, *Jesus*, 206. "The norms of intelligibility and coherence demand that one reconciles the universal relevance of Jesus with the conviction that other religions have a role in world history under God's providence" (Haight, *Jesus*, 50).

How does Christology relate to this? Haight first distinguishes between four fundamental positions and then places his own approach within this scheme:[53]

a) The first position assumes a soteriological 'exclusivism', according to which there is salvation only in Christ or in (explicit) faith in Christ. This view restricts the will or ability of God to enact salvation for all and therefore contradicts the New Testament testimony to Christ.

b) 'Constitutive inclusivism' sees Christ as the source and the one *single* mediator of all salvation but assumes that humans without explicit faith in Christ can also participate in this salvation process. These humans are then declared to be 'anonymous' or 'latent' Christians. Haight rejects this Christocentric universalism because it does not take seriously religions' own self-understanding, defies the theocentric focus of Jesus' proclamation (by declaring Jesus Christ himself to be the origin of salvation), and ignores the historical particularity of the Christ-event by considering it an 'eternal' event (so that it can be regarded as relevant to humans who lived before Christ).

c) The 'normative non-constitutive position' assumes the universality of God's salvific action and regards Jesus Christ as the norm or criterion by which this salvation *can be recognized*. This is the position that Schubert Ogden advocates; it also corresponds to the representational Christology of the current volume.

d) Soteriological 'pluralism' postulates multiple mediators of salvation who stand on an equal footing with Jesus Christ. The relationship of these mediators of salvation to the divine foundation of all being can be established either meta-religiously, i.e., based on a trans-religious philosophy of religion (as in the case of Hick), or within the framework of a specific religious tradition (as is the case with Panikkar, who interprets other religions' mediators of salvation as incarnations of the divine Logos).

Haight places his own Christological approach between the third and fourth positions, though he is closer to the fourth position above (d) than he is to (c). His thesis is "that the normativity of Jesus does not exclude a positive appraisal of religious pluralism, and that Christians may regard other world religions as true, in the sense that they are mediations of God's salvation".[54] This quotation shows that Haight represents a pluralism from a theology of religions perspective, adhering to the normativity of Jesus Christ in order to identify what is in accordance with God in other religions and thus also to assess religious phenomena. At the same time, however, Haight's pluralism also assumes a plurality of normative mediators of salvation. The positive view of religious diversity

---

53 Haight, *Jesus*, 399–423.
54 Haight, *Jesus*, 411.

should not diminish the normative significance of Jesus; neither should the normative significance of Jesus diminish the theological appreciation of non-Christian religions. For Haight, the basic problem with soteriological exclusivism and inclusivism is the assumption that Jesus Christ is the *cause* of human salvation, i.e., a constitutive Christology. The third and fourth positions mentioned above reject this assumption. Haight shares Paul Knitter's view that "Jesus is the 'true' but 'not the only' bearer of God's salvation".[55]

The normativity of Jesus is related less to his person as such and more to the salvific grace of God symbolized and mediated by this person. Wherever grace appears, it can be traced back to the presence of God. According to Haight, this criterion can be considered already fulfilled if the form of religion in question does not contradict God's unconditional love for humanity—rather than only if it agrees with the words or ministry of Jesus. It should therefore be applied negatively rather than positively. Furthermore, its application is not limited to Christian use but applies universally, even if it is not actually used by followers of other religions. They too can be guided by it, just as Christians can be inspired by the normative centers of other religious traditions.

To justify the conviction that there are other religious mediations besides Jesus that truly symbolize God's creative and salvific presence and are therefore normative, Haight refers to Jesus' theocentric orientation. The God of Israel, whom Jesus calls his 'Father', is the creative and redeeming foundation of all reality. The mode of his presence in cosmic reality is the Spirit of God; this Spirit makes use of historical media to realize itself. Haight agrees with Rahner's view that God's activity does not take place in the mode of ahistorical spirituality. God works in history and through history. Humanity's relationship with God is also historically specific, i.e., mediated by a particular religion in a particular context. For Haight, it follows from this "that the religions are de facto channels of God's saving grace".[56]

5.2.2.3 The Divinity of Jesus Christ

Haight refers throughout *Jesus, Symbol of God* to the plurality of Christological forms of thought, beginning with the New Testament and continuing through the history of theology to the diverse forms of inculturation of the Christian faith and Christological reflection at present. His own answer to the question of the divinity of Jesus Christ is pluriform in its own right. It consists of a Logos- and a Spirit-Christological approach; he sees both as fulfilling the three criteria that he requires of a valid Christology. Firstly, they are in harmony with

---

55   Haight, *Jesus*, 395. With reference to Knitter, *Jesus*, 72–83.
56   Haight, *Jesus*, 412.

the biblical tradition and with Early Church theology; secondly, they are intelligible in the present intellectual and cultural context; and thirdly, they provide impulses to live the Christian life in intellectual, spiritual, and ethical terms.[57] Haight sees the two approaches less as elaborate concepts and more as "schematic representations of paradigms of Christology".[58] Indeed, this characterization also applies to the triad of Logos-, Spirit- and Wisdom-Christological approaches I presented in chapter 4 of this volume.

In developing these two "working models",[59] Haight first critiques Karl Rahner's Logos theology,[60] which represents a form of 'constitutive inclusivism'. It starts 'from above' with God's self-communication and insists on the uniqueness of the Incarnation of the Logos in Jesus. Haight sees this as a 'modern' inculturation of Logos-Incarnation Christology, which requires revision if its concerns are to be addressed in a postmodern setting.[61] He seeks to replace the underlying Alexandrian paradigm of the Incarnation of the Word of God (in the sense of a hypostatic union of divine and human nature) with the Antiochian idea of the assumption of the human Jesus by the Logos (through his indwelling in him). This would permit Logos Christology to begin 'from below' with the human Jesus and to understand him as a symbol of "God as Logos".[62] Jesus is "God's Word about God, the world, and human existence".[63] According to Haight, a Logos Christology which had been revised in this way would deconstruct Rahner's anthropocentrism, relate redemption more strongly to socio-political conditions, and allow symbolizations of the Logos of God in other religions to be accepted.

Haight juxtaposes Logos Christology with Spirit Christology in *Jesus, Symbol of God*,[64] as indeed he had already in earlier publications.[65] He sees it as one of the strengths of the Spirit-Christological approach that it can serve as a basis for integrating the diversity of New Testament interpretations of Christ, whereas Logos Christology tends to exclude other interpretations. It is therefore more inclusive than exclusive.[66] A further strength lies in its ability to

---

57   Haight, *Jesus*, 425–27.
58   Haight, *Jesus*, 431.
59   Haight, *Jesus*, 431.
60   Haight, *Jesus*, 431–35.
61   Haight, *Jesus*, 435–45.
62   Haight, *Jesus*, 439.
63   Haight, *Jesus*, 440.
64   Haight, *Jesus*, 445–65.
65   Haight, *The Case for Spirit Christology*, 257–87.
66   Haight, *Jesus*, 451.

connect with current 'experiences of grace': of self-transcendence, of being filled with spiritual energy and counterfactual hope, of creativity, healing, inspiration, 'enlightenment', etc. Haight prefers the term 'empowerment' as a metaphorical expression for the effect of the Spirit of God.[67] In contrast to the term 'indwelling', it emphasizes the dynamic effect that does not suppress human freedom but activates it. A third strength lies in the fact that this approach does not run the risk of downplaying Jesus' humanity. The Spirit of God takes Jesus, who is fully human, and fills him with the power of God's presence. To express this without relying on a weak understanding of 'inspiration', Haight is quite open to using the terminology of Incarnation theology within a Spirit-Christological framework:[68] "Jesus is a manifestation and embodiment of the reality of God".[69] This indicates that God not only acts *through* Jesus but is *in* him.[70]

One of the consequences of the Spirit-Christological approach is that the uniqueness of Jesus, i.e., his difference from humanity, can no longer be thought of as a categorical or qualitative difference (at least not without further definition of this term). It consists in the extent to which he, unlike other humans, is filled with the Spirit of God: "God as Spirit was present to Jesus in a superlative degree".[71] The assertion of a categorical difference would not be compatible with the assumption that he is of the same nature as humanity, i.e., a real human being. This approach therefore locates the understanding of Jesus' uniqueness as a point along a continuum. It expresses a gradual understanding of divinity.

The Spirit-Christological approach seems to Haight to be particularly suitable for articulating the biblically attested universality of God's saving action in the entire cosmos throughout all time. At the same time, it preserves the

---

67 Haight, *Jesus*, 454.
68 Haight, *Jesus*, 458–60.
69 Haight, *Jesus*, 462.
70 John Hick objects to Haight for having transformed mediatorial Christology (according to which God's love occurs *through* Jesus Christ) back into an ontological concept of incarnation (according to which God's Logos is *in* Jesus Christ). Hick sees this as a concession to the teaching of the Catholic Church (Hick, *The Metaphor*, 168–9). Hick's own rejection of incarnational Christologies comes across in this objection. For Haight, on the other hand, there is no tension between the two relational definitions denoted by the prepositions "through" and "in". Because God's Logos and God's Spirit are *in* Jesus Christ, God can work *through* him. Haight can also equate "through" and "in": "God is encountered in or through him" (Haight, *Jesus*, 239). This is also the position taken in the representational Christology advocated here.
71 Haight, *Jesus*, 464.

normativity of Jesus Christ for the Christian faith. Yet "Jesus is not constitutive of salvation universally";[72] the Spirit of God reaches further than its symbolization in Jesus and creates other symbolizations in other religions.

5.2.2.4 Trinity

In his reflections on how the Trinity is to be understood in relation to Christology, Roger Haight also looks at history starting 'from below', in this case with the historical development of the doctrine of the Trinity from Christological questions in the Early Church.[73] Here too, his direction of thought goes from the world to God and not from God to the world. It is not a theology of revelation, but a 'theology of history' in the broadest sense. All theologies (including theologies of revelation) are the result of experience-based human reflections that take place in a specific historical context, swim in the flow of historical developments, and exist in a plurality of approaches. However, these reflections have their epistemological foundations in the real self-communication of God in history. The doctrine of the Trinity arises from a process of reflection on these foundations. For Haight, as for Schleiermacher, it stands at the *end* of the long chain of reflection, not at its beginning as for Barth. As the *conclusion* of implications and inferences, it can only to a very limited extent become the starting point for further conclusions. The linguistic form of the doctrine of the Trinity, too, is that of symbolic speech. It must not be understood as a definition of the nature of God but rather as expressing the experience of God's threefold *commitment* toward us (from which arises the doctrine of the economic Trinity). It sees this commitment as anchored in the *nature* of God (from which arises the doctrine of the immanent Trinity).

In developing his doctrine of the Trinity, Haight starts 'from below' in a second respect. He understands this doctrine as the structure of the Christian faith or the experience of God mediated in Christ: "the doctrine rests on and derives from the experience of salvation and has as its point to assert and protect the economy of that experience of salvation".[74] It describes the self-communication of God that underlies this experience: the connection between the subject of this self-communication (God the 'Father'), the 'objective' historical medium of Jesus Christ, and its 'subjective' reception and interpretation in the faith of Christians. In epistemological terms this connection can be understood as a revelation of a saving transformation of existence—and in soteriological terms as an impulse toward this transformation. The doctrine

---

72 Haight, *Jesus*, 456.
73 Haight, *Jesus*, 471–80.
74 Haight, *Jesus*, 485.

of the Trinity thus allows us to think of a threefold presence of God in the world: the creative omnipresence, the salvific presence in Jesus as Christ, and the presence in the power of the Spirit which reaches into a person's inner being and brings forth spiritual communion. These reflections all center on the doctrine of the *economic* Trinity; Haight is more reserved toward the doctrine of the *immanent* Trinity, which seems to him to be too speculative.

5.2.3 *Questions*

The representational Christology of this book is largely consistent with Haight's concept. I will highlight only two points of difference.

The first relates to Haight's approach to religious pluralism. He claims that, by emphasizing the normativity of Jesus, he is occupying a middle position between the 'normative non-constitutive' and the 'pluralist' position. But the normativity of Jesus is not denied in religious pluralist approaches either; rather, it is pluralized by assuming multiple normative mediators of salvation, just as Haight does.[75] However, in not elaborating on this idea, he leaves many questions unanswered, questions such as: Are these normative centers of identity valid only to the followers of different religions, or do they have universal validity? Haight appears to claim universal validity for the mediation of God in Jesus.[76] This also applies to the other mediators of salvation. But what then is the relationship between these different normativities and mediators of salvation? Haight writes, "Jesus is [the] salvation bringer not for a certain group in history but for all human beings"[77] But different religions offer different ways to salvation and different understandings of it. Does Jesus bring a 'general' salvation to all humans or the specific 'Christian' one?

The fundamental conviction on which the pluralist position is based is that religious statements from different religious traditions ultimately refer to the same divine reality and therefore cannot ultimately contradict each other: "pluralism means differences within a *wider unity*".[78] This is also reflected in Haight's understanding of 'faith' (as opposed to 'belief'): "faith is a universal form of religious experience [...] that entails an awareness of and loyalty to an ultimate or transcendent reality".[79]

Haight seeks to maintain that religious statements make a cognitive, propositional claim to truth; that is to say, they not only express a subjective feeling,

---

75 Haight, *Jesus*, 395, 422.
76 "Jesus is normatively true for the whole human race" (Haight, *The Case for Spirit Christology*, 280); Haight, *Jesus*, 417.
77 Haight, *Jesus*, 421.
78 Haight, *Jesus*, 425 (my emphasis).
79 Haight, *Jesus*, 4.

but also claim to capture divine reality or its revelation accurately. For cognitive and propositional truth claims, however, the principle of non-contradiction applies. If it is now assumed that these different truth claims ultimately refer to the same reality, then the differences (and even the contradictions) must be dissolved into complementarities and the deep differences between the religious traditions seen as only a provisional expression of an ultimate unity. To this end, Haight refers on the one hand to the historical specificity and contextuality of religious statements, i.e., to their integration into the lifeworld of the subject and the wider community. On the other hand, he reminds us that religious statements refer to a transcendent reality that can only ever be expressed in analogical and interpretative language. Therefore, contradictions between religious statements should not be seen as insurmountable. They should be made fruitful as impulses toward a deeper engagement with other religious traditions.[80]

The turn towards this way of thinking is already predetermined by the premise that different religious traditions ultimately refer to the same divine reality. However, I believe that this premise does not have sufficient epistemological foundation. In any case, religious traditions cannot be taken as a foundation for such a claim, even if there are certainly representatives within them who promote this view. Each religion is oriented towards *its* respective center of identity and, at best, sees the ultimate reality which *it* propagates at work in other religions as well. In justifying an appreciative attitude towards other religions, it is not necessary to assume that the center of identity of one's own religion is on an equal footing with those of other religions and that these are equal paths to salvation. All that is needed is an interpretation of the center of identity of one's own religion as a representation of divine reality that does not exclude other representations. The concession of such a possibility is a sufficient basis for interreligious appreciation.

A second point of difference concerns Haight's Christology. As much as I appreciate his 'from below' approach to the person and life of Jesus, as attested above all in the Synoptic Gospels, the question arises as to how the central themes of Pauline theology (the cross and 'resurrection') and the 'high-Christology' of the Johannine writings feature in this approach. In terms of the doctrine of the three offices, Haight foregrounds Jesus' prophetic office, while the priestly and kingly offices largely or completely recede. However, this leaves under-defined the interpretative perspectives which are particularly important for soteriology; and Haight's entire Christology refers back to

---

80   Haight, *Jesus*, 405–408.

the experience of salvation mediated by Jesus. The negative forces are named (ignorance, sin, guilt, suffering, and death, in terms of individuals; injustice, oppression, and strife, in terms of society) but how does God's symbol Jesus relate to these negative forces? Is it enough to place the effort to overcome such forces in the hands of human beings who are 'empowered' to do so by the Spirit of God? There is a need for greater emphasis on the real presence of God amid suffering, his actions bringing justice in the face of sinful transgressions, and his eschatological rule over history: in other words, everything that is symbolized by the Jesus symbol.

In my presentation and discussion of Ogden's and Haight's representational approaches to Christology, I did not intend to claim that my own approach is superior to theirs. Rather, I sought to honor them as precursors who (besides others) paved the way for my own project. I built upon their efforts, aiming to strengthen the biblical and theological foundations of a representational Christology and to develop it in a direction that extends beyond their concepts.

CHAPTER 6

Conclusions and Further Reflections

This final chapter will offer some conclusions on the Christological approach presented in this book. The first two address the question of how we should materially (6.1) and linguistically (6.2) understand exclusivist Christological and soteriological claims, which have been and still are connected with belief in Christ. The third applies the Christological approach developed here to a case study: the question of whether the Qur'an can also be regarded as a representation of God (6.3).

6.1 Soteriological Exclusivism?

If God's all-encompassing, unconditional commitment is represented in Jesus Christ, then it is hardly conceivable that an exclusion principle should be established of all things concerning faith in Christ. That would entail a contradiction between the *repraesentandum* and the mode of its representation. The content of the message of Christ would be called into question by the way it is realized: the Christ-content called into question by the way the Christ-event is proclaimed and understood. If this content consists of God desiring the salvation of all (1 Tim. 2:4), then salvation cannot be bound exclusively to a path that is not in fact accessible to all. If it is granted unconditionally, then there can be no historical conditions of access.

This does not mean that the idea of the exclusivity of salvation should be abandoned. Indeed, it is indispensable, because in all religious walks of life there are offers and promises of salvation that fob off human beings with illusions, turn them into tools or instruments, make them addicted, exploit or abuse them, etc. This danger also existed, and continues to exist, in the Christian religion. 'Salvation' is a gift from *God* that does not become a religious possession and therefore must not be used to ban adherents of other religious traditions from being in a salvific relationship with God. Soteriological exclusivism should not be applied to the representative of God, nor to relationships with him, nor faith in him, nor the community that follows him, and certainly not to religious practices, institutions, and authorities that claim to represent the representative. The justification of these lies solely in their referential function and thus in self-relativization: religious authorities must relativize themselves in regard to their foundational basis (i.e., to the representative of God) in the same way that this representative has relativized himself to God.

The claim to exclusivity should not be related to the representative and certainly not to its representations, but to that which is represented (the *repraesentandum*, the saving presence of God) and thus ultimately to the one who is represented in it: to the God who brings about salvation. The claim to exclusivity thus does not mean that there is no existential, salvific relationship with God outside of the Christ-event and the history of its reception, or outside of the Christian faith and the church. Rather, it means that salvation originates exclusively from God. Wherever a human being lives out a relationship with the divine ground of all being, they can experience a salvific orientation of existence. The relationship with God that brings about salvation can also appear in "manifestations of grace"[1] that are not related to Christ, are not mediated in the Christian faith, and are not the subject of church proclamation. It is not the content [*Gehalt*] that is different, but the form [*Gestalt*]. Its form is particular, its content universal. Both sides of that polarity are important and should not become underdefined. In my questions to Haight I emphasized the importance of taking seriously the particularity of the 'ways of salvation'. Now I stress the universality of salvation.

Biblical testimony indicates that God is not an indeterminate absolute. God is the creative ground of all being—one who is not unrelated to its existence, but who exercises upon it the divine will of salvation and brings about in finite reality the divine presence of salvation. By what right can we deny God the freedom to work through the media of non-Christian religions and beyond them? We must at least concede the *possibility* of this. According to Siegfried Wiedenhofer, "in the mode of *potentialis* and hope, the believer can therefore also speak of revelations in other religions".[2] This is also Schubert Ogden's position and the position represented in this volume.

For those who participate in the presence of God in him, *Christ* is the one and only realization of God. This possibility of participation is open to all human beings. But even those who do not make use of it are not excluded from God's love. God can also make Godself present in other times and spaces, and in other ways and media, in order to manifest the divine, universal, and unconditional presence of salvation and to be 'there' for humans. Even biblical testimony has it that God's self-communication goes beyond the revelation in Christ. In its universality, it occurs not only in the "works of creation"

---

1 Translated from Tillich, *Protestantische Gestaltung*, 57–61.
2 Translated from Wiedenhofer, "Offenbarung", 297.

(Rom. 1:18–20), in events in the history of Israel, and in the believing Christian community, but also in the entire cosmos, in world history, and thus, potentially, in the sources and streams of multiple religious traditions.

Whether one should apply the theological term 'revelation' to such self-communications remains to be seen. For the time being, I prefer to speak only of *experiences* of the presence of the sacred and *testimonies* of revelations in the religions. However, merely on the basis of these experiences and testimonies, non-Christian religions deserve to be valued as sources of inspiration for theological knowledge. In normative terms, from the perspective of Christian theology, they are not of equal value to the Holy Scriptures of the Old and New Testaments, but they can be seen as illuminative contexts in which these scriptures can be interpreted. Just as theology has always developed within the frame of reference of particular cultural histories, philosophies, and contemporary contexts of experience, so too can it and should it reflect on the content of the Christian faith in relation to other religious traditions. How fruitful such reflections can be is shown by many theological dialogs on religion, whether they are actually interreligious exchanges or 'inner dialogs' of Christian theologians. This is not a plea for an 'interreligious theology' that draws equally from the sources of different religious traditions and seeks to create a 'world theology' from them; rather, it is a call for Christian theology and Christian theologians to listen to non-Christian voices.

The conclusion that Karl-Josef Kuschel drew from his reflections on the "Uniqueness of Christ in Conversation with the World Religions" applies to my Christological approach:

> Christ's normativity without claiming absoluteness, finality without exclusivism, definiteness without superiority can be theologically justified on the basis of the New Testament and the Early Church councils (understood within the framework of contextual exegesis and dogmatic hermeneutics).[3]

In the Christian understanding, Christ is the *focus*, but not simultaneously the *limit*, of God's relationship to the world. So he represents God's universal and unconditional will for salvation, which can also be represented elsewhere in other religious traditions in different shapes.

---

3 Translated from Kuschel, *Christologie und interreligiöser Dialog*, 401; reprinted in: *id.*, *Christentum*, 152.

Christian theology must therefore be open to the possibility that human beings can enter into relationship with the divine ground of being in ways that do not have a Christian label and that may not correspond with Christian convictions and practice. From the perspective of the Christian faith, such formations can be defined in relation to the 'Christ-content' as represented in Jesus. This reference can be established 'positively' (by demonstrating similarities or resonances). But it can also be established 'negatively': that is to say that a way of living and believing that does not obviously contradict the Logos, the Spirit, and the Wisdom of God with which Jesus was filled, but which gives human beings existential support and orientation, deserves recognition and appreciation.

6.2   Solus Christus?

Representational Christology still holds a place for the meaning of *solus Christus* (i.e., the confession of the uniqueness of Jesus' mediation of salvation). However, it is important to clarify what kind of language is being used in any such statements. Considerations arise from hermeneutics, linguistic analysis, and the philosophy of religion. This is less about clarifying *what* the Christian faith says and more about *how* we are to understand the way it articulates its self-understanding—in this case, its statements on the revelation of God in Jesus Christ and its salvific significance.

In the 'language of faith', such statements should not be understood as metaphysical, propositional, and factual truths, but as personal, existential, and relational ones: as *testimonies* of faith in Jesus Christ, as *confessions* about him and the presence of God represented by him. They express *certainties* of truth that must not be shifted to *claims* of being universally valid propositional truths. That there is no other way to God is an existential statement, rooted in a promise and verified by experiences; it must not be transformed into a conditional proposition ('only if one believes in Jesus Christ can salvation be gained'). This would turn the existential statement into an exclusivist definition (a word which contains the Latin word 'finis' = limit), a 'soteriological *numerus clausus*'. As such, it would contradict *what* is represented in Jesus Christ: the unconditionality and universality of God's saving presence.

In the statement 'there is no other way to God', faith in Jesus Christ is articulated in the mode of a promise, as an *assurance* of salvation, not as the establishment of an entry requirement for accessing salvation. Such statements of faith are unconditionally valid for those concerned. Yet such statements should not give rise to any claim to 'absolute' validity, i.e., claims detached ('ab-solvere') from the faith of those concerned. These are statements from the participant's perspective (the grammatical 'first person'), not the observer's (the 'third person').

The fact that these are personal, confessional truths does not entail understanding them as merely subjectivist and non-cognitive. They are embedded in the community of believers and in the tradition of faith. They certainly have a content that goes beyond expressing subjective religiosity: they express the promise and the certainty, based on the experience that a *truly* sustainable path to communion with God has been opened up in Jesus Christ.

In Reformation theology, the *solus Christus* concept was originally positioned within soteriology or the doctrine of justification. It means that the justification of human beings before God has happened 'in Christ alone', so that they must not, and cannot, make any contribution of their own. This statement has a kerygmatic, pastoral character; it should convey certainty of salvation and solace in living and dying.

In his theology of the Word of God, Karl Barth extended the *solus Christus* beyond soteriology to theological epistemology: Christ should be the *sole* source of the Christian faith. The first thesis of the Barmen Declaration likewise mandates this. However, this does not mean that there *is* no other Word of God, but that 'we' (i.e., Christians!) should not *hear* any other Word of God. For those who know that they are included in this 'we' or 'us', Jesus *is* the single, definitive Word of God. However, this conviction cannot simply be elevated to the level of a theological proposition without hermeneutical reflection.

The confession of the uniqueness of the revelation of God and mediation of salvation in Jesus Christ is an expression of the uniqueness in which believers know they are addressed by him. It is an expression of faith that points to the foundation of faith, the representative of God, and through him to the presence of God. As such, the confession is accompanied by the conviction that this foundation of faith is also existentially significant for other human beings. However, such a conviction must not be dogmatically or rationally reified into a universally valid, ahistorical doctrine that is independent of faith and experience. Statements of faith express an awareness of being unconditionally tied to God. However, if they are reflected upon as statements of faith, then it becomes apparent that they cannot be set apart from the person (and cultural and religious background) of the believer. This does not diminish their significance. The *solus Christus* is therefore above all an assertion of faith. As such, it is to be understood less as a propositional and more as a doxological statement.

6.3 An Application: the Qur'an as a Representation of God?

As I conclude the train of thought developed in this volume, I would like to apply these reflections, by way of example, to a question which is of fundamental importance for defining Christianity's theological relationship to Islam. Namely, whether the Qur'an can also be seen as a representation of God's self-communication and thus of Godself. In light of what I have said so far, the answer is positive, but it must be formulated *in potentialis*: the Qur'an *can* be seen in such terms.

There is no theological basis upon which we can draw directly for this statement. However, we can deduce such a theological basis from the basic conviction that God is not distant even from those who do not have a relationship with God through Christ (according to Acts 17:27). This promise of God's closeness is even intensified in the Qur'an (Q. 50:16). According to Q. 6:12, mercy is an essential attribute to which God is committed. The Qur'an mentions God's mercy almost 600 times, and refers to God as the 'All-Merciful' almost 170 times. So, for example, Q. 7:56 understands mercy in terms of God's nearness. This *can* be seen as an expression of God's unconditional and universal salvific will.

But does the Qur'an really speak of the *unconditionality* of God's mercy? Is it not rather a mercy *conditioned* by human obedience or disobedience to the will of God, i.e., a mercy of the *judging* God? This is undoubtedly the message of many verses of the Qur'an (as indeed it is in the Old and even the New Testament!). However, a distinction must be made between the *application* of mercy and its *constitution*. The talk of unconditionality refers to the constitution. As an essential characteristic of God, mercy is eternally prior to and above all human acts of obedience and disobedience. This applies, in precisely the same way, to Christian discourse on the unconditional salvific will of God; it is also the meaning of the Reformation's 'sola gratia' ('by grace alone').

Despite the parallels noted, there are also profound differences between Islam and Christianity, especially in the understanding of God and Jesus Christ. The Qur'anic emphasis on the unity and 'oneness' of God is opposed to the Christian faith's Trinitarian understanding of God and to all talk of Jesus as 'Son of God'. One can certainly ask whether the Quranic criticism is directed against the Christian doctrine of God, Christology, and soteriology in general, or only against era-specific formulations of these beliefs (e.g., Alexandrian theology with its talk of Mary as the 'Mother of God' [*theotokos*] or the teachings of heterodox Christian groups in Muhammad's environment).

Justified though it certainly is, such contextualizing within theological history does not solve matters, since the problem also concerns the biblical traditions themselves, especially the Christology of Paul and the Johannine writings. The Islamic critique of Christology refers not only or even mainly to the teachings of heterodox Christian groups, and not only or not even primarily to the orthodox doctrines of the early church, but also to the ways in which the Pauline and Johannine writings understand Jesus Christ.

I will limit myself to a comparison with Paul and only mention a few points of difference:

- While Paul places Christ and Adam in a contrasting relationship to each other, the Qur'an emphasizes their creaturely equality. According to Q. 3:59, Jesus, like Adam, was created by God from the earth. God said to him 'be' and he was.
- Calling Jesus the 'son of Mary' contradicts Paul's use of the term 'son of God'.
- Although the Qur'anic title used for Jesus, 'Messenger of God', echoes Paul's statements that the Son of God is 'sent', it refers to the message to be delivered by the *human* Jesus: "he has given me the Scripture, and made me a prophet".[4]
- Jesus describing himself as a "servant of God" in Q. 19:30 stands in contrast to the exalted title 'Lord' which Paul uses. According to the Qur'an, only *God* is the Lord whom human beings are to serve.

These points, and the many others which could be added, can be summarized thus: the Qur'an emphasizes the humanity of Jesus while Paul's Christology relates to the exalted Christ.

At the same time, however, the Qur'an also de-historicizes and de-contextualizes the humanity of Jesus. The only mention of his lineage is to Mary and the virgin birth. All other allusions to the historical context of his life are omitted. The miracles he is recorded as performing receive only mentions; they are neither narrated in detail nor situated in time and place as they are in the Gospels. On the one hand, therefore, Jesus' humanity is emphasized, yet on the other he appears strangely unworldly. In addition, exalted titles are ascribed to him. He is not only described as a prophet, servant of God, and messenger of God, but also as Messiah and healer, and indeed as the Word and Spirit of God. He is the "Word of truth" (Q. 19:34) and "sign [of God] for humanity" (Q. 19:21 and elsewhere).[5] Statements such as these are obviously compatible with a representational Christology.

---

4 Q. 19:30 (translation by Talal Itani: https://www.clearquran.com/) (accessed: 02/02/2025).
5 Reynolds, *The Islamic Christ*, 183–98.

In terms of the Christian doctrine of the three offices, one could say that the Qur'an portrays Jesus as fulfilling the 'prophetic office'. In view of his eschatological return, which is implied in Q. 4:159f. and in some hadiths, and which is particularly emphasized in Shiite Islam, one can even speak, to a certain extent, of a 'kingly office' (subordinated to Mohammed!). The 'priestly office', on the other hand, the Qur'an clearly rejects.

The differences between the Islamic and Christian understandings of the person and significance of Jesus cannot and must not be reduced. However, they also do not need to be exaggerated in a polemical spirit as being mutually exclusive opposites. From a Christian perspective, the significance of Jesus Christ in the Qur'an and in Islamic traditions remains underdefined. But underdefined does not mean false.

On the contrary: Islamic criticism contains important caveats. It warns against overstating the Christian understanding of Jesus' person and significance to the point of turning him into an idol. It calls to mind the fundamental Jewish-Christian-Islamic confession of the unity and 'oneness' of God, as reiterated by Jesus himself in Mk. 12:29. This emphasizes the distinction between God and Jesus—a distinction expressed in the twofold difference that I detailed in chapter 4.3. In Christian theology, and even more so in the history of piety (including the practice of prayer), this distinction has often been suppressed and completely denied in bold confessional statements made by Christians who claimed an exceptional strength of their faith.

If Christians assume that the only authentic and definitive revelation of God took place in Jesus Christ, then they must deny even the *possibility* that God's unconditional and universal salvific will is also represented in the Qur'an. If it were assumed that God is not only revealed differently in the Qur'an but also that the author of this revelation is a completely different God (or no God at all), then the Qur'an would be, at best, interesting as a religious document, but would have no theological relevance. However, since monotheistic religions believe that there is only *one* God, this would call into question the divinity of the God to which the Qur'an testifies.

If, on the other hand, one concedes the possibility that the Qur'an can also be a medium of representation of God, then a foundation is laid for critical yet constructive theological debates on the Christian and Muslim understandings of God. This foundation consists of an elementary theological appreciation that also includes respect for difference and the otherness of other forms of faith.

The reason for interreligious openness, regarding the Qur'an and Islam as well as the sources and expressions of other religions, lies in contemplating God's universal and unconditional 'openness' toward creation—or, in theological terms, 'revelation' as self-representation. This contemplation results in an attitude of openness in defining and shaping relationships with people of other faiths. Hand in hand with this attitude is the hope that representations of God and of God's grace might also be discovered in non-Christian forms of religion.

6.4 Closing Remarks

Over the course of outlining my arguments here I have sought to articulate the significance of Jesus Christ in the context of religious plurality and the theological reflections arising from such plurality. The aim has not been to pass a theological judgment on other religions, or on their sources, traditions, teachings, and forms of practice. Rather, my intent has been to show that the Christian faith, and Christology as the center of its thinking, does not necessarily need to lead to *a priori* negative judgments of the centers of identity of other religions; it can instead be linked to a theologically based appreciation of other faiths (which by no means excludes critical judgments of individual phenomena). This does not, and should not, answer the question of how we are to view such other faiths theologically. Such a question must ultimately remain open: it can only be answered from an eschatological perspective. Since we cannot adopt such a perspective, my view is that the representation of God in Jesus Christ makes it imperative to sing the praises of the greatness of God's grace, which sovereignly transcends religious boundaries (and indeed all other boundaries). This song of praise includes the possibility that God could also have represented Godself in a comparable way in the normative centers of other religions. To me, more than such a cautious answer *in potentialis* does not seem responsible considering the limitations of what we know and can confidently conclude. However, if we look back at the history of the relationship between Christianity and other religions, the position I hold poses a clear 're-vision' that also has an impact on the practical shaping of interreligious relations.

Answers *in potentialis* do not satisfy the need for unambiguous clarity. Rather, they contain a critique of this need. The demand for a theology of religions that is as robust as possible and that does not speak *in potentialis* but *in realis* therefore seems to me to be just as misguided as a Christology that does not even attempt to refer to religious diversity.

However, whereever such references are made in the sense of a theologically justified appreciation, the foundation is laid for an approach to interreligious encounters that can search for "manifestations of grace"[6] in other religions with critical openness. Where it finds what it is looking for, the *potentialis* becomes a *realis*. However, this is then no longer a matter of theology, but of mutual experiences of the interreligious encounter—not the subject of *a priori* assertions, but rather of *a posteriori* exploration.

The understanding of truth that Franz Rosenzweig described in *The Star of Redemption* can guide our approach to such interreligious encounters:

> truth must therefore be veri-fied, and just in the way in which it is generally denied: namely by letting the 'whole' truth rest on itself and yet taking the share that we comply with for eternal truth.[7]

---

6 Translated from Tillich, *Protestantische Gestaltung*, 57–61.
7 Rosenzweig, *The Star of Redemption*, 416.

Bibliography

Baillie, Donald M. *God Was in Christ*. Faber & Faber, 1948.
Barth, Karl. *Church Dogmatics*. Translated by G. W. Bromiley and T. F. Torrance. T. & T. Clark, 1957–1988.
Barth, Karl. *Die christliche Lehre nach dem Heidelberger Katechismus: Vorlesung gehalten an der Universität Bonn im Sommersemester 1947*. Evangelischer Verlag, 1948.
Barth, Karl. *Erklärung des Johannesevangeliums (Kapitel 1–8)*. Karl Barth Gesamtausgabe II/4. Theologischer Verlag Zürich, 1976.
Barth, Karl. *Unterricht in der christlichen Religion. Vol. 1: Prolegomena (1924)*. Karl Barth Gesamtausgabe II/17. Theologischer Verlag Zürich, 1985.
Baruch de Spinoza. "73. Letter to Heinrich Oldenburg (1675)." *Sacred Texts*. Accessed 02/02/2025. https://sacred-texts.com/phi/spinoza/corr/corr18.htm.
Becker, Adam H., and Annette Yoshiko Reed, eds. *The Ways that Never Parted: Jews and Christians in Late Antiquity and the Early Middle Ages*, Texts and Studies in Ancient Judaism, 95, 2nd edn. Mohr Siebeck, 2020.
Becker, Jürgen. *Johanneisches Christentum: Seine Geschichte und Theologie im Überblick*. Mohr Siebeck, 2004.
Beintker, Michael. "Creator Spiritus. Zu einem unerledigten Problem der Pneumatologie." *Evangelische Theologie* 46 (1986): 12–26.
"Bericht: Das Filioque aus ökumenischer Sicht". In *Geist Gottes—Geist Christi. Ökumenische Überlegungen zur Filioque-Kontroverse*, ed. Lukas Vischer. Lembeck, 1981.
Berkhof, Hendrikus. *Theologie des Heiligen Geistes*. Neukirchener Verlag, 1968/1988.
Bernhardt, Reinhold. *Ende des Dialogs? Die Begegnung der Religionen und ihre theologische Reflexion*. Theologischer Verlag Zürich, 2006.
Bernhardt, Reinhold. *Inter-Religio: Das Christentum in Beziehung zu anderen Religionen*. Theologischer Verlag Zürich, 2019. DOI: https://doi.org/10.34313/978-3-290-18290-8.
Bernhardt, Reinhold. *Jesus Christus—Repräsentant Gottes. Christologie im Kontext der Religionstheologie*. Theologischer Verlag Zürich, 2021. DOI: https://doi.org/10.34313/978-3-290-18437-7.
Bernhardt, Reinhold. *Klassiker der Religionstheologie im 19. und 20. Jahrhundert: Historische Studien als Impulsgeber für die heutige Reflexion*. Theologischer Verlag Zürich, 2020. DOI: https://doi.org/10.34313/978-3-290-18332-5.
Bernhardt, Reinhold. *Monotheismus und Trinität. Gotteslehre im Kontext der Religionstheologie*. Theologischer Verlag Zürich, 2023. DOI: https://doi.org/10.34313/978-3-290-18526-8.
Bernhardt, Reinhold. "'Da wurden ihre Augen geöffnet' (Lk. 24:31)—Offenbarung als Wahrnehmungsereignis." In *Zwischen Glaube und Wissenschaft: Theologie in Christentum und Islam*, ed. by Esnaf Begic et al., 143–56. Friedrich Pustet, 2015.

Bernhardt, Reinhold. "Offenbarung als Selbstmitteilung Gottes." In *falsafa: Jahrbuch für islamische Religionsphilosophie / Yearbook for Islamic Philosophy of Religion*, Vol. 2: *Vernunft und Offenbarung*, ed. by Milad Karimi, 87–106. Verlag Karl Alber, 2019.

Bernhardt, Reinhold. "Zur theologischen Bedeutung des Judeseins Jesu." In *Christologie zwischen Judentum und Christentum: Jesus, der Jude aus Galiläa, und der christliche Erlöser*, ed. by Christian Danz, Kathy Ehrensperger, and Walter Homolka. Mohr Siebeck, 2020.

Bernhardt, Reinhold. "Monotheism. Christianity. Modern Europe and America." *Encyclopedia of the Bible and Its Reception* (EBR). Online publication, forthcoming.

Bockmuehl, Markus. "Offenbarung. IV. Neues Testament." In *Religion in Geschichte und Gegenwart*, 4th ed., Vol. 6, 470–73. Mohr Siebeck, 2001

Bolz, Norbert. "Interlinearversionen der geoffenbarten Wahrheit." In *Wahrheitsansprüche der Religionen heute*, ed. by Willi Oelmüller. Schöningh, 1986.

Bonhoeffer, Dietrich. *Dietrich Bonhoeffer Works* (= DBWE), 16 vols. Fortress Press, 2013.

Bonhoeffer, Dietrich. *Letters and Papers from Prison: The Enlarged Edition*. Macmillan, 1972.

Bornkamm, Günther. "Mysterion." In *Theologisches Wörterbuch zum Neuen Testament*, Vol. 4: 825–28, W. Kohlhammer. 1942

Bornkamm, Günther. "Das Problem der Toleranz im 16. Jahrhundert." In *Das Jahrhundert der Reformation: Gestalten und Kräfte*, 342–79. Vandenhoeck & Ruprecht, 1961.

Boyarin, Daniel. "The Gospel of Memra: Jewish Binitarianism and the Prologue of John." *Harvard Theological Review* 94 (2001): 243–284.

Bultmann, Rudolf. "Offenbarung, IV. Im NT." In *Religion in Geschichte und Gegenwart*, 2nd ed., Vol. 4: 661–664, Mohr Siebeck, 1930.

Bultmann, Rudolf. *Glaube und Verstehen: Gesammelte Aufsätze*, Vol. 2. Mohr Siebeck, 1993.

Burkhardt, Armin. "Geballte Zeichen. Das Symbol und seine Deutungen." *Semiotik* 18 (1996): 461–482.

Busch, Eberhard. *Barth—ein Porträt in Dialogen: Von Luther bis Benedikt XVI*. Theologischer Verlag Zürich, 2015.

Calvin, John. *Institutes of the Christian Religion*. Ed. by John T. McNeill. Translated by Ford Lewis Battles. Westminster Press, 1960.

Campbell, John McLeod. *The Nature of the Atonement*. Macmillan, 1856, 1959.

Camus, Albert. *The Rebel. An Essay on Man in Revolt* (1951). Translated by Anthony Bower. Vintage Books, 1991.

Congregation for the Doctrine of the Faith. *Declaration: "Dominus Iesus" On the Unicity and Salvific Universality of Jesus Christ and the Church*, §10. Accessed 02/02/2025. www.vatican.va/roman_curia/congregations/cfaith/documents/rc_con_cfaith_doc_20000806_dominus-iesus_en.html.

Congregation for the Doctrine of the Faith. *Notification on the Book "Jesus Symbol of God" by Father Roger Haight s.j.* Accessed 02/02/2025. https://www.vatican.va/roman_curia/congregations/cfaith/documents/rc_con_cfaith_doc_20041213_notification-fr-haight_en.html.

Conzelmann, Hans. *Outline of the Theology of the New Testament.* SCM Press, 1969.

Cornille, Catherine. "Soteriological Agnosticism and the Future of Catholic Theology of Interreligious Dialogue." In *The Past, Present, and Future of Theologies of Interreligious Dialogue*, ed. by Terrence Merrigan and John Friday, 201–215. Oxford University Press, 2017.

Crisp, Oliver D. "John Owen on Spirit Christology." *Journal of Reformed Theology* 5 (2011): 5–25.

Crossan, John Dominic. *The Dark Interval: Towards a Theology of Story.* Polebridge Press, 1975.

Cyprian of Carthage. *Über die Einheit der katholischen Kirche (On the Unity of the Catholic Church).* Bibliothek der Kirchenväter (= BKV) 34/1. Kösel & Pustet, 1918.

Dalferth, Ingolf. "Der Mythos vom inkarnierten Gott und das Thema der Theologie." *Zeitschrift für Theologie und Kirche* 84 (1987): 320–344.

Del Colle, Ralph. *Christ and the Spirit: Spirit-Christology in Trinitarian Perspective.* Oxford University Press, 1994.

Denzinger, Heinrich, and Peter Hünermann. *Enchiridion Symbolorum: A Compendium of Creeds, Definitions and Declarations of the Catholic Church* (= DH). Ignatius Press, 2012.

Deuser, Hermann. *Gott: Geist und Natur. Theologische Konsequenzen aus Charles S. Peirce' Religionsphilosophie.* De Gruyter, 1993.

Deuser, Hermann. *Gottesinstinkt. Semiotische Religionstheorie und Pragmatismus.* Mohr Siebeck, 2004.

Deuser, Hermann. *Kleine Einführung in die Systematische Theologie.* Reclam, 1999.

Dirscherl, Erwin. "Die Herausforderung für eine Christologie im Angesicht von Jesu Judentum. Das theozentrische Beten und Fragen Jesu als bleibende Herausforderung des christlichen Glaubens an den einen Gott." In *Christologie zwischen Judentum und Christentum. Jesus, der Jude aus Galiläa, und der christliche Erlöser*, ed. by Christian Danz, Kathy Ehrensperger, and Walter Homolka, 209–227. Mohr Siebeck, 2020.

Dunn, James D. G., ed. *Jews and Christians. The Parting of the Ways A. D. 70 to 135. The Second Durham-Tübingen Research Symposium on Earliest Christianity and Judaism (Durham, September 1989).* Mohr Siebeck, 1992.

Dunn, James D. G. "Let John be John." In *Das Evangelium und die Evangelien*, ed. by Peter Stuhlmacher, 309–339. Mohr Siebeck, 1983.

Dunn, James D. G. *Christology in the Making: A New Testament Inquiry into the Origins of the Doctrine of the Incarnation.* Wm.B. Eerdmans, 1980, 2003.

Dunn, James D. G. *The Parting of the Ways: Between Christianity and Judaism and Their Significance for the Character of Christianity*. SCM Press, 1991, 2006.
Dunn, James D. G. *The Theology of Paul the Apostle*. Wm.B. Eerdmans, 1998.
Dupuis, Jacques. "'Die Wahrheit wird euch frei machen'. Die Theologie des religiösen Pluralismus—noch einmal betrachtet." *SaThZ* 10 (2006): 12–64.
Dupuis, Jacques. *Christianity and the Religions: From Confrontation to Dialogue*. Orbis, 2002.
Dupuis, Jacques. *Toward a Christian Theology of Religious Pluralism*. Orbis, 1997.
Ebert IV, Daniel J. *Wisdom Christology: How Jesus Becomes God's Wisdom for Us*. P & R Publishing, 2011.
Eusebius of Caesarea. *Praeparatio Evangelica (Preparation for the Gospel)*. Translated by E. H. Gifford. Clarendon Press, 1903.
Evangelische Kirche in Deutschland (Protestant Church in Germany). *Christlicher Glaube und religiöse Vielfalt in evangelischer Perspektive*. Gütersloher Verlagshaus, 2015.
Evangelische Kirche in Deutschland. *Declaration of the 12th Synod of the Evangelical Church in Germany in its 3rd Session*. Hannover, 2015. Accessed 02/02/2025. https://www.ekd.de/en/Declaration-of-the-12th-Synod-of-the-Evangelical-Church-in-Germany-in-its-3rd-Session-815.htm.
Feckes, Carl. *Das Mysterium der heiligen Kirche. Dogmatische Untersuchungen zum Wesen der Kirche*. Ferdinand Schöningh, 1934, 1951.
Feldtkeller, Andreas. "Religionswissenschaftliche Perspektiven zur Trinitätslehre." In *Trinität*, ed. by Volker Henning Drecoll, 221–243. Mohr Siebeck, 2011.
Fischer, Johannes. "Vom Geheimnis der Stellvertretung." *EK* 21 (1988): 165–167.
Fischer, Johannes. *Glaube als Erkenntnis. Zum Wahrnehmungscharakter des christlichen Glaubens*. Kaiser, 1989.
Frankemölle, Hubert, ed. *Juden und Christen im Gespräch über 'Dabru emet—Redet Wahrheit'*. Bonifatius, 2005.
Frankemölle, Hubert. *Das jüdische Neue Testament und der christliche Glaube: Grundlagenwissen für den jüdisch-christlichen Dialog*. W. Kohlhammer, 2009.
Ganoczy, Alexandre. "Trinität—vom Heiligen Geiste reflektiert. Eine Skizze." In *Der eine Gott in vielen Kulturen. Inkulturation und christliche Gottesvorstellung*, ed. by Konrad Hilpert and Karl-Heinz Ohlig, 90–98. Benziger, 1993.
Gerhard, Johann. *Loci theologici*. 9 vols. (1610–1622). Schlawitz, 1863–85.
Gestrich, Christof. "Unterscheidung zwischen göttlicher und menschlicher Stellvertretung. Zur Präzisierung des Verständnisses des 'wunderbaren Tauschs' und der Sündenvergebung." *Una Sancta* 46 (1991): 229–244.
Gestrich, Christof. *Die Wiederkehr des Glanzes in der Welt. Die christliche Lehre von der Sünde und ihrer Vergebung in gegenwärtiger Verantwortung*. Mohr Siebeck, 1996.

Ginzburg, Carlo. "Repräsentation—das Wort, die Vorstellung, der Gegenstand." *Freibeuter* 53 (1992): 2–23.
Graham, Jeannine Michele. *Representation and Substitution in the Atonement Theologies of Dorothee Sölle, John Macquarrie, and Karl Barth*. Peter Lang, 2005.
Grillmeier, Alois. *Jesus der Christus im Glauben der Kirche*. Vol. 1. Herder, 1979.
Haight, Roger. "The Case for Spirit Christology." *Theological Studies* 53 (1992): 257–287.
Haight, Roger. *Dynamics of Theology*. Orbis, 1990, 2001.
Haight, Roger. *Jesus Symbol of God*. Orbis, 1999, 2005.
Haight, Roger. *The Future of Christology*. A&C Black, 2005.
Hartenstein, Karl. "Die Kirche und die Religionen." emz 1 (1940): 6–21.
Heidelberg Catechism. Reformed Church in the United States. Accessed 02/02/2025. https://rcus.org/confessions-2/.
Hempelmann, Reinhard. *Sakrament als Ort der Vermittlung des Heils: Sakramententheologie im evangelisch-katholischen Dialog*. Vandenhoeck & Ruprecht, 1992.
Herder, Johann Gottfried. *Ideen zur Philosophie der Geschichte der Menschheit*. Wissenschaftliche Buchgesellschaft, 2002.
Herzgsell, Johannes. *Das Christentum im Konzert der Weltreligionen: Ein Beitrag zum interreligiösen Vergleich und Dialog*. Friedrich Pustet, 2011.
Hick, John H. "An Inspiration Christology for a Religiously Plural World." In *Encountering Jesus: A Debate on Christology*, ed. by Stephen T. Davis, 5–22. Westminster John Knox, 1988.
Hick, John H. "Christology at the Crossroads." In *Prospects for Theology*, ed. by Francis George Healey, 137–66. James Nisbet, 1966.
Hick, John H. *God and the Universe of Faiths*. Macmillan, 1973, 1975.
Hick, John H. *The Metaphor of God Incarnate: Christology in a Pluralistic Age*. Westminster John Knox, 1993, 2006.
Hick, John H. *The Myth of God Incarnate*. scm Press, 1977.
Hoff, Gregor Maria. "Wer ist Christus? Das Symbol von Chalkedon als Grammatik des Glaubens." In *Stichproben: Theologische Inversionen. Salzburger Aufsätze*, ed. by Gregor Maria Hoff, 187–200. Tyrolia, 2010.
Hoff, Gregor Maria. *Aporetische Theologie: Skizze eines Stils fundamentaler Theologie*. Schöningh, 1997.
Hofmann, Hasso. *Repräsentation: Studien zur Wort- und Begriffsgeschichte von der Antike bis ins 19. Jahrhundert*. Duncker und Humblot, 1974.
Hölscher, Andreas, and Rainer Kampling, eds. *Die Tochter Gottes ist die Weisheit: Bibelauslegungen durch Frauen*. lit, 2003.
Homolka, Walter, and Magnus Striet. *Christologie auf dem Prüfstand: Jesus der Jude—Christus der Erlöser*. Herder, 2019.
Homolka, Walter. *Der Jude Jesus—Eine Heimholung*. Herder, 2020.

Homolka, Walter. *Jesus von Nazareth: Im Spiegel jüdischer Forschung.* Hentrich & Hentrich, 2017.

Horn, Friedrich Wilhelm. *Das Angeld des Geistes: Studien zur paulinischen Pneumatologie.* Vandenhoeck & Ruprecht, 1992.

Hurtado, Larry W. *One God, One Lord: Early Christian Devotion and Ancient Jewish Monotheism.* Fortress Press, 1988, 1998.

Huxley, Aldous. "Knowledge and Understanding, Part 1 (1956)." In *Complete Essays: 1939–1956*, ed. by Robert S. Baker and James Sexton. Ivan R. Dee, 2000. Accessed 02/02/2025. https://vedanta.org/2002/monthly-readings/knowledge-and-understanding-part-1/.

International Theological Commission. *Selected Questions on Christology* (1979). Accessed 02/02/2025. www.vatican.va/roman_curia/congregations/cfaith/cti_documents/rc_cti_1979_cristologia_en.html.

Irenaeus of Lyon. *Against Heresies.* Christian Classics Ethereal Library. Calvin University. Accessed 02/02/2025. https://ccel.org/ccel/schaff/anf01.html.

Janowski, Bernd. "'Hingabe' oder 'Opfer'? Zur gegenwärtigen Kontroverse um die Deutung des Todes Jesu." In *Mincha (FS R. Rendtorff)*, ed. by Erhard Blum, 93–119. Neukirchener Verlag, 2000.

Jaspers, Karl. *Der philosophische Glaube angesichts der Offenbarung.* 3rd ed. Ex Libris, 1984.

Jervell, Jacob. "Bild Gottes I. Biblische, frühjüdische und gnostische Auffassungen." *TRE* 6: 491–498. De Gruyter, 1980.

Joest, Wilfried. *Dogmatik I.* Vandenhoeck & Ruprecht, 1987.

Joest, Wilfried. *Ontologie der Person bei Luther.* Vandenhoeck & Ruprecht, 1967.

Johnson, Elizabeth A. "Die Weisheit ward Fleisch und wohnte unter uns. Christologie aus feministischer Perspektive." *EvTh* 66 (2006): 142–155.

Johnson, Elizabeth A. *Ich bin, die ich bin. Wenn Frauen Gott sagen.* Patmos, 1994.

Jüngel, Eberhard. "Das Sakrament—was ist das?" *EvTh* 26, no. 6 (1966): 32–336.

Jüngel, Eberhard. "Die Kirche als Sakrament?" *ZThK* 80 (1993): 432–457.

Jüngel, Eberhard. "Hoffen, Handeln—und Leiden." In *Beziehungsreich: Perspektiven des Glaubens*, ed. by Eberhard Jüngel, 13–40. Radius-Verlag, 2002.

Jüngel, Eberhard. *God as the Mystery of the World: On the Foundation of the Theology of the Crucified One in the Dispute between Theism and Atheism.* Bloomsbury, 2014.

Justin Martyr. *The Dialogue with Trypho.* Translated by A. Lukyn Williams. The Macmillan Co., 1930.

Justin Martyr. *The First & Second Apology of Justin. The Fathers of the Church: Saint Justin Martyr.* Translated by Thomas B. Falls. The Catholic University of America Press, 2008.

Kamlah, Wilhelm. *Der Mensch in der Profanität: Versuch einer Kritik der profanen durch vernehmende Vernunft.* W. Kohlhammer, 1949.

Karrer, Martin. *Jesus Christus im Neuen Testament*. Vandenhoeck & Ruprecht, 1998.
Keener, Craig S. *The Gospel of John: A Commentary*. Vol. 1. Hendrickson Publishers, 2003.
Keller, Catherine. *On the Mystery: Discerning Divinity in Process*. Fortress Press, 2008.
Kellerhals, Emanuel. *Der Islam: Seine Geschichte, seine Lehre, sein Wesen*. Verlag der Basler Missionsbuchhandlung, 1945.
Khodre, Georges. "An Orthodox Perspective of Inter-Religious Dialogue." *Current Dialogue* 19 (1991): 25–31.
Klappert, Bertold, ed. *Diskussion um Kreuz und Auferstehung*. Aussaat, 1967.
Knitter, Paul F. *Jesus and the Other Names: Christian Mission and Global Responsibility*. Orbis, 1996.
Knitter, Paul F. *One Earth Many Religions: Multifaith Dialogue and Global Responsibility*. Orbis, 1995.
Korsch, Dietrich. *Dialektische Theologie nach Karl Barth*. Mohr Siebeck, 1996.
Kraus, Hans-Joachim. "Eine Christologie des Heiligen Geistes." In *Jesusbekenntnis und Christusnachfolge*, ed. by Bertold Klappert et al., 37–46. Kaiser, 1992.
Kraus, Hans-Joachim. *Systematische Theologie im Kontext biblischer Geschichte und Eschatologie*. Neukirchener Verlag, 1983.
Küng, Hans. *Credo. Das Apostolische Glaubensbekenntnis—Zeitgenossen erklärt*. Piper, 1992, 2018.
Kuschel, Karl-Josef. "Christologie und interreligiöser Dialog. Die Einzigartigkeit Christi im Gespräch mit den Weltreligionen." *StZ* 209 (1991): 387–402. Reprinted in *Christentum und nichtchristliche Religionen*, ed. by Karl-Josef Kuschel, 135–54. Wissenschaftliche Buchgesellschaft, 1994.
Lampe, Geoffrey W. H. "The Holy Spirit and the Person of Christ." In *Christ, Faith and History: Cambridge Studies in Christology*, ed. by Stephen W. Sykes and John P. Clayton, 111–130. Cambridge University Press, 1972.
Lampe, Geoffrey W. H. *God as Spirit*. Clarendon, 1977.
Lévinas, Emmanuel. "Die Spur des Anderen." In *Die Spur des Anderen: Untersuchungen zur Phänomenologie und Sozialphilosophie*, ed. by Emmanuel Lévinas, 209–35. Karl Alber, 2007.
Lévinas, Emmanuel. "Gott und die Philosophie." In *Gott nennen: Phänomenologische Zugänge*, ed. by Bernhard Casper, 81–123. Karl Alber, 1981.
Liefeld, Walter L. "Salvation." In *The International Standard Bible Encyclopedia*, Vol. 4, 287–95. Wm.B. Eerdmans, 1988.
Link, Christian. "Das menschliche Gesicht der Offenbarung. Bemerkungen zum Religionsverständnis Karl Barths." *KuD* 26 (1980): 277–302.
Link, Christian. "Das sogenannte Extra-Calvinisticum. Die Entscheidung der Christologie Calvins und ihre theologische Bedeutung." *EvTh* 47 (1987): 97–119. Reprinted in *Prädestination und Erwählung*, 145–70. Neukirchener Verlag, 2009.

Link, Christian. *Schöpfung*. Vol. 1. Gütersloher Verlagshaus, 1991.
Loeb Classical Library (= LCL). Harvard University Press. Accessed 02/02/2025. https://www.loebclassics.com/.
Lüpsen, Focko, ed. *Neu Delhi Dokumente. Berichte und Reden auf der Weltkirchenkonferenz in Neu Delhi 1961*. Luther-Verlag, 1962.
Luther, Martin. "Christmas Sermon on Isaiah 9." In *Festival Sermons of Martin Luther: The Church Postils*. Translated by Joel R. Baseley, 62–101. Mark V Publications, 2005.
Luther, Martin. *D. Martin Luthers Werke. Kritische Gesamtausgabe*. 120 vols. Weimarer Ausgabe (= WA), 1883–2009. Hermann Böhlau, 2000–2007.
Luther, Martin. *Luther's Works* (= LW). 75 vols. Concordia Publishing House, 1955ff.
Luther, Martin. *The Large Catechism by Dr. Martin Luther*. Translated by F. Bente and W. H. T. Dau. In *Triglot Concordia: The Symbolical Books of the Ev. Lutheran Church*, 565–773. Concordia Publishing House, 1921. Accessed 02/02/2025. https://sacred-texts.com/chr/luther/largecat.htm.
MacKinnon, Donald. "The Relation of the Doctrines of the Incarnation and the Trinity." In *Themes in Theology, The Three-Fold Cord: Essays in Philosophy, Politics and Theology*, ed. by Donald MacKinnon, 145–67. T&T Clark, 1987.
Macquarrie, John. "Jesus Christus, VII. Dogmatic." *TRE* 17: 43–64. De Gruyter 1988.
Macquarrie, John. *Principles of Christian Theology*. SCM Press, 1977.
Marxsen, Willi. *Die Auferstehung als historisches und als theologisches Problem*. Gütersloher Verlagshaus, 1966.
Marxsen, Willi. *Die Sache Jesu geht weiter*. Gütersloher Verlagshaus, 1976.
Masuzawa, Tomoko. *The Invention of World Religions: Or, How European Universalism was Preserved in the Language of Pluralism*. University of Chicago Press, 2005.
Melanchthon, Philipp. *Loci communes 1521*. Translated by Charles Leander Hill. Meador, 1944.
Merian, Katharina. *Repräsentation: Ein neues christologisches Modell im Kontext der Religionen*. Theologischer Verlag Zürich, 2025.
Miletto, Gianfranco. "Philo of Alexandria." In *WiBiLex* Accessed 02/02/2025. https://www.bibelwissenschaft.de/ressourcen/wibilex/altes-testament/philo-von-alexandrien.
Moltmann, Jürgen. *The Trinity and the Kingdom: The Doctrine of God*. SCM Press, 1981.
Moltmann, Jürgen. *The Way of Jesus Christ: Christology in Messianic Dimensions*. Fortress Press, 1993.
National Jewish Scholars Project. *Dabru Emet: A Jewish Statement on Christians and Christianity*, 2000. Accessed 02/02/2025. https://www.ccjr.us/dialogika-resources/documents-and-statements/jewish/dabru-emet.
Naumann, Friedrich. *Briefe über Religion. Mit Nachwort „Nach 13 Jahren"*. De Gruyter, 1916.

Naumann, Thomas. *Ismael. Studien zu einem biblischen Konzept der Selbstwahrnehmung Israels im Kreis der Völker aus der Nachkommenschaft Abrahams*. Vandenhoeck & Ruprecht, 2018.

Nicholas of Cusa. "De dato Patris luminum / On the Gift of the Father of Lights" (1446). In *Nicholas of Cusa's Metaphysics of Contraction*, translated by Jasper Hopkins, 372–86. J. Banning, 1983.

Nöth, Winfried. *Handbuch der Semiotik*. J. B. Metzler, 2000.

O'Keeffe, Michael E. "The Spirit Christology of Piet Schoonenberg." In *Christology—Memory, Inquiry, Practice* (*The Annual Publication of the College Theology Society* 48), ed. by Anne M. Clifford and Anthony J. Godzieba, 116–40. Orbis, 2003.

Oberman, Heiko. "Die 'Extra'-Dimension in der Theologie Calvins" (1966). In *Die Reformation. Von Wittenberg nach Genf*, ed. by Heiko Oberman, 253–82. Vandenhoeck & Ruprecht, 1986.

Ogden, Schubert M. *Christ without Myth: A Study Based on the Theology of Rudolf Bultmann*. Harper & Brothers, 1961.

Ogden, Schubert M. *Is There Only One True Religion or Are There Many?* Southern Methodist University Press, 1992.

Ogden, Schubert M. *On Theology*. Harper & Row, 1986.

Ogden, Schubert M. *The Notebooks of Schubert M. Ogden*. Accessed 02/02/2025. https://uknow.drew.edu/confluence/display/ogden/.

Ogden, Schubert M. *The Reality of God and Other Essays*. Harper & Row, 1966.

Ogden, Schubert M. *The Understanding of Christian Faith*. Cascade, 2010.

Ogden, Schubert M. "Problems in the Case for a Pluralistic Theology of Religions." *Journal of Religion* 68 (1988): 493–507.

Ogden, Schubert M. "The Point of Christology." *Journal of Religion* 55 (1975): 375–95.

Oxford Latin Dictionary. Oxford University Press, 2012.

Panikkar, Raimon. *The Unknown Christ of Hinduism: Towards an Ecumenical Christophany*. Orbis, 1981.

Panikkar, Raimon. *Trinität: Über das Zentrum menschlicher Erfahrung*. Kösel, 1993.

Pannenberg, Wolfhart. *Grundzüge der Christologie*. Gütersloher Verlagshaus, 1982.

Pannenberg, Wolfhart. *Problemgeschichte der neueren evangelischen Theologie in Deutschland: Von Schleiermacher bis zu Barth und Tillich*. Vandenhoeck & Ruprecht, 1997.

Pannenberg, Wolfhart. *Systematic Theology*. Vols. 2–3. T&T Clark, 2004.

Patrologia Graeca (= PG). 161 vols. J. P. Migne's Imprimerie Catholique, 1857–1866.

Patrologia Latina (= PL). 221 vols. J. P. Migne's Imprimerie Catholique, 1841–1855.

Peirce, Charles S. *Collected Papers*, ed. by Charles Hartshorne and Paul Weiss. Vol. 1. Harvard University Press, 1931.

Peirce, Charles S. *Philosophical Writings of Peirce*. Dover, 1955.

Pesch, Otto Hermann. *Katholische Dogmatik. Aus Ökumenischer Erfahrung.* Vol. 1: *Die Geschichte der Menschen mit Gott.* Sub-volume 1/1: *Wort Gottes und Theologie. Christologie.* Matthias Grünewald, 2008.

Pesch, Otto Hermann. *Thomas von Aquin: Grenze und Größe mittelalterlicher Theologie. Eine Einführung.* Matthias Grünewald, 1988.

Petrus Lombardus. *Sententiae in Patrologia latina* vol. 192. Jacques Paul Migne. Ateliers Catholiques, 1855. English Translation: Peter Lombard. The Sentences, Books 1–4. Translated by Giulio Silano. Pontifical Institute of Mediaeval Studies, 2007–2010.

Petuchowski, Jakob J., and Clemens Thoma. *Lexikon der jüdisch-christlichen Begegnung: Hintergründe, Klärungen, Perspektiven.* Herder, 1997.

Pinnock, Clark H. *Flame of Love: A Theology of the Holy Spirit.* InterVarsity Press, 2016.

Plotinus. *The Enneads*, ed. by Lloyd P. Gerson et al. Cambridge University Press, 2018.

Pontifical Council for Promoting Christian Unity / Commission for Religious Relations with the Jews. "The Gifts and the Calling of God are Irrevocable" (Rom. 11:29): A Reflection on Theological Questions Pertaining to Catholic-Jewish Relations on the Occasion of the 50th Anniversary of *Nostra Aetate*. Vatican, 2015.

Pope John Paul II. *Redemptoris Missio: On the Permanent Validity of the Church's Missionary Mandate*, December 7, 1990. Accessed 02/02/2025. https://www.vatican.va/content/john-paul-ii/en/encyclicals/documents/hf_jp-ii_enc_07121990_redemptoris-missio.html.

Pratzner, Ferdinand. *Messe und Kreuzesopfer: Die Krise der sakramentalen Idee bei Luther und in der mittelalterlichen Scholastik.* Herder, 1970.

Pröpper, Thomas. *Erlösungsglaube und Freiheitsgeschichte: Eine Skizze zur Soteriologie.* Kösel, 1991.

Pseudo-Dionysius the Areopagite. *De coelesti hierarchia / De ecclesiastica hierarchia / De mystica theologia*, ed. by Günter Heil and Adolf Martin Ritter. De Gruyter, 1991.

Rahner, Karl. *Foundations of Christian Faith: An Introduction to the Idea of Christianity.* Translated by William V. Dych. Crossroad, 1987.

Rahner, Karl. *Kirche und Sakramente.* 2nd ed. Herder, 1960.

Rahner, Karl. *Sämtliche Werke.* 32 vols., ed. by Karl Kardinal Lehmann et al. Herder, 1995–2018.

Rahner, Karl. *Schriften zur Theologie.* 16 vols. Benzinger, 1954–84.

Rahner, Karl. *Was ist ein Sakrament? Vorstöße zur Verständigung.* Herder, 1971.

Ratzinger, Joseph / Pope Benedict XVI. *Truth and Tolerance: Christian Belief and World Religions.* Ignatius Press, 2004.

Reynolds, Gabriel Said. "The Islamic Christ." In *The Oxford Handbook of Christology*, ed. by Francesca Aran Murphy, 183–98. Oxford University Press, 2015.

Robinson, James M. *Jesus: According to the Earliest Witness.* Fortress Press, 2007.

Robinson, John A. T. *The Human Face of God.* SCM Press, 1974.

Rosenzweig, Franz. *Der Mensch und sein Werk. Gesammelte Schriften 1: Briefe und Tagebücher*. Vol. 1. Martinus Nijhoff, 1979.

Rosenzweig, Franz. *The Star of Redemption*. Translated by Barbara E. Galli. University of Wisconsin Press, 2005.

Ryle, Gilbert. *The Concept of Mind*. Penguin, 1949.

Schaede, Stephan. "Jes 53, 2 Kor 5 und die Aufgabe systematischer Theologie, von Stellvertretung zu reden." In *Stellvertretung: Theologische, philosophische, und kulturelle Aspekte*, ed. by J. Christine Janowski et al., 125–48. Neukirchener Verlag, 2006.

Schaede, Stephan. *Stellvertretung: Begriffsgeschichtliche Studien zur Soteriologie*. Mohr Siebeck, 2004.

Schäfer, Peter. *Die Geburt des Judentums aus dem Geist des Christentums: Fünf Vorlesungen zur Entstehung des rabbinischen Judentums*. Mohr Siebeck, 2010.

Schäfer, Peter. *Zwei Götter im Himmel: Gottesvorstellungen in der jüdischen Antike*. C. H. Beck, 2017.

Scheerer, Eckart, et al. "Repräsentation." *Historisches Wörterbuch der Philosophie* 8 (n.d.): 790–853. Schwabe Verlag, 1992. Accessed 02/02/2025. https://doi.org/10.24894/HWPh.5675.

Scheffczyk, Leo. "Die Kirche—das Ganzsakrament Jesu Christi." In *Christusbegegnung in den Sakramenten*, ed. by Hubert Luthe, 63–120. Butzon und Bercker, 1982.

Scheffczyk, Leo. "Jesus Christus—Ursakrament der Erlösung." In *Christusbegegnung in den Sakramenten*, ed. by Hubert Luthe, 9–61. Butzon und Bercker, 1982.

Schillebeeckx, Edward. *Christ the Sacrament of the Encounter with God*. Sheed and Ward, 1963.

Schillebeeckx, Edward. *Jesus. Die Geschichte von einem Lebenden*. Herder, 1975, 1992.

Schmidt-Leukel, Perry. "Buddha and Christ as Mediators of the Transcendent: A Christian Perspective." In *Buddhism and Christianity in Dialogue: The Gerald Weisfeld Lectures 2004*, ed. by Perry Schmidt-Leukel, 151–75. SCM Press, 2005.

Schmidt-Leukel, Perry. "Buddha und Christus als Inkarnationen." In *Gottesdenken in interreligiöser Perspektive*, ed. by Bernhard Nitsche, 202–19. Otto Lembeck, 2005.

Schmidt-Leukel, Perry. *Gott ohne Grenzen: Eine christliche und pluralistische Theologie der Religionen*. Gütersloher Verlagshaus, 2005.

Schmidt-Leukel, Perry. *Grundkurs Fundamentaltheologie: Eine Einführung in die Grundfragen des christlichen Glaubens*. Don Bosco, 1999.

Schmidt-Leukel, Perry. *Theologie der Religionen: Probleme, Optionen, Argumente*. Ars Una, 1997.

Schoonenberg, Piet. *Der Geist, das Wort und der Sohn: Eine Geistchristologie*. Friedrich Pustet, 1992.

Schöttler, Heinz-Günther. "Mose und Jesus—zwei unterschiedliche soteriologische 'Karrieren'." In *Christologie zwischen Judentum und Christentum: Jesus, der Jude aus*

Galiläa, und der christliche Erlöser, ed. by Christian Danz, Kathy Ehrensperger, and Walter Homolka, 377–398, Mohr Siebeck, 2020.

Schrage, Wolfgang. "Theologie und Christologie bei Paulus und Jesus auf dem Hintergrund der modernen Gottesfrage." *Evangelische Theologie* 36 (1976): 121–154.

Schüssler Fiorenza, Elisabeth. *Jesus—Miriam's Child, Sophia's Prophet: Critical Issues in Feminist Christology*. Continuum, 1994.

Schweizer, Eduard. *Jesus, das Gleichnis Gottes: Was wissen wir wirklich vom Leben Jesu?* Vandenhoeck & Ruprecht, 1995.

Scott, Martin. *Sophia and the Johannine Jesus*. A&C Black, 1992.

Semmelroth, Otto. *Die Kirche als Ursakrament*. Knecht, 1955.

Sherry, Patrick. "Modes of Representation and Likeness of God." In *Christ, Ethics and Tragedy*, ed. by Kenneth Surin, 34–48. Cambridge University Press, 1989.

Siecienski, Anthony Edward. *The Filioque: History of a Doctrinal Controversy*. Oxford University Press, 2010.

Sölle, Dorothee. *Atheistisch an Gott glauben*. DTV, 1994.

Sölle, Dorothee. *Christ the Representative: An Essay in Theology after the "Death of God."* Fortress Press, 1967.

Spence, Alan. *Incarnation and Inspiration: John Owen and the Coherence of Christology*. T&T Clark, 2007.

Stockmeier, Peter. "'Offenbarung' in der frühen Kirche." In *Handbuch der Dogmengeschichte* I/1a (*Offenbarung: Von der Schrift bis zum Ausgang der Scholastik*), 27–87. Herder, 1971.

Suggs, M. Jack. *Wisdom, Christology, and Law in Matthew's Gospel*. Harvard University Press, 1970.

Sumner, Darren O. *Karl Barth and the Incarnation: Christology and the Humility of God*. Bloomsbury, 2014.

Tertillian. *Adv. Marcionem*. Ante-Nicene Christian Library, ed. Alexander Roberts and James Donaldson, Vol. VIII: Tertullianus against Marcion. T&T Clark, 1868.

Tertullian. *Apology*. De Spectaculis. Minucius Felix: Octavius. Translated by T. R. Glover, Gerald H. Rendall. LCL 250. Harvard University Press, 1931.

The Holy See. *Ad Gentes: On the Mission Activity of the Church*. Vatican, 1965. Accessed 02/02/2025 https://www.vatican.va/archive/hist_councils/ii_vatican_council/documents/vat-ii_decree_19651207_ad-gentes_en.html.

The Holy See. *Dogmatic Constitution on the Church: Lumen Gentium*. Vatican, 1964. Accessed 02/02/2025 https://www.vatican.va/archive/hist_councils/ii_vatican_council/documents/vat-ii_const_19641121_lumen-gentium_en.html.

Theobald, Michael. *Die Fleischwerdung des Logos: Studien zum Verhältnis des Johannesprologs, zum Corpus des Evangeliums und zu 1. Joh*. Aschendorff, 1988.

Theobald, Michael. *Studien zum Corpus Iohanneum*. Mohr Siebeck, 2010.

Thomas Aquinas. *Summa Theologica* (= **STh**), 61 vols. Eyre & Spottiswoode, 1964–80.

Tillich, Paul. "A Reinterpretation of the Doctrine of the Incarnation." *Church Quarterly Review* 147 (1949): 133–148. Reprinted in *Paul Tillich Main Works / Hauptwerke*, vol. 6, ed. By Gert Hummel, 305–318. De Gruyter, Evangelisches Verlagswerk, 1992.

Tillich, Paul. "Offenbarung v. A. Religionsphilosophisch". RGG 2nd ed. Vol. 4: 664–669, J.C.B. Mohr (Paul Siebeck), 1930.

Tillich, Paul. "The Religious Symbol". *Daedalus* 87, no. 3 (1958): 3–21.

Tillich, Paul. "The Significance of the History of Religions for the Systematic Theologian" (1965). In *The Future of Religions*, ed. Jerald C. Brauer, 80–94. Harper & Row, 1966. Reprinted in: Main Works / Hauptwerke. Vol. 6. ed. Gert Hummel, 431–446. De Gruyter 1992, 2020.

Tillich, Paul. *Christianity and the Encounter of the World Religions*. Columbia University Press, 1964.

Tillich, Paul. *Die Überwindung des Religionsbegriffs in der Religionsphilosophie* (1922). (Gesammelte Werke. Vol. 1). Evangelisches Verlagswerk, 1959.

Tillich, Paul. *Protestantische Gestaltung* (1929) (Gesammelte Werke. Vol. 7). Evangelisches Verlagswerk, 1962.

Tillich, Paul. *Rechtfertigung und Neues Sein*, ed. Christian Danz. Evangelische Verlagsanstalt, 2018.

Tillich, Paul. *Systematic Theology*. 3 vols. University of Chicago Press, 1951, 1957, 1963.

Tillich, Paul. *Wesen und Wandel des Glaubens* (Gesammelte Werke, Vol. 8). Evangelisches Verlagswerk, 1970.

Veenhof, Jan. "Pneumachristologie." *Theologische Zeitschrift* 59 (2003): 312–334.

Vernant, Jean-Pierre. *Mythe et pensée chez les Grecs. Études de psychologie historique*. La Découverte, 1966.

Vetter, Martin. *Zeichen deuten auf Gott: Der zeichentheoretische Beitrag von Charles S. Peirce zur Theologie der Sakramente*. Elwert, 1999.

Vischer, Lukas, ed. *Geist Gottes—Geist Christi: Ökumenische Überlegungen zur Filioque-Kontroverse*. Lembeck, 1981.

Vollenweider, Samuel. "Christus als Weisheit. Gedanken zu einer bedeutsamen Weichenstellung in der frühchristlichen Theologiegeschichte". In *Horizonte neutestamentlicher Christologie*, ed. Samuel Vollenweider. Mohr Siebeck, 2002: 29–52.

von Rad, Gerhard. *Old Testament Theology*. Vol. 2: The Theology of Israel's Prophetic Traditions, Westminster John Knox Press, 2001.

Wengert, Timothy J. *The Augsburg Confession: Renewing Lutheran Faith and Practice*. Fortress Press, 2020.

Wengst, Klaus. *Jesus zwischen Juden und Christen: Re-Visionen im Verhältnis der Kirche zu Israel*. Kohlhammer, 2004.

Werbick, Jürgen. *Vom entscheidend und unterscheidend Christlichen*. Patmos, 1992.

Wiedenhofer, Siegfried. "Offenbarung". In *Neues Handbuch theologischer Grundbegriffe*, ed. Peter Eicher. Vol. 3., 283–301. Kösel, 2005.

Wiles, Maurice. *Remaking of Christian Doctrine. The Hulsean Lectures 1973*. SCM Press, 1974.

Willis, E. David. *Calvin's Catholic Christology. The Function of the so-called Extra Calvinisticum in Calvin's Theology*. E. J. Brill, 1966.

World Council of Churches (WCC). *The San Antonio Report: Your Will Be Done Mission in Christ's Church*, ed. F. R. Wilson. WCC Publications, 1990.

Yong, Amos. *Discerning the Spirit[s]. A Pentecostal-Charismatic Contribution to Christian Theology of Religions*. Wipf and Stock, 2019.

Yong, Amos. *The Spirit Poured Out on All Flesh. Pentecostalism and the Possibility of Global Theology*. Baker Academic, 2005.

Zwingli, Ulrich. *Ulrich Zwingli Werke (Collected Works)*. VI/5 = *Corpus Reformatorum* (= CR) 93/4. Theologischer Verlag Zürich, 1991.

Index of Names

Abelard, Peter   172*n*207
Anselm of Canterbury   3, 49, 81, 84, 168, 171
Apollinaris of Laodicea   102–103, 137
Aristotle   155
Arius   112
Athanasius   168
Augustine   28, 49, 64

Baillie, Donald M.   124, 137
Balthasar, Hans Urs von   25
Barth, Karl   64, 69, 77–78, 90, 117, 120–122, 181–183, 195*n*35, 204, 212,
Becker, Jürgen   114–115
Beintker, Michael   149
Berkhof, Hendrikus   137
Biedermann, Emanuel   91, 182, 191,
Bockmuehl, Markus   78
Bolz, Norbert   159
Bonhoeffer, Dietrich   2, 92*n*15, 176, 182–183
Boniface VIII   66
Bornkamm, Heinrich   15–16
Buber, Martin   35
Bultmann, Rudolf   186, 189–192
Burkhardt, Armin   73
Busch, Eberhard   120

Calvin, Jean   7*n*9, 25–26, 66, 89–90, 117–122, 138, 168
Camus, Albert   177
Colle, Ralph del   137
Conzelmann, Hans   111
Cornille, Catherine   163
Crossan, John Dominic   63
Cyril of Alexandria   102

Dalferth, Ingolf   124
Deuser, Hermann   2, 43–44, 74
Dirscherl, Erwin   36
Dunn, James D. G.   85, 100, 111, 115, 153
Dupuis, Jacques   10, 127–128

Ehrenberg, Rudolf   35
Eliade, Mircea   196
Eusebius of Caesarea   31

Feckes, Carl   65
Frei, Hans   19*n*7

Gerhard, Johann   89*n*3
Gestrich, Christof   44, 58, 81

Haight, Roger   13, 71, 95, 127–128, 186, 194–207, 209
Hamann, Johann Georg   160
Hartenstein, Karl   7
Hegel, Georg W. F.   50, 78
Herder, Johann Gottfried   160
Herzgsell, Johannes   8
Hick, John H.   117, 122–124, 200
Hoff, Gregor Maria   46
Huxley, Aldous   161

Ignatius of Antioch   138
Irenaeus of Lyon   28, 115, 137, 147
Iwand, Hans   174

Jacobi, Friedrich Heinrich   160
Janowski, Bernd   170
Jaspers, Karl   68
Jervel, Jacob   62*n*29
John of Damascus   119
Johnson, Elizabeth A.   150, 152
Jüngel, Eberhard   65
Justin Martyr   28, 30, 112

Kant, Immanuel   160
Keener, Craig S.   107
Kellerhals, Emanuel   7
Khodre, Georges   147*n*161
Kierkegaard, Søren   182
Knitter, Paul F.   147*n*161, 192, 201
Korsch, Dietrich   183
Kraus, Hans-Joachim   134, 137–138
Küng, Hans   139
Kuschel, Karl-Josef   210

Lampe, Geoffrey W. H.   124, 137, 139–140
Lévinas, Emmanuel   94, 161
Lindbeck, George   19*n*7

Link, Christian   117–118, 121–122
Luther, Martin   7n9, 49–50, 52–53, 64, 85, 89, 102–103, 118–119, 166, 168, 189

MacKinnon, Donald   186
Macquarrie, John   30, 186
Marheineke, Philipp Konrad   78
Marxsen, Willi   187
Melanchthon   90
Moltmann, Jürgen   117, 137–138, 149, 195n35

Naumann, Friedrich   160
Nicholas of Cusa   131

Oberman, Heiko A.   118
Ogden, Schubert M.   13, 186–194, 200, 207, 209,
Origen   28
Owen, John   138, 140

Panikkar, Raimon   126, 200
Pannenberg, Wolfhart   4, 29, 90, 181
Pascal, Blaise   159
Peirce, Charles Sanders   44, 69, 74
Pesch, Otto Hermann   136, 170
Petrus Lombardus   119
Petuchowski, Jakob J.   138
Philo of Alexandria   105, 108–111, 148–149, 152
Plotinus   108
Pröpper, Thomas   173
Pseudo-Dionysius the Areopagite   161n189

Rahner, Karl   8, 30, 65, 69, 83n89, 125, 170, 193, 196, 201–202
Ratramnus of Corbie   68
Ratzinger, Joseph / Pope Benedict XVI   14, 195
Ricœur, Paul   196
Ritschl, Albrecht   81, 169, 182–183,
Robinson, James   153

Robinson, John A. T.   63
Rosenzweig, Franz   35, 217
Ryle, Gilbert   76

Schaede, Stephan   45, 79–81, 83–84
Scheerer, Eckart   39
Scheffczyk, Leo   65
Schelling, Friedrich W. J.   183
Schillebeeckx, Edward   196n40
Schleiermacher, Friedrich D. E.   2, 50, 95, 167, 169, 204,
Schmidt-Leukel, Perry   117, 125
Schoonenberg, Piet   137
Schöttler, Heinz-Günther   94
Schrage, Wolfgang   63
Schüssler Fiorenza, Elisabeth   153
Sölle, Dorothee   82, 85
Spinoza, Baruch de   103, 113
Suggs, M. Jack   151

Tertullian   30, 64, 66, 137
Theobald, Michael   106, 115–116
Thoma, Clemens   138
Thomas Aquinas   88, 119, 170
Thumm, Theodor   118
Tillich, Paul   2–3, 11–12, 28, 40, 50, 69–74, 90–91, 137, 143, 162, 182–184, 186, 195–197
Troeltsch, Ernst   4

Vernant, Jean-Pierre   43
Vetter, Martin   74n74

Wengst, Klaus   35
Wesley, John   189
Wiedenhofer, Siegfried   209
Wiles, Maurice   186

Yong, Amos   148n161

Zwingli, Ulrich   28